Judges

Judges

Jack Batten

Macmillan of Canada
A Division of Canada Publishing Corporation
Toronto, Ontario, Canada

First printing August, 1986
Reprinted October, 1986

Canadian Cataloguing in Publication Data

Batten, Jack, date.
  Judges

ISBN 0-7715-9729-0

1. Judges — Canada.   I. Title.

KE395.B37 1986   347.71'014'0922   C86-093816-6

DESIGN: Don Fernley

Macmillan of Canada
A Division of Canada Publishing Corporation
Toronto, Ontario, Canada

Printed in Canada

For two fine men of the law,
Reg Soward and John Robinette

CONTENTS

ACKNOWLEDGMENTS

A nne Holloway was partly responsible for thinking up this book, and for editing it, and she supplied me with encouragement and friendship. Doug Gibson came through with his customary enthusiasm for the project. Garry and Julian Clarke provided the refuge in Vancouver. James G. Snell and Frederick Vaughan wrote an excellent book, *The Supreme Court of Canada*, which yielded fresh insights into the judges who sit on that court. Jacques Monet translated some indispensable French material. The Ontario Arts Council was once again generous with its financial support. Peter Russell, Ed Sexton, Ed Ratushny, and Maggie Siggins were unselfish with their help and advice. Marjorie Harris gave her love and she never once yawned when I told her my judges stories. To all, I send my gratitude.

PREFACE

The lot of the Canadian judge is tough and getting tougher. That's one truth I learned in the two years I spent researching and writing this book. It wasn't that the judges I interviewed and watched in courtrooms across the country complained about their jobs; on the contrary, they were almost unanimous in expressing the pleasures and satisfactions they found in work on the bench. The conclusion about the ever-increasing demands on judges' time and energy and intelligence is my own. On any average day in court, I discovered, a judge is routinely called on to exhibit the tact of a diplomat, the wisdom of Solomon, the patience of a peace negotiator. And it helps, when he gets around to putting his judgment on paper, if he can write with the clarity and grace of E. B. White. A judge under our system doesn't have to be perfect, but he or she had better come awfully close.

Some of the burdens of the judge's job go with the territory. His or her role, after all, is to make hard decisions. They come in two varieties — decisions at the trial level and decisions at the appellate level. In the first, a judge must rule on the guilt or innocence of an accused person in a criminal trial, or must choose between the contending arguments of two parties, plaintiff and defendant, in a civil trial. Sometimes, almost exclusively in criminal proceedings, the judge has the assistance of a jury. On those occasions, the judge's duty is to make the law clear to the jury members, and they become the arbiters who arrive at the case's final verdict under the judge's shepherding hand.

At the appellate level—in the appeal courts of all the provinces and in the Supreme Court of Canada—the judge operates in a different, more isolated way. Only lawyers appear in such courts. They argue the merits of a decision that has been reached by a judge at the trial level. Did the trial judge correctly interpret the law as it had been established in earlier cases? Or had he made errors that needed to be straightened out? The arguments grow intricate and esoteric, and when the appeal court judge finally retires to his chambers to write his judgment, he carries the heavy responsibility of the umpire. He considers the lawyers' points, analyses past case law, puts his own spin on matters, and out of his deliberations he nudges the law in one direction or another. It's a creative process, and what the judge creates is new law which affects us all — lawyers, lower courts, and humble citizens.

The other explanation for the difficulty of the tasks that today's Canadian judge faces, apart from the inherent nature of his post, is more contemporary and political. It has to do with the arrival in 1982 of our constitution. With it, and its Charter of Rights, a whole new set of arguments and possibilities and areas of decision has opened up. In a sense, the elected politicians have abandoned much of the deciding about the future and direction of the country to the appointed —not elected—judges. It's the judiciary who has been handed the problem of defining the meaning and extent of the multitude of freedoms and rights that the Charter has bestowed on Canadians. Censorship, abortion, the claims of abandoned wives, of minority groups, of native peoples, and of men and women who feel cheated by the system—all of these and many more are the stuff of fresh litigation which the courts must address and resolve. The Charter of Rights has put our courts on the cutting edge of policy and change.

The good news is that the judges, as I saw them in action, are up to the challenge. Perhaps I can best explain my own confidence in our judiciary by describing how I felt after I'd spent a few days in November 1985 hanging around the Supreme Court of Canada in Ottawa, listening to arguments in the courtroom, reading judgments, chatting with the justices in their chambers on the second floor of the Supreme Court Building. I felt proud. I felt that these nine judges were splendid Canadians. They were courteous, bright, determined, and industrious. The eight men and one woman on the court shoulder a staggering weight of obligation to the law and to the country, and they bear it with impressive dignity and intelligence.

I admired almost all of the judges I called on in the course of putting this book together. I covered judges who sit at every level of the judiciary in the country, from the Provincial Court, where the scrappy, visceral stuff takes place, to the Supreme Court in Ottawa, where the lofty judgments are delivered. I went across much of Canada, speaking to the Chief Justice of British Columbia, to a retired judge of the Court of Criminal Sessions in Montreal, to a professor of international law at Dalhousie University in Halifax who sits, of all unlikely places, on the European Court of Human Rights in Strasbourg, France, representing the nation of Liechtenstein. I talked to them, watched them in court, and admired them and their work.

All of which may give the idea, correctly, that this book is *not* about a number of things. Except incidentally, it is not a book about the philosophical underpinnings of the judicial process. It is not about the ways in which judges get appointed in Canada. It is not about judicial accountability. And it is not about several other weighty and academic matters that affect the country's judges.

What it *is* about is something that is more human, more
fun, and, perhaps in the long run, more enlightening. It is
about Canadian judges as people and Canadian judges at
work. As I called on them, I found they were delighted to talk
to me about both subjects—their lives and their work. At the
beginning, starting out on the book, I was afraid that judges
might be remote characters, private and close-mouthed. That
turned out to be the exact reverse of the truth. All of the judges
I encountered were extraordinarily generous with their time
and opinions and recollections. Sometimes, it seemed to me,
they were relieved to have someone come along and ask a
few questions. Maybe it gets a little lonely back there in chambers. Maybe they welcomed the chance to break from their
duties for some conversation.

I also discovered that many judges from different parts of
the country have connections with other judges that reached
far into the past. Perhaps that's not so surprising, but the
revelations of these relationships always delighted me. Sandy
MacPherson, a retired judge from the Saskatchewan Court
of Queen's Bench, and Chief Justice Brian Dickson of the
Supreme Court of Canada, were in the same high school class
in Regina. Ron Macdonald, the Dalhousie man on the European Court of Human Rights, once hired Ken Lysyk, now a
British Columbia Supreme Court justice, as a lecturer at the
University of Toronto Law School. And when Judge Stephen
Borins of the District Court of the Judicial District of York
graduated from law school in the early 1960s, he went to work
for a year as the clerk to Chief Justice James McRuer of the
Ontario Supreme Court. I chose all of these judges to write
about without knowing of their connections which, for me,
somehow gave the judiciary and this book an extra dimension.

When I visited James McRuer in his Toronto apartment in
the spring of 1985, he was ninety-four years old and long
retired from the bench. But, as with all of the judges in the
book, he was happy to talk about his career. McRuer's mind

was sharp and his memory was unclouded. His body, however, was growing frail.

"When'll this book of yours be out?" he asked me as I was leaving his apartment after our last conversation.

I told him the fall of 1986.

"Oh, well," he said, "I won't be around to see it."

He was right.

James Chalmers McRuer died on October 6, 1985. He'd been a remarkable judge, one of many in Canada.

JACK BATTEN
March 1986

CHAPTER ONE

A Year of Trials

One murdered Vietnamese. A businessman from Thorold, Ontario, who claimed that the CTV program *W5* had libelled him and thereby ruined his health and reputation. Assorted divorces and other pieces of marital grief. A video-tape shot in a London, Ontario, hospital that began with the routine examination of a young woman and ended a few minutes later with the young woman's agonized death. A fire insurance company charging that an insured set fire to his own house. One paraplegic. And a young black man with a long criminal record who added to it by shooting a store-keeper in the back.

"It's been a fairly typical year in my business," Doug Carruthers was saying. It was June of 1985 and Carruthers was looking back over the list of cases he'd dealt with since the beginning of the judicial year in the previous September. His full title is the Honourable Mr. Justice Douglas Henry Carruthers of the High Court of the Supreme Court of Ontario, one of fifty-one judges who sit on that court, and his "business" is conducting trials.

The year started for Carruthers with a blitz in Ottawa. It's a judges' word, "blitz", and it's a recent innovation for the Ontario Supreme Court. A small band of judges organize

1

their schedules to descend together on a city or town where the case list has grown desperately long. The judges sit in separate courtrooms through an intensive three weeks of hearings on cases that have been waiting as long as three years for trial. The objective is to clear up the backlog, and in September 1984 it was Ottawa's turn for the treatment.

Carruthers is in favour of the blitz technique. He likes efficiency and speed in his courtroom and in most of life's other activities. He doesn't waste much time over a meal. He talks quickly. He doesn't suffer fools gladly. When he was a student at the University of Toronto, he played basketball, a sport that puts a premium on swift acceleration and clever moves. It was Carruthers' kind of game.

He and four other judges checked into the Four Seasons Hotel in Ottawa just after Labour Day, and for the following three weeks, except for the day when the Pope came through on tour and closed down operations at the Carleton County Courthouse, they adjudicated on a steady flow of cases. Carruthers handled mostly civil actions, bitter arguments over disputed contracts and contested property rights. It was grinding work without much surprise or colour. Carruthers himself supplied the most exciting moment in his courtroom when he unloaded a blast at the state of the century-old Carleton Courthouse, a stolid limestone building on Daly Street in downtown Ottawa.

"This courthouse is a monument to the local politicians' short-sighted approach to the administration of justice," he said one day to the counsel, litigants, jurors, and spectators in his courtroom. "People in elected office would rather put a new layer of blacktop on some remote highway than fix up a courthouse. They think the blacktop'll get them more votes. But what they're doing is showing their contempt for the way justice is carried out in Ontario. I'm not complaining just because I have to work in buildings like this. I'm complaining because every citizen who expects a fair hearing is adversely affected when he comes into such a terrible court-house."

Carruthers is more direct and vocal both on and off the bench than most of his brethren on the Ontario court. He doesn't mind unorthodoxy; in one 1981 case, he held court for three days in rooms at the Westin Hotel in Toronto in order to take examination-in-chief and cross-examination from a plaintiff who was dying of cancer. "It worked fine," Carruthers says. "A maid came in to make up the room one day, but she didn't bother us and we didn't bother her." And he's different in other ways. Physical fitness is one. At least three times a week after court, he takes off on four-mile runs. He lifts weights. He plays tennis regularly at the Boulevard Club in Toronto, and in winter he skies at the Georgian Peaks Club near Collingwood, Ontario. "My good physical condition helps my mental condition on the bench," he says. He's in his mid-fifties but looks ten years younger, a tall, trim man with light-brown hair, even features, an attractive smile, and, in any good cause, a quick lip.

"One — eight — five," he said, very content, when the Ottawa blitz ended and he returned to his home base in Toronto. "That's how many cases we disposed of. One hundred and eighty-five. Not a hell of a lot of dramatic stuff except for the terrible murder case, a cop killing, that Nick McRae had in front of him. Not dramatic but damned happy for everybody in Ottawa — the lawyers, the litigants, the court officials, and the judges who go in there after us and find a nice tidy case list."

The drama for Carruthers escalated at the courthouse on University Avenue in Toronto when he began the hearing of a libel action in early October. The plaintiffs were a man named Norris Walker and his company, Walker Brothers Quarries, of Thorold, a town in the Niagara peninsula. Walker Broth-

ers has been in business for several decades, a family operation, and in the past dozen or more years the business has
consisted mainly of disposing of industrial waste. In the
spring of 1980, *W5*, the investigative program that is shown
on Sunday nights on the CTV network, caught whisperings
that Walker Brothers was negligent, maybe even illegal, in
the methods it used in burying the industrial waste. *W5*
dispatched one of its crack reporters, Henry Champ, to
check out the rumours. He returned with an eighteen-minute
segment for the show, including an interview which Norris
Walker cheerfully granted. The segment came down mainly
on the side of the rumours. It said Walker Brothers might be
misleading the Ontario Ministry of the Environment about
its disposal techniques, that the waste left around by the
company could harm the surrounding countryside, that the
situation created by Walker Brothers was "a potential time
bomb". The eighteen-minute item ran on *W5* on the night of
October 26, 1980, and on January 1, 1981, Norris Walker and
his company sued CTV for libel.

When the case reached court in front of Carruthers, Julian
Porter appeared for the plaintiffs, Bill Somers for the defendant, a pair of formidable adversaries. Somers is a bulky,
red-haired man in his early fifties, seasoned in the courtrooms, armoured with a quick and caustic wit. Porter, a few
years younger, has striking good looks and a high profile
around Toronto. He belongs to the inner councils of Tory politics, serves as working chairman of the Toronto Transit Commission, and knows everybody who counts in media and
publishing circles. Libel is his specialty.

Porter led Norris Walker through his testimony. He is a
slim, fussy man in his fifties, and he said that after the *W5*
broadcast, he suffered terrible stomach pains. His health dete-
riorated. So did relations and business with his company's
customers. The jury listened attentively but kept their faces
blank. A libel suit is one of the last remaining civil actions in

Ontario in which a jury is still mandatory, a six-person jury rather than the twelve-person juries required in most criminal trials. For *Norris* v. *CTV*, the jury was made up of four women and two men. Porter gave them all his charm and persuasive treatment. The point he kept returning to was that the *W5* segment had created an untrue picture of Walker Brothers' operations through slanted film editing. Parts of interviews which didn't fit the program's thesis that the company was a dangerous polluter were snipped from the tapes. The show referred to talk in the Thorold community that Walker Brothers were up to no good, and yet, in the interview with Norris Walker, Henry Champ never put the local gossip to Walker. Not fair, Porter said, libellous. He paraded witnesses to the stand to underline his point, but he wasn't certain whether the jury was going for it.

"The way I read this case," Porter said, part way through the trial, "I could set a record for the amount of damages my man is going to get or else it'll be the kind of case I'll want to wipe from my mind for all time."

Carruthers was having fun.

"Hey, it's great. I've never heard a good libel case before," he said in his chambers one afternoon when court had adjourned for the day. "That's the thing, a judge should be prepared to take every kind of case. He goes into court with some knowledge of the law in all areas, with good judgment and a lot of common sense. Then the counsel get up and give him the facts and the law in the specific case—murder, civil action, libel, whatever it happens to be. The judge listens and makes decisions. If there's a jury, he makes sure they're getting everything straight. What the judge doesn't do is say to the lawyers, look, you guys, I'm the expert here and I'll tell you all about the law. No way. Lawyers do their job, judges do theirs. Sounds simple but it doesn't always work that way. Sometimes you get judges who set themselves up as gurus in one branch of the law, criminal law often, and they start making decisions before the lawyers have even given their pitch. One thing sure, I'm no expert in libel. I'm learning a lot from those guys out there."

The trial entered its third week. Bill Somers for CTV pressed in defence that the *W5* item had presented a straightforward account of the situation at Walker Brothers as the facts revealed it to be. It was responsible journalism, and in any event the law permitted both the print and the electronic media to comment fairly in matters of public concern. If the situation were otherwise, he argued, it would "put a crimp in investigative journalism".

By Wednesday morning, October 18, all of the witnesses had been heard, and Julian Porter began his address to the jury. He worked without notes as he prowled in front of the jury-box. He outlined the case for the plaintiff and reviewed the testimony of his witnesses. He began on a relatively light note. This is a solemn business, his manner implied, but we're allowed a little comic relief. He made a small joke. "Mr. Somers told you that a judgment for the plaintiff would put a crimp in investigative journalism," Porter said. "I don't want to put a crimp in it. I want to put a *cramp* in it." The jury smiled.

Porter had been talking for forty-five minutes. His voice took a step up in pitch and emotion. His body language signalled that something serious was on its way. He crouched in front of the jury-box. He listed accusations that *W5* had zinged at Norris Walker and his business, and after each accusation, Porter spoke the same two words.

"Not true."

"*W5* said Walker Brothers poisoned the ground," Porter told the jury. "Not true."

By the time Porter reached *W5*'s tenth accusation, his voice had risen to a shout that echoed off the ceiling of the court-room.

"*Not true!*"

Two of the women jurors pushed back in their chairs as if they'd been punched.

Carruthers called a recess to allow the jury to take its customary eleven-thirty coffee break.

"Porter's having a hell of a good time out there," Carruthers said in his chambers behind the courtroom. "That's what I liked to do as a counsel." In his own practice before he accepted an appointment to the bench in August 1977, Carruthers practised mostly litigation law. He handled work for insurance companies, the sort of cases that frequently involved jury trials. "I think I had a knack with a jury. I loved it, really letting fly with everything you've got. Maybe there's a little ham in it. But the ham stuff, that's a very effective element in persuading a jury to accept your line of argument."

Just before noon, Porter resumed his jury address. He began at measured pace. Calm but intense. "This case," he said, "gets into the deepest valley of malice." The jury straightened up. "*W5* took its hours of tapes and edited them down to a few minutes that would make their show into something sensational and popular and that would attract hundreds of thousands of viewers, and when they did all of that, they said that Norris Walker was negligent and crooked."

Porter was building to a climax, and it came thirty minutes later with the last two sentences of his address.

"When a man dies," Porter said, his voice husky with pleading, something close to sorrow, "all he leaves behind is his reputation and his good name."

Porter was standing to the right of the jury-box, between it and Carruthers. He was hunched forward, his shoulders quivering.

"Won't you," he said, his voice breaking. "Won't you" — now his voice was a rasp, his face contorted — "won't you" — Porter was closing in on a sob — "won't you let Norris Walker die with his name cleared of this infamy?"

Porter was finished, but he held his clutched pose, arms

slightly outstretched, head bent. No one in the jury-box moved. No one in the courtroom moved or spoke, not a guard or counsel or a spectator or a clerk or Carruthers. Five seconds went by. Porter walked to his seat at the counsel's table. His footsteps banged like small thunderclaps in the silence of the courtroom.

Carruthers broke the mood.

"We'll adjourn until two-thirty," he said.

Porter left to meet his friend Allan Fotheringham, the journalist, for lunch at Winston's, the Toronto restaurant favoured by men with faces and names that get in the papers. Carruthers went to his chambers and changed out of his crimson and black gown.

"Incredible," he said. "I've had people weep in my courtroom, but this is the first time the person who wept was a counsel. That was a fantastic address."

The jury retired to make its decision on the case at two o'clock on Thursday afternoon, October 18, and during the wait for their return, Carruthers passed some of the time in the courtroom kibitzing with Porter and Somers and their juniors.

"What'd you think?" one of the juniors asked Carruthers. "What'll the verdict be?"

"Maybe they'll give the plaintiff something," Carruthers said. "I think they'll find he was libelled and award him about twenty-five thousand dollars. That's just a guess. Shouldn't be higher than twenty-five because the program doesn't really seem to have cost the company any appreciable loss of business."

At six o'clock the next afternoon, Friday, the jury returned to the courtroom with its verdict. The foreman handed to the court clerk two sheets of paper on which the decision had been written, and the clerk passed the sheets up to Carruthers. The verdict in a libel case takes the form of answers to a short list of questions, and for two or three minutes, Carruthers studied the answers on the sheets in front of him.

"I looked at the numbers on the paper," Carruthers said later, "and what I wanted to do was lift my head and say to the counsel, 'You guys should see what *I'm* looking at!'"

Until that moment, the largest award in a Canadian libel action had been the $125,000 which Richard Vogel, the Deputy Attorney General of British Columbia, had won from the CBC in 1982. The award which Carruthers was staring at on the pieces of paper in front of him topped that figure by more than one million dollars.

The jury had found that *W5* libelled Norris Walker and his company. It calculated the damages for the libel in a variety of categories: $25,000 in personal damages to Walker, $50,000 in exemplary damages as punishment to *W5* for its offensive journalism, a whopping $883,000 in damages to the Walker Brothers company computed at the rate of one dollar for every person who was watching the *W5* show on the night the libellous segment was broadcast, and interest on the award dating from January 1981 when the lawsuit was initiated.

Total: $1,372,048.

Bill Somers was stunned. "For openers," he said later, "the damages are so excessive, they can't stand." He was planning an appeal. Norris Walker wasn't thinking of the future. He left the courtroom to drink a couple of bottles of champagne with friends. Julian Porter had his own small celebration, and Carruthers hurried away on a mission of different importance. He was booked into a game of tennis doubles at the Boulevard Club.

Carruthers had a beef.

"Look," he said in the courtroom at the University Avenue Courthouse in mid-November, "we put a man on the moon fifteen years ago. So why can't we straighten out a little technical problem like running two translations at once without all this terrible babble?"

The translators were required for the three accused whose

trial was about to start before Carruthers. The three were charged with first-degree murder, and none of them admitted to entirely understanding English. They were Vietnamese, but that fact didn't end the language complications. Two of the accused spoke conventional Vietnamese, while the third spoke a Chinese dialect. That called for two interpreters. As soon as the trial began, there was instantly a racket of three languages in the courtroom, English from Carruthers, the counsel, and almost everyone else, Vietnamese from the female interpreter who sat in the prisoners' box feeding the two Vietnamese-speaking accused, and Chinese from the male interpreter sitting outside the box and muttering to the third accused. It might have been a scene from a Marx Brothers movie — except that the subject was murder.

"Until you figure a way to straighten this out," Carruthers told the crown attorney, "I'm adjourning court."

The problem was solved two days later by installing an arrangement of steno masks and earphones. The interpreters wore the masks and communicated through them and a wiring system to the accused, who wore the earphones. Relative silence fell over the courtroom.

"This arrangement cost eighteen hundred dollars, my lord," the crown attorney told Carruthers. He looked proud.

"I'll write the Attorney General's department and tell him I'm grateful," Carruthers answered, though his expression seemed to be asking why the Attorney General's office hadn't looked after the difficulty before it reached his courtroom.

The second problem wasn't so speedily resolved. It concerned exactly what happened after eleven o'clock on the night of Saturday, September 17, 1983, near the corner of Bellevue and Oxford avenues in downtown Toronto. That was the time and place where a nineteen-year-old named Hong Trieu Thai died when someone fired a bullet from a .38 revolver that severed his spinal cord and made him a dead man before he hit the sidewalk.

Everyone agreed that the trouble had originated on the previous Saturday night after a dance that was held two blocks east of the murder site in a second-floor dance hall over a car wash at Oxford and Spadina avenues. The surrounding neighbourhood has been the headquarters for successive waves of immigrants ever since the turn of the century. First came Jews from a variety of middle-European countries, then Hungarians and Portuguese, later the Chinese, and, in the early 1980s, the Vietnamese. At the end of the war in Vietnam, after the Americans pulled out, many of the country's citizens fled to North America. "Boat people" is what they were called, and though the Canadian government settled them across the country, the majority soon headed for Toronto. They moved into homes in the College-Spadina neighbourhood and arranged social events like the dance over the car wash on Saturday night, September 10, 1983.

The highlight of the evening was a disco contest. After hours of drinking, dancing, and judging, the contest winner and a pair of his friends were buttonholed in the washroom by a crowd of young guys who hung out with Hong Trieu Thai, the fellow who ended up dead a week later. The Thai bunch told the winner that he was no John Travolta. A lousy dancer, they said. The insults boiled into a confrontation of curses and threats and pushes and shoves. The contest winner and one of his friends pulled guns and the other friend waved a mean-looking stick. Thai's crowd vacated the washroom in a hurry. The other three, victors in the showdown, were the men who would go on trial two years later for first-degree murder.

The Thai bunch held a council of war early on the evening of September 17 at the Quoc-Te Restaurant. They were mad. They planned to get even with the three guys who'd challenged them the previous Saturday. They piled into a van and drove a few blocks north through Kensington Market, teeming with outdoor stalls and shops selling exotic foods, to the St. Stephens Community House on Bellevue Avenue. A birthday party was being held at the hall. The three villains from the dance over the car wash were sure to be present. When Thai and his pals hopped out of the van, they weren't empty-handed. Some had machetes, and one man was packing a contemporary version of the fearsome swords that fifteenth-century Vietnamese warriors carried into battle. The sword was curved into a hook at the tip, just right for yanking out an opponent's stomach.

What happened next has been forever shadowed in that night's darkness, in lies and faulty memories. The one fact that's certain is the reality of the clash between the Hong Trieu Thai group and their three adversaries. The action took place on Bellevue Avenue's east sidewalk and on the walkway that leads between a picket fence and a chain-link fence to the front door of St. Stephens House. Two of the Thai group ended the brief but bloody skirmish with bullet wounds. Thai himself ran south on Bellevue Avenue, pursued by another man according to some witnesses, and it was at the corner of Bellevue and Oxford where Thai took the bullet through the spine that killed him.

By the time the police arrived, many of the parties to the battle — most notably the three men who were the objects of the Thai gang's wrath — had scattered. Still, the cops turned up several witnesses who had seen at least parts of the struggle, and they found a machete lying under a car on Bellevue and the ferocious sword in the alleyway leading into St. Stephens House. Neither weapon seemed to have blood on the blade. The police came across no guns at the scene, but they had something almost as helpful — the names of the three suspects who'd possibly done the shooting.

When the men's names appeared in a Toronto paper on Sunday, they jumped into an Oldsmobile that one of them owned and set out for Vancouver. None of the three had any notion of the distance to Vancouver. A short hop, they thought, not so far that the owner of the Olds couldn't drop off the other two in Vancouver and drive back in time for work on Wednesday or Thursday. He didn't bother to pack a change of clothes. On Tuesday, the three men were arrested in Sault Ste. Marie, Ontario, and returned to Toronto. The police charged all three with first-degree murder, though their roles in the killing were alleged to be different and not yet specifically defined.

Asau Tran was thirty years old and the acknowledged leader of the trio. He had been the principal target of the Thai group, the man who'd done most of the threatening, insulting, and gun-waving in the washroom after the disco contest on September 10. Tran didn't hold down a conventional job, but he collected a salary for his duties as a guard at a Vietnamese gambling house on Spadina Avenue. He was diligent about his illegal chores and had purchased a gun from a black man whom he met in a bar on Cecil Street in the neighbourhood. The gun showed he meant business around the gambling house. Tran didn't bother to pay income tax or unemployment insurance on his guard's salary.

Van-Nghiep Truong was the alleged shooter of Hong Trieu Thai. He was twenty-two and appeared to be the most upstanding citizen of the three accused. He was the man with the Olds. He had a wife and three children, and a job at a factory. He didn't own a gun.

Sang-Minh Nguyen was twenty-seven and he had a gun for the same reason that Tran packed his pistol. Nguyen, too, worked as a guard at the Spadina Avenue gambling house, and he got his gun from the same mysterious black man in the Cecil Street bar. Nguyen also ignored such incidentals as income tax and unemployment insurance.

In court, the three counsel who were defending the accused, all receiving a minimum fee from the Legal Aid fund, made up a veteran, skilled, determined, gaudy, sometimes difficult, occasionally unorthodox group. Carruthers suspected that he might have been assigned to the case in order to keep these particular defence lawyers in line. Some judges grow impatient with counsel who don't always go by the book. Others lose control of a tough murder trial and let it drift on for too many weeks. Carruthers had no such problems, and he relished the chance to preside over a trial that featured counsel with minds of their own.

John Rosen acted for Tran, the accused trio's leader. Rosen is a husky man in his mid-forties, dark and sleek, articulate, and usually one step ahead of the crown attorney in a murder trial. Rosen took his first murder case in 1975, and by November 1984 his murder-trial total had reached almost forty. He'd lost only one.

Jack Pinkofsky has a reputation as the aging *enfant terrible* of the criminal courts. In person, he's a greying, rumpled, engaging fellow. In court, he's a tiger. Two Supreme Court justices have reprimanded him for his intransigent tactics at trial, but nothing, not even a pair of heart attacks, has slowed down Pinkofsky in his drive to win a case for the client. He likes underdogs and frequently acts for people from Toronto's black community. He had his hands full in the trial before Carruthers. Pinkofsky's client was Truong, the alleged shooter of Thai.

Wally Rose, Nguyen's counsel, was the most senior of the defence lawyers, the "Silver Fox", as he's universally known, a man with a thousand stories, most of them outrageous. He acquired his early fame in the 1950s when he developed a defence for women charged with prostitution that was ingenious and foolproof. "After that," Rose says, "the girls brought in their boyfriends for me to defend. The boyfriends were all safe-crackers." Rose's practice flourished in many fields of criminal law until the 1970s, when his life underwent a rapid series of changes in direction. He married a beautiful Scottish woman nineteen days after he met her. Gave up law. Opened an inn in the Scottish Highlands. Lost his eyesight. Regained most of his eyesight. Got divorced. Returned to Toronto and his criminal-law practice in May 1983. "I went into the courts," he says, "and my old youthful idealism came back."

The crown attorney in the Vietnamese trial was Glen Orr, a man in his mid-forties who's made his career in the crown's office. The line on Orr is that he's the sort of crown who keeps a spare set of keys to the courthouse and is likely to turn up in the court library at midnight on a Saturday. He's a diligent worker, and his record of successful prosecutions reflects his tenacity. He has also developed a distinctive courtroom schtick. He is a ruffled, folksy man, and with juries he keeps his considerable courtroom experience and his moxie as a prosecutor partly concealed under a down-home, just-plain-fellas approach.

Carruthers opened the trial with the customary judge's instructions to the jury. The purpose of the remarks is to impress on the jury members their duties and responsibilities. "Best opening to a jury I've ever heard," John Rosen said later. "Carruthers just looked them in the eye, told them why they were there, and he treated them like real people and not idiots."

Glen Orr began his presentation of the crown's case, and it became transparently clear that Orr's style and Carruthers' style mixed like oil and water. Orr took pains over the evidence. He summoned a police witness to the stand to identify several photographs of the streets and alleys around the murder scene. With every photo, Orr elicited the policeman's description, then passed the photo to each of the jury members, then repeated the policeman's description of the scene in the photo. It was a laborious process, and Carruthers, the judge who demands efficiency and momentum in his courtroom, stepped in.

"Mr. Orr," he said, "instead of going through this rigamarole of proving every single photograph, can't we just ask defence counsel to agree to allow the pictures to go in evidence? Wouldn't that be simpler and faster?"

The matter of the photos was taken care of, but the pace of the crown's case never shifted to high gear. Partly it was Orr's insistence on a presentation of breath-taking orderliness. Partly it was the necessity for much of the evidence to be sifted through the interpreters before it reached Carruthers, counsel, and the jury, since the Vietnamese witnesses from the night of the shooting delivered their testimony in languages that excluded English. The trial inched forward, and Carruthers didn't like the dragging rate of progress. He encouraged the crown to more expeditious measures, and on a few occasions handed out admonishments to Orr.

"My lord," Orr replied to one of Carruthers' remarks, "I feel like the little boy who's been told by his father to climb into a hole and pull the hole in after him."

Carruthers stared down from the bench until Orr put his next question to the witness on the stand.

Carruthers' attitude to Orr caught the attention of a group of kids from Westwood Secondary School whose teacher had brought them to the courtroom on the last Monday in November for a day's educational outing. After Carruthers adjourned court in the afternoon, he stayed behind to answer the students' questions, and one of the first was about the crown attorney. Wasn't Carruthers a little rough on Orr?

"Stick around, you haven't seen anything yet," Carruthers answered. The kids laughed and so did Carruthers. "Seriously," he went on, "he is a professional. He can take it. It's just that some lawyers get to the point right away. They're incisive. This one happens to be more of a plodder."

Carruthers fielded other questions from the kids.

How much did he earn?

"About ninety thousand dollars a year," Carruthers answered. The kids gasped and whistled. "A defence lawyer," Carruthers added, "makes an awful lot more than that." Louder gasps and more whistles.

Did Carruthers ever get bored?

"Bored? *Bored*? Of course not. I'm dealing with people every day. I move around the province always meeting new people and new situations and hearing all sorts of cases. How could I get bored?"

Orr pressed on with his construction of the crown's case. He called dozens of witnesses — policemen, Vietnamese who knew the victim and the accused and the circumstances that led up to the killing, a handful of independent observers of the fatal night's action. The crown's case took a shape of an awkward but plausible sort. Tran and Nguyen owned guns from their guard jobs at the gambling club. The two of them and Truong had an ongoing grudge against Thai and his gang after the run-in at the disco contest. When Thai's crowd swooped down at St. Stephens House, the three men attacked them. Tran probably fired the shots that wounded two of their opponents. Truong somehow came into possession of one of the guns and sprinted down Bellevue in chase of Thai. It was the crown's case that he caught up to him at the corner of Oxford and Bellevue and shot through Thai's spine from a distance of no more than twelve inches. If Truong, Tran, and Nguyen were acting in consort throughout the clash, then all were equally guilty of first-degree murder.

The defence counsel hammered at the crown witnesses in cross-examination and thought they were scoring big points. "We massacred those witnesses," Rosen said. The defence questions undoubtedly shook the credibility of some of the Vietnamese who testified for the crown. And the questions also established a number of key points that favoured the defence. It emerged that there were probably ten or twelve men in Thai's group, armed with machetes, when they set out on their assault of the three accused. Twelve against three? The numbers laid the grounds for a self-defence argument.

The crown called a young Vietnamese student who had been the last person in Thai's company before the shooting. He testified for the crown that Thai had run down Bellevue with someone running after him. The witness heard shots. He couldn't make out what had happened to Thai. The street was a muddle of running and shouting people. The witness went to Thai's house and waited for him. When Thai didn't show up, he left for his own home. Next morning, he said, another friend phoned to tell him that Thai was dead.

John Rosen, acting for Tran, the leader among the accused, cross-examined the student witness, who, like all of the Vietnamese witnesses, was testifying in Vietnamese. Rosen questioned him about his education. The witness had been in a Toronto high school at the time of the shooting and was now studying engineering at an Ontario community college. In what language had he taken his high school courses? English. How about his college courses? English. What was the language of his textbooks? English. Of his examinations? English.

"Well, wait," Carruthers interrupted, "why is this witness testifying in Vietnamese?"

"It's the language he prefers, my lord," Orr answered.

"Mr. Rosen, what do you say about that?" Carruthers asked.

"My lord," Rosen said, stringing out his words, "I say it's for the jury to decide whether they believe this witness's testimony or not."

"You're probably right," Carruthers said.

Rosen picked up the cross-examination of the student. How far away was Thai's house from St. Stephens House? Just one block. That fact hadn't come out in the witness's examination-in-chief, and Rosen made the most of the new detail. Well, if the student was the last person to see his friend Thai alive and if there was shooting that seemed to involve Thai and if Thai didn't turn up at his own house, why didn't the student walk the one short block back to St. Stephens House and find out what had happened to Thai? Simple enough question, Rosen said. The student mumbled an answer and looked and sounded evasive in the witness-box. His testimony, for what it was worth, seemed in shreds.

Rosen had a theory about the student, which may also have applied to some of the other young Vietnamese who had resisted testifying in English.

"The kid lived a double life," Rosen explained outside the courtroom. "At home with his parents, everything was traditional. He spoke the language of his parents. But out in the world, he ran with a bunch of guys who hung out in poolrooms. He lived a home life and a street life, and he didn't want his people at home to know about the street life. Understanding that, I had a grip on the way to go at him in cross-examination. Why did he flee the shooting? Why didn't he run back to find out about Thai? Why didn't he go to the police with what he knew? Why did he wait until the police came to him weeks later? Why? Because he didn't want his parents to know. That's the real reason, but cross-examining him, I could use my knowledge to show the jury that he wasn't a credible, believable witness."

Wally Rose, defending Nguyen, had his innings — and his small joke — with another witness. Her name was Dr. Cheryl Wagner, an attractive woman who lived at 96 Bellevue Avenue across the street from St. Stephens House. She testified for the crown that she had seen a man, possibly Nguyen, run down the east side of Bellevue firing shots as he ran. If that were the case, Rose said, wouldn't there be a trail of cartridge shells on the sidewalk down the lower part of Bellevue? Dr. Wagner agreed. But, Rose closed in, the police found only two cartridge shells and they lay on the sidewalk much further north on Bellevue.

Then came Rose's fun. Many weeks earlier, between the case's preliminary hearing and the trial, he had gone to the South Riverdale Community Health Centre for a checkup. A receptionist ushered him into a doctor's office. The doctor was Cheryl Wagner.

"As far as the doctor is concerned," Rose went on in court, "the lady is mistaken about the gunshots. That's understandable under the circumstances of the darkness and the speed with which events occurred that night. I'm not going to say more than that. I wouldn't want to arouse her displeasure. I may see more of her in the future."

Carruthers' eyes shot up.

"She might be my doctor," Rose finished.

One of Jack Pinkofsky's jokes in court almost backfired. Pinkofsky, representing Truong, the alleged shooter, was cross-examining a witness named Chung, and he wasn't having much success in moving Chung off the testimony he'd given to Orr on examination-in-chief. Pinkofsky, a man with a terrier-like grip on cross-examination, finally approached the moment of surrender with Chung. He decided to go out with a gag line. Earlier in the trial, there had been several references to another man named Phuc, pronounced to rhyme with "book". Since the Vietnamese equivalent of the English "mister" is Ah, the gentleman referred to was Ah Phuc.

"Well," Pinkofsky said to the recalcitrant Chung, "if I can't get you to agree with me, then *Ah Phuc.*"

Pinkofsky sat down and wore a tiny grin.

It was time for the lunch recess, and Carruthers dismissed the jury.

"My lord," Orr said after the jury had filed out, "I don't think Mr. Pinkofsky should resort to such a tactic as we've just heard in the courtroom."

"I'll let you know what I think about it after lunch," Carruthers said.

Orr had correctly anticipated the jury's reaction to Pinkofsky's crack. The jury foreman sent a note to Carruthers during the lunch break. The note asked for an apology from Pinkofsky.

When court resumed at two-fifteen in the afternoon, Carruthers passed on the jury's request, and Pinkofsky, a model of graciousness, begged the jury members' pardon. The looks on their faces seemed to say he had it.

Orr wound up the crown's case, and the three defence counsel had a choice to make. Should they call the accused men to the witness-box? It was an easy decision.

"What you have here," Wally Rose said, "are three guys with guns and they dispose of them and get in a car to drive to Vancouver even though they seem to think Vancouver's some place over near Lake Huron. Okay, you got to put them in the witness-box to explain what they were up to."

"A jury likes to hear from the accused in a murder trial," John Rosen said. "If they're going to acquit, they want to feel comfortable about it. In the case of Jack's client, who's the shooter according to the crown, they want to know they've given an acquittal to someone who's probably an all-right person, not someone who's got a previous criminal record or something. Jack's guy, Truong, was clean as a whistle."

The defence lawyers were banking on the jury's acceptance of their version of the case. In the cross-examinations, they had set out to make the point that Truong was without a gun during the skirmish on Bellevue. No one could say for a certainty that Truong had been seen with a gun. He couldn't have shot Thai. Whatever action he took was in self-defence. And the other two, Tran and Nguyen, acted in similar self-defence. Thai's group outnumbered them by four to one, and the three accused were under siege from guys who carried vicious weapons. Maybe they fought back, Truong and Tran and Nguyen, but no one could swear precisely what happened that night on Bellevue Avenue. Certainly there was no evidence that any of the three accused had gone at Thai with intent to kill.

Truong took the stand. Pinkofsky instructed him to testify in English and to use the interpreter only if an English word or phrase eluded him. English testimony, Pinkofsky reasoned, would impress the jury after the crowd of crown witnesses who chose Vietnamese over English. Truong's story had no frills. He testified that, yes, he may have been the man whom several witnesses had seen running down the east side of Bellevue at about the time Thai was fleeing in the same direction. But Truong insisted he was running for his life. Two or three men had approached him. They wanted to fight. He took off down Bellevue toward Oxford. At the corner, more guys threatened him. He raced back up Bellevue. He found his two friends, and the three sped away in his Oldsmobile. In all the turmoil, he didn't shoot anyone. How could he? He didn't own a gun.

Tran also testified in English with fall-back help from the interpreter. Sure, he had a gun. He needed it to wave around at the gambling club. But he hadn't killed anyone with it that night outside St. Stephens House. Anything he did was in reaction to the men who attacked him. He was in fear of his own life.

Glen Orr cross-examined Tran.

"Didn't it bother your conscience that you had a gun illegally?" he asked at one point. "Didn't it bother you that you paid no income tax on the salary from the gambling house?"

Wally Rose's client, Nguyen, testified in Vietnamese. His story was that he'd arrived on Bellevue Avenue just as the fighting broke out. Someone pulled a knife on him. He reached for his gun, but when he pulled the trigger, the gun jammed. No shots came out of the barrel. At that moment, his pal Tran grabbed him and led the way from the scene of the battle. He left with Tran and Truong in the Olds.

Orr stood up to cross-examine Nguyen.

"When I give the signal," Pinkofsky whispered to Rosen, "slip me a dollar bill."

"Didn't it bother your conscience . . ." Orr started to ask during his cross-examination.

"Okay, now," Pinkofsky said to Rosen.

Rosen slid out the dollar bill and put it in Pinkofsky's palm.

"I think about three or four jurors saw what we were up to," Rosen said later. "They understood we were making a bet that Orr would ask that particular question. It was a little gimmick to show we were on top of the crown's case."

When the defence had finished with its witnesses and after all four lawyers, Orr and the three defence counsel, had made their arguments to the jury, Rosen, Pinkofsky, and Rose felt confident that the tide of the trial was running their way.

"All of us had the impression that Carruthers was leaning to the defence's side during the trial," Rose said. "And rightly so, we thought. Carruthers was very fair. He had this kind of wry humour that helps in a long trial, and he always went with the knife straight to the point. But all the way, I felt he was having doubts about some of the crown witnesses' credibility and that he was pro-defence for that reason."

The three defence counsel made a small readjustment in their assessment after Carruthers' charge to the jury. The charge took about two hours on the morning of Monday, December 17, and though it may have had a slight slant to the defence, it stuck mainly to the middle of the road. It explained the principle of reasonable doubt to the jury, emphasizing that the jury must be satisfied of the accused men's guilt beyond any reasonable doubt before it could convict them. And the charge was careful in picking out the highlights in the arguments raised by both crown and defence.

Pinkofksy was disappointed. He told Rosen that if the defence hadn't called any evidence, Carruthers would have given a strongly defence-oriented charge. He would have had to, Pinkofsky argued, because there was no convincing case for the crown. By calling witnesses, the defence had given Carruthers more to talk about than the crown's weak case.

"Listen," Rosen said, putting the best light on things, "Carruthers may be the living end, but he's not our co-counsel. He has to do what he has to do — give both sides of the argument."

The jury started deliberations after lunch that day, Monday, and ran into its first obstacle within thirty minutes. There were seven smokers on the jury and five non-smokers, and the second group refused to allow the first group to light up in the jury room. The jury appealed to Carruthers, who told them to solve the dilemma on their own. It'd be good practice in reaching decisions. They took care of the problem by agreeing to break at the end of each hour while the smokers puffed in an outer room.

At six o'clock in the evening, the jury signalled that it had reached a verdict of sorts. Everyone assembled in the courtroom, and the jury revealed that it was twelve to none against conviction on first-degree murder. But the jury members were at an impasse, eleven to one, on the alternative that was open to them — a conviction on second-degree murder, a lesser offence but one that still carried a long jail sentence.

"It's got to be eleven to one for acquittal," Rose said. "I can feel it. The jury's got one holdout."

Carruthers told the jury members to stick at their deliberations. They'd be put up overnight in rooms at the Holiday Inn behind the courthouse and could start in again at nine o'clock the next morning.

Just before noon on Tuesday, Carruthers received a long note from the jury foreman. They were still stuck at eleven to one, the note said, and it went on to spell out in detail the nature of the deadlock. The note gave Carruthers a small concern. The Criminal Code places restrictions on the publication in any form of a jury's secret discussions. The very explicit note may have come close to putting this jury in violation of the Code.

Carruthers decided to say nothing to the jury about the ways it was flirting with trouble. But after lunch he gathered them in the courtroom for a pep talk.

"Nobody knows the evidence in this case better than you twelve," he said. "I'd like you to try just a little longer and a little harder to find a verdict."

To the jury, Carruthers came across like Vince Lombardi.

The jury foreman got to his feet. He was a middle-aged man in a sweater, and he had a down-home look.

"We had the feeling we were just spinnin' our wheels in there," he said to Carruthers. "But after what you say, we'll go at it again."

The jury didn't come back until a quarter past five that afternoon. It had already reached the acquittal verdict on the charge of first-degree murder. Now, at last, it had a verdict on the remaining possibility of second-degree murder.

Asau Tran: not guilty.

Sang-Minh Nguyen: not guilty.

Van-Nghiep Truong: not guilty.

The three men were free.

The usual custom in a case where the jury has delivered an acquittal is for the judge to dismiss the jury members before he discharges the accused. Carruthers didn't follow the custom. He thanked the jury. "I don't think you could have reached any other verdict on the evidence," he said. Then he had them remain in the courtroom to hear him express his feelings about Tran, Truong, and Nguyen.

"Canada gave you people refuge when you couldn't find it in your own country," he said to the three men. "You repaid this act of kindness by cheating on your income tax and unemployment insurance, working for an illegal business, and carrying guns. I don't like any of this one bit."

"My lord," Pinkofsky broke in. "I submit that my client, Mr. Truong, is a dedicated and hard-working factory worker, the kind of immigrant we can all be proud of."

"One wonders about the ability of a person to pick his friends," Carruthers answered icily.

It was the end of the case.

A week later, the three accused men, now acquitted, invited their counsel out to a lunch of thanks. They ate in a Vietnamese restaurant near Spadina Avenue. The hosts presented each of the guests with a small gift. Wally Rose had a gift of his own for Jack Pinkofsky. It was an exquisite little Buddha, and on its base Rose had arranged for two words to be engraved in black letters against the gold background.

"Ah Phuc."

The Supreme Court of Ontario operates out of three buildings on University Avenue in Toronto. They're lined up in a row from north to south. At the top is the University Avenue Courthouse, a plain, modern, workaday building which holds twenty-six courtrooms and a variety of court administrative offices. Directly south, across a small, undecorated square, is Osgoode Hall. Among the architectural prides of Toronto, it probably claims first place. It dates from the mid-nineteenth century, and combines the sort of grandeur and elegance that invites hushed awe. The Ontario Court of Appeal sits in Osgoode Hall, and so do justices of the High Court when they're hearing procedural motions and other matters that require the presence of counsel without their clients. Osgoode also provides, in the sequestered rear of the building, the permanent chambers, meeting rooms, dining hall, and other quarters required by the justices. South of Osgoode, on the opposite side of Queen Street, is the third building where Supreme Court trial judges hold forth. It's particularly drab, a saltbox of a structure that once housed Ontario civil service workers. The tiny lobby is equipped with a machine that checks people passing through the door for weapons. The building is given over exclusively to family law cases, and the security system in the lobby was installed a few years ago after a man shot and killed his estranged wife's lawyer in a fifth-floor corridor.

Carruthers began January 1985 with a tour of duty in the Queen Street building. He was assigned to hear motions on divorce, custody, and maintenance cases that hadn't yet reached court. He set up shop in an office on the fourth floor which had a noisy heating system and a portrait of Queen

Elizabeth looking glum. Carruthers sat behind a desk in one of his smart business suits — he dresses in stylish good taste — and dealt with a parade of lawyers who came through seeking variations on custody orders, alimony payments, privileges of access to children of a broken marriage. Carruthers needed about ten minutes to dispose of each matter. He was decisive and not inclined to put up with any second-guessing.

"Your lordship, my client is the wife in this action," one lawyer began. "She is very firmly opposed to her husband taking the child out on weekends."

"Why's that?" Carruthers asked.

"You have to understand, my lord, that the husband is of Czechoslovakian background."

"Okay," Carruthers said. "What's that got to do with it?"

"My client is afraid that if her husband is allowed to have the son for a weekend, he'll take him away to Czechoslovakia."

"Wait a minute," Carruthers said. "He's going to run off to *Czechoslovakia* when he can live in Canada? Impossible."

"That's her fear, my lord."

"It's not a reasonable enough fear for me to stop a father from having time with his own son," Carruthers said. "I'm not going to vary the access order."

"Thank you, my lord."

A man and woman entered the office. They were a separated husband and wife appearing without counsel. Carruthers' manner changed. Where he was brisk with the lawyers, he slowed down his pace with the man and woman. Both were in their early thirties. She wore a pink outfit and chewed gum. He was a strapping fellow, handsome in a square-jawed way.

Carruthers looked over the file on the couple's case.

"How are things going?" he asked.

"Fine," the woman snapped, nodding at her husband, "since *he* left."

"I see you're a policeman," Carruthers said to the man.

"That's right," the man answered in a low, hesitant voice.

"I don't want him to see my daughter," the woman said, talking rapidly. "She's eleven and she's terrified of her father."

"That's when I was drinking," the man said. "I'm better now. I took the cure at Donwoods Clinic for alcoholics."

"He looks pretty steady to me," Carruthers said to the woman.

"Well . . ." the woman said, leaving her doubt hanging over the conversation.

"I haven't touched a drop in three months," the man said, his voice still subdued.

"It's important for a young girl to have contact with her father," Carruthers said to the woman.

"Well . . ."

Carruthers guided the discussion for another fifteen minutes. The woman grew more conciliatory, the man less cowed. Her anger and his timidity began to recede.

"I'll tell you what," Carruthers said. "There's an empty office down the hall. Why don't you two use it for as long as you need to. Talk things out and see if you can't find an answer to this problem of visiting rights with your daughter. Come back here if you feel like it. I'll be around all day, okay? I don't want to impose my solution on you if you can figure out a better way. I'm no social worker. I'm only a judge."

The couple left, and Carruthers turned to other cases. By four o'clock he had heard the last of the motions. There was no sign of the policeman and his gum-chewing wife.

"I guess they resolved the thing," Carruthers said. "All they needed was someone to give them an overview of their situation and then work from there. They did what everybody should in a family law problem: talk it over without getting some fire-breathing lawyer in the picture."

On a Sunday in early February, Carruthers loaded his car and drove down Highway 401 to London for a scheduled three weeks of sittings. He packed running-shoes, small barbells, and tennis gear. When Carruthers hits a new town on the judicial circuit, he sends out word to the local bar that he's available for a couple of sets of tennis any night of the week. He always finds a game. He also packed his copy of the judges' guide to food and accommodation in Ontario towns and cities. It comes in a loose-leaf binder, and begins with a quote from the American food writer M. F. K. Fisher: "A well-made martini, correctly chilled and properly served, has been more often my friend than any two-legged creature," and it offers a constantly updated listing of the best hotels and restaurants around the province. The guide first appeared in 1979, and it was the joint brainstorm of Carruthers and Bill Anderson, another member of the Ontario High Court.

"We put it together because we were appalled at the lousy places some of our guys were using for eating and sleeping," Carruthers says. "Life is hard enough for trial judges on the road without upset stomachs and beds with rocks in them."

In London, he checked into the downtown Holiday Inn and was installed in the Summit Club, which is what the hotel calls its VIP section. "Not bad," Carruthers said. "Pay TV and Pears soap in the bathroom." He went to bed early Sunday night.

Next morning he walked the mile to London's courthouse. It's housed in a faceless skyscraper that was put up a few years ago to replace the aging but handsome former courthouse which carries on as a tourist attraction. Carruthers rode the elevator to the judges' office on the fourteenth floor and summoned the assistant court registrar. He was a heavy, bearded, slow-talking man, and he had bad news. Some civil actions that Carruthers was slotted to hear had been settled over the weekend. The list was temporarily stalled and empty.

"Well, what have you got for today?" Carruthers asked.

"This sexual assault might take a day and a half."

"Yeah."

"Or it might be a guilty plea."

"*Guilty plea*?" Carruthers stood out of his chair. "Holy Hannah, man, when did this come up?"

"Just now."

"If he pleads guilty, we'll be through in thirty minutes and I'll be left with nothing."

"That's true, your lordship."

Carruthers looked exasperated.

"Send the crown in here," he said. "And the defence counsel. And in the meantime get on the phone to counsel and rustle up some more cases. I didn't come down here to sit on my ass."

"Lots of cases," the assistant registrar murmured hesitantly. "Don't know if counsel are ready."

A few minutes later, two men in gowns, vests, and dickeys arrived at the office, the crown attorney and the defence counsel in the sexual assault case. Both were in their early thirties and had slender builds and eager expressions.

"What's happening with your man?" Carruthers asked the defence counsel.

"It came as a surprise to me, my lord," the defence counsel answered. "He told me just this morning that he wants to change his plea to guilty and I've been trying to explain the ramifications to him."

"From what I've read in the documents," Carruthers said, "it's not the sort of case that should be wasting the Supreme Court's time anyway. I know the newspapers get mad when they hear judges say so, but the fact is this doesn't look like a serious sexual assault."

The crown spoke up.

"On a scale of one to ten," he said, "this is about a one and a half."

"Well, talk it over," Carruthers said, "and I'll see everybody in court."

At ten-fifteen, the man charged with sexual assault was led into the courtroom. He had gaunt cheeks, sunken eyes, and

slumped shoulders. He seemed out of contact with his surroundings, and when the court clerk asked how he pleaded
to the sexual assault charge, his counsel answered for him.

"Guilty."

The crown attorney recited the case's facts. The accused
man had grown up in foster homes. He was thirty-six years
old and had never worked. He had psychiatric problems, not
serious enough to put him in an institution but defeating
enough to keep him on medication and disability benefits. At
the time of the assault, he was living in an apartment at the
back of a house which was owned and occupied by a single
mother with two daughters. One night the mother asked the
man to keep an eye on the youngest daughter, an eight-year-
old. He went into the little girl's bedroom, lifted her nightie,
and touched what the girl later described to police as her
"private spot". When she asked the man to stop, he went away.
The girl told her mother, who phoned the police.

"Let me say this for the accused, my lord," the defence counsel said. "At the time of this incident he had stopped taking
his medication for a reason no one can explain, least of all
the accused. This behaviour is quite foreign to him. He has
no criminal record, and as for the little girl, my lord, the
mother says she sees no bad effects on her as a result of what
happened."

Carruthers turned to the slumped, blank man in the prisoners' box.

"You've led a deprived life," he said. His voice had taken
on the inflections of a schoolteacher instructing a backward
child. "But you've also committed a serious offence. Do you
understand that?"

No expression crossed the man's face. He said nothing.

"Okay." Carruthers started again in his teacher's voice. "I
don't see that prison would help you or the little girl. I'm
putting you on a year's probation. But I'm going to insist on
several conditions. Understand?"

No reaction.

"You've got to stay away from the little girl and her family," Carruthers continued. "You've got to take your medication. You've got to see your psychiatrist every week. And you've got to keep appointments with your probation officer. You understand all of this?"

The man was frozen in silence.

"I'll explain it to him, my lord," the defence counsel said.

"I just hope you can," Carruthers said.

He looked troubled.

There were no more cases that day for Carruthers, and on his walk back to the Holiday Inn, he stopped at a Records On Wheels store. He headed for the jazz section. After ten minutes of flipping through the albums, he pulled out a remaindered record by Johnny Hodges and Charlie Shavers. "Only four bucks," he said. "Hell of a bargain. I knew something had to break right today." He bought the Hodges-Shavers album.

Jazz has been a passion for Carruthers since he was a kid growing up in the Parkdale and Swansea neighbourhoods in the west end of Toronto. When he was eleven, he found a job as an usher at the Club Kingsway, a dance spot that booked in touring American bands. "I go way back," he says. "I even heard the famous John Kirby little band with all the original guys." Carruthers kept his Club Kingsway job for almost twelve years. It helped pay his way through university and Osgoode Hall Law School.

"I was the first person in the family to graduate from university," he says. "My father had a disappointing life, always working at jobs that were never very satisfying. He was in the hospital when I was writing exams in first-year law school and I went to see him. 'Douglas,' he said, 'you're going to live the kind of life I wanted to live.' My father died a couple of days later. Those were the last words he spoke to me."

In his first years of practice, Carruthers specialized in motor vehicle litigation. "Not the most fascinating work," he says. "But I learned how to talk in a courtroom without making a fool of myself." By the time he reached his early forties, he was a partner in a firm concentrating on insurance cases. It was a demanding but satisfying field, and Carruthers hit his courtroom stride. Eventually, though, the demands outweighed the satisfactions.

"I felt like a halfback in the National Football League," he says. "The halfback can run through the line only so many times, then his knees go, his back starts to ache, the zip is lost. That was me. I'd had enough of combat, enough of always looking two weeks down the road, wondering what court I'd be in next, what kind of case I'd have to argue."

When the chance arrived to move to the bench, Carruthers grabbed it. For him, the date is set in stone. August 8, 1977.

In his room at the Holiday Inn, Carruthers opened a fat file and began to write on a pad of unlined paper. He had brought with him the documents and notes he needed to work on a judgment which he had reserved in a case argued before him in Toronto during the two weeks before his assignment in London. The case's details were tangled. A woman signed an offer to purchase a house in the tony Forest Hill section of Toronto for $425,000. As the deal moved toward its closing date, the purchaser's eagle-eyed husband discovered that a chunk of the house's property was an ancient road allowance which the City of Toronto owned. For years the city had neither noticed nor cared that its road allowance was being used by successive residents of the Forest Hill house. The city's interest was still minimal. But the prospective purchaser demanded an abatement on her purchase price. The vendor insisted that she close the deal at the agreed price, $425,000, and the transaction degenerated into a squabble which encompassed the vendor, the purchaser, two real estate firms, individual real estate agents, and assorted other parties. Carruthers needed to write forty pages of judgment before he could straighten out the mess. "I take a lot of pride in my writing," he says. "If I have to go slow to be clear, okay, that's how I write." In the real estate hassle, Carruthers' judgment made the frustrated purchaser into the principal winner.

When he wasn't picking his way through the writing of the judgment, Carruthers was answering the phone. Bud Estey called. So did Sonny Nemetz. Estey is a justice of the Supreme Court of Canada and Nemetz is Chief Justice of British Columbia. Both were calling about the same pressing subject, the meeting that summer of the Canadian Institute for Advanced Legal Studies at Trinity College in Cambridge, England.

The institute was founded in 1977 for the purpose of promoting education in law, legal science, and law reform. And every other July, about two hundred Canadian lawyers, judges, and legal academics swing over to Cambridge for a week of talks, seminars, formal dinners, and a little fun. Doug Carruthers has been the institute's president since its early days, and he is on the receiving end of a steady barrage of phone calls from men like Estey and Nemetz who sit on the institute's board.

"They get antsy as the conference comes closer," Carruthers says. "No problem. I can handle it."

Tight organization is one of Carruthers' long suits. When he was a practising lawyer, he took a lead in planning trips for the Advocates' Society, a high-powered club of Ontario litigation lawyers who take off every couple of years to spend several days checking out the workings of other common-law countries. Carruthers got the logistics of such excursions down pat.

"So one afternoon in 1978 I walk into the office of the chief justice of my court and get a surprise," Carruthers says. "He's sitting around with a bunch of other chief justices from all over the country trying to make a bunch of decisions about the Canadian Institute's first trip. I'm the kid in the room, but I say, hey, you're missing the boat on a few things here."

The chief justices paid attention, and, not long after, they arrived at the logical choice. They asked Carruthers to assume the institute's presidency. He's held the job ever since.

"I'm good on details," he says. "It isn't just making the agenda and rounding up the speakers and panelists. It's small things. When the lawyers and judges arrive in Cambridge with their wives and husbands, I've already got the flowers and the bottle of Scotch in their rooms."

The list of cases in London continued to drag. Trials were short, cases got delayed, and Carruthers grew restless with the inactivity. The restlessness turned to anger, and he gave an interview to Chip Martin, the court reporter for the *London Free Press*. "Maybe I'll go elsewhere in the province where I'm needed," Carruthers told Martin. "Everybody likes to feel needed." Carruthers let loose a complaint that the local litigation bar might be dragging its feet. Martin wrote his story, and it appeared on the front page of the next day's *Free Press*. "Judge demands fuller caseload or he'll quit city," the headline read. A couple of days later, business in Carruthers' courtroom began to pick up.

Lawrence Taylor's case came before Carruthers. He was a polite, soft-spoken man in his late twenties who carried a load of grief, and he wanted compensation from the hospital and the medical people whom he blamed for his burdens. Taylor was a widower. When his late wife, Veronica, was twelve years old, someone hit her on the head with a baseball bat. She developed epileptic seizures. In her early twenties, married and with a baby son, her seizures grew worse. Doctors at University Hospital in London thought her condition might be cured by a relatively new surgical technique, and in the late summer of 1980, Veronica Taylor went into the hospital for tests that would determine whether the technique could safely be used in her case. During the tests, on September 5, 1980, Veronica Taylor died. Lawrence Taylor sued, alleging negligence on the part of the defendants, and his suit named as defendants the hospital and everyone who took part in the tests on his wife—three doctors, two technicians, and a nurse.

Almost immediately after the case opened in front of Carruthers, he was surprised by two pieces of evidence. One was introduced into court on videotape. While Veronica Taylor was being put through the tests at University Hospital, the proceedings were recorded on tape. The same test was tried on Taylor three separate times. Its purpose was to discover if the proposed surgery might wipe away her memory function; if so, the surgery would be abandoned. The test called for one doctor to inject Taylor with a mixture of sodium amytal in a concentrated saline solution and for all the doctors in the room to put her reactions under close scrutiny. Each of the three tests lasted about fifteen minutes, and the tapes of the three were run in the courtroom for Carruthers while a woman psychologist, standing in the witness-box, described the events he was watching. The first two tests went by without anything unusual showing up on the screen. But during the third test, shortly after the doctor injected the solution into Veronica Taylor, she began to behave in strange and frightening ways. Moans broke from her mouth. Her arms and legs quivered. Her body thrashed in horrible convulsions.

"Wait a minute!" Carruthers broke in. "Stop the tape!"

He spoke to the woman psychologist in the witness-box.

"Pardon me," he said, "but in the first two tapes, did we see the patient injected?"

"Yes."

"Did we see her react the way I've just seen the woman react on the third tape?"

"No."

"Is this injection, the one on the third tape, what is really at issue in the case?"

"I guess so, my lord."

"Do you mean I've just seen that woman beginning to die?"

"Yes."

Carruthers was shaken.

"Holy Hannah!" he said later in his office. "I wasn't pre-pared for *that*."

The second surprising piece of evidence turned on the mat-ter of liability. There were two principal defence counsel in court representing two different insurers. One counsel spoke for the company that insured the hospital and its employees, and the second counsel spoke for the Canadian Medical Pro-tective Association, which insured the three doctors. The lia-bility issue was confused and centred on the procedure that led up to the injection of the fatal fluid. The doctor who injected Veronica Taylor didn't prepare the mix of sodium amytal and saline solution. He accepted the filled syringe from one of the technicians and shot Taylor with the injection that killed her. That series of events raised the question, Where did the fault lie? With the technician who presumably pre-pared the deadly mixture? With the doctor for failing to check the mixture? With some other party to the process? And another question: When the technician filled the syringe and handed it to the doctor, did she cross over the line between being an employee of the hospital and becoming a member of the doctors' team? The answers to the questions were essen-tial in deciding which insurer, the insurance company for the hospital and its employees or the CMPA for the doctors, would be most responsible in paying damages for Veronica Taylor's death. At that early point in the trial, no one had admitted liability, but the issue loomed over the proceedings.

Then came the surprising piece of evidence — an admis-sion, in fact — that broke the liability log-jam.

"My lord," the counsel for the hospital and its employees said in court, "I am admitting liability on the part of one party, the nurse."

The *nurse*?

After he adjourned court that day, Carruthers changed into his shorts and running-shoes and set off on a jog through Lon-don's streets. He knew that the plaintiff, Lawrence Taylor, was now home free. Taylor had an admission of liability on behalf of one of the defendants. That was all he needed to collect from at least one of the insurers, the company for the hospital and its employees. But the *nurse*? It seemed the hospital wasn't going to admit liability on the part of the technicians, and the doctors weren't admitting anything. Where did that leave the nurse? What had she done wrong during the tests?

Next morning in court, Carruthers raised the question with the counsel.

"I'm bothered about something," he said. "In fact, it caused me to run an extra mile last night. Yesterday, liability was accepted on behalf of the nurse. But, look, did I miss something? Did anybody tell the court what the nurse did that was so negligent?"

No! All three counsel spoke up, the counsel for the plaintiff and for the two defendant insurers. No, they said emphatically, Carruthers had not heard anything about the nurse's negligence.

"Thank God," Carruthers said. "I was beginning to wonder if I'd slept through part of the trial and didn't hear the answer."

He was never to hear the answer in court. Perhaps the nurse had been responsible for handing to the technician the ingredients that went into the mixture for the syringe and perhaps she'd chosen the wrong ingredients. Maybe she reached for a bottle of sodium chloride for the saline solution and picked a bottle with a stronger dose than the technician required. Maybe. But the answers to those perplexing questions didn't surface in the courtroom because, after three days of trial, the case was settled out of court.

Carruthers had been pushing the counsel to settle from the beginning. He thought it was cruel and ridiculous that Lawrence Taylor had waited five years from the time of his wife's death to receive compensation. Carruthers thought the sys-

tem had not worked for Taylor. He saw no need for the trial
to go on further if counsel could arrive at a settlement among
themselves. He talked to the lawyers in his office and he tried
to nudge them toward a bargain.

"These are top-notch counsel," he said while he waited for
the lawyers to negotiate. "These are reliable guys. They're
just doing the job for their clients. What's at fault in this kind
of case is something that can only be fixed by legislation.
There ought to be a law that says a hospital is solely responsible for patients like Mrs. Taylor who go into the place alive
and come out dead. That'd get rid of the protracted litigation
and disputes between doctors and technicians and the poor
nurses and everybody else as to who's to blame and who
should pay."

The lawyers arrived at a settlement which their clients
accepted. They returned to the courtroom and announced the
news. Lawrence Taylor would be compensated. That left
Carruthers with one more duty. Since the dead woman's son
was an infant, Carruthers had to approve the part of the settlement that affected him. How much was allotted to the
child? Fifty thousand dollars, the lawyers told Carruthers.

"That sounds appropriate to me," Carruthers said.

He hesitated a moment. Should he ask the lawyers how
much the total settlement added up to, the amount that Lawrence Taylor would receive as compensation for the death of
his wife? Since the case had been settled out of court, the
court might not, strictly speaking, have been entitled to such
information. For their part, the lawyers weren't volunteer-
ing a thing.

"Okay, I guess that's it," Carruthers said. He closed the
case.

"I was in my rights to ask them to tell me the whole figure," Carruthers said later in his fourteenth-floor office.
"That's because I should see if the infant, with his fifty thousand dollars, is getting a fair proportion of the total settle-

ment. But those lawyers are honest guys, trustworthy guys, and if they didn't want to tell me, I wasn't about to force them."

Rumours went around the courthose about the final settlement figure. Chip Martin, the *Free Press* court reporter, heard it came close to five hundred thousand dollars. A lawyer who'd been sitting in court on the last day said word was that the Canadian Medical Protective Association had agreed to chip in twenty per cent of the amount and the hospital's insurer swallowed the rest. Nobody was entirely sure what the nurse had done wrong and why she was the single party pinned with liability. In a sense it didn't matter — except to the nurse — since the larger problem had been resolved. Lawrence Taylor and his son, the man and the boy so tragically deprived, had at last received their measure of justice.

Carruthers loaded his car and drove back along the 401 and home.

Carruthers thought the case that came before him in the University Avenue Courthouse in early March promised a few skyrockets. It was a battle between a home owner and the insurance company that held the fire policy on his house. When the house burned down, the owner looked to the company for payment. Nothing doing, the company answered after its investigators filed their report. It accused the owner of either setting the fire himself or hiring an arsonist to do the job. The argument reached Carruthers for resolution, and, alas for him, it delivered none of the heat and battle he'd hoped for.

"This case is going thud every day," he said at the end of the first week in court. "It's the lawyers' presentations. They're dull."

But a peripheral matter intrigued Carruthers.

"One of the counsel," he said, "every time I look at him, I

think Shecky Green. He's a dead ringer for Shecky Green, the comedian you see on the Johnny Carson Show, places like that. Been around a long time, very funny guy, Shecky Green."

After two and a half weeks of trial, Carruthers delivered an oral judgment from the bench. He found in favour of the home owner, who was represented by the Shecky Green look-alike. Carruthers ruled that the insurance company had not satisfied the double onus that lay with it to prove that the fire had been deliberately set and that the insured had caused it to be deliberately set.

Later that afternoon, Carruthers and his wife flew to Aspen, Colorado, for a ski holiday, and on the first morning in Aspen, Carruthers poured a cup of coffee and settled in front of the television set. The Phil Donahue Show flicked on. Three guests were discussing their experiences with alcoholism. One was Grace Slick, the rock singer, another was a New York writer, and the third — Carruthers almost spilled his coffee — was Shecky Green.

"Hey," Carruthers called to his wife, "I've been looking at this guy for two and a half weeks and he's followed me all the way to Colorado."

The first witness to testify in the civil trial that Carruthers heard in the University Avenue Courthouse in mid-April was a man from New Zealand who explained the mysteries of the sport of rugger. He talked of scrums and hookers and tight head props. The second witness was a good-looking twenty-two-year-old named David Shannon who had once played rugger. He was the plaintiff in the case, and he testified from a wheelchair.

Almost four years earlier, at the beginning of the school year in September 1981, David Shannon had been taking part in a rugger practice at the University of Waterloo in Kitchener-Waterloo, Ontario. He was in the middle of an eight-man scrum playing the tight-head-prop position. That meant seven other players were lined up behind him as the battle over the ball began. Something went wrong in the scrum. Players piled on top of one another. Shannon came out of the scrum a quad-riplegic.

He explained in court that he had no feeling below his chest. He had taught himself to write by clenching a pencil between his teeth. He lived in a facility for disabled people in Thunder Bay, Ontario, and took classes in English literature at Lakehead University. He needed help to get through life's routines — combing his hair, shaving, brushing his teeth. He was suing the University of Waterloo and the coaches in charge of its rugger program for damages. When he testified, his voice was matter-of-fact and without a hint of bitterness.

"Practically speaking, it looks like there are only two questions to be answered," Carruthers said in his chambers after David Shannon's testimony. "How much money does that fine young man need to be looked after for the rest of his life and who's going to pay?"

The two lawyers in the case were apparently of the same mind. They sent a message to Carruthers' chambers on the morning of the trial's third day, April 17, asking that the beginning of court be delayed. They had things to talk about. Shortly before eleven, the lawyers showed up in person in the chambers, Paul Shannon for the plaintiff, a placid man with a handsome black moustache, no relation to his client, and Wendell Wigle for the defendants, big and genial, a basketball star at the University of Western Ontario in the 1950s. Both men wore their gowns, and they were accompanied by a third, ungowned lawyer. He was Bruce Lawson, short, compact, and poker-faced. Though Wigle was handling the defendants' presentation in court, Lawson seemed to be pulling the strings for their side behind the scenes.

"We've almost got the damages worked out, your lordship," Shannon told Carruthers.

"Well, why not?" Carruthers smiled. "A bunch of pros like you guys."

"The sticking point is the OHIP payments," Wigle said. "OHIP's already paid out forty-seven thousand dollars on the plaintiff's hospitalization, and it'll probably hit seventy-five thousand when all the bills are in."

"The defendants have made us an offer we can live with," Shannon explained. "But we're not going to pay the OHIP bill."

"We've got our figure and we're not going a nickel beyond it," Lawson said sharply. He sounded as if he'd put up a stone barrier.

"We'll take the figure as long as we don't have to pay anything over it," Shannon answered in a level voice.

Everyone in the room understood what Shannon meant. Either OHIP would have to waive repayment of the money it had spent on David Shannon or the defendants would absorb the costs. Bruce Lawson was having none of the second alternative.

"We've got a figure and that's the end of it," he said.

"Charlie Gordon's on his way down to the courthouse," Wigle said to Carruthers. Wigle's voice had an easy, mellow roll. He was playing good cop to Bruce Lawson's bad cop.

"Charlie Gordon." Carruthers repeated the name. "That man, he's been OHIP's claims manager for as long as I can remember."

"We've just been on the phone to him," Wigle said. "When he gets here, we'll see what he says about giving a pass on the money OHIP's owed."

"Keep me posted," Carruthers said, and as the men left the room, he reached for the phone.

"It's Doug Carruthers, Mary," he said into the receiver. "I think you'd better come up here and bring your list."

Mary Dayton runs the working life of each of the Supreme Court trial judges. She draws up the judges' assignments and moves them around the courthouses to cover the cases that are ready for trial. The job is akin to plotting a plan of battle — except that this battle never ends. The case list never runs out of cases.

"I'm down for four weeks on the Shannon trial," Carruthers told Dayton in his chambers. "But I think these guys are going to wind it up by tomorrow latest."

"I'll keep you busy," Dayton said. She's an elegant woman with an alive enthusiasm to her. "Uh-huh, there're some small civil cases I can get ready," she went on as she shuffled through a thick file folder. "And there's an attempted murder."

"Yeah?"

"Sounds nasty," Dayton said. "John Osler was trying it for three weeks before Christmas, but he had to call a mistrial. Jury heard some evidence it wasn't supposed to. This'll be the second time around."

"I'm game."

"That'll take you into June."

"Ah, it isn't like the old days," Carruthers said. "It used to be a judge'd get an assignment for a week's trial in Orangeville, the thing'd end on Tuesday and the judge would disappear for the rest of the week. Gone fishing."

"The problem now is there are too many cases in our court that shouldn't be there," Dayton said. She has a positive, ringing voice. "Criminal cases especially. If the Criminal Code says the accused is entitled to a trial in the Supreme Court if he chooses, we have to take him, even though he could just as easily be tried in a lower court. All those darned sexual assault cases."

"I had one of them in London."

"And drug cases." Dayton pressed her point. "The District Court has jurisdiction on them as well as us, but the cases keep coming to our court. Counsel like to use the Supreme Court because of the prestige, I suppose, and because they know they'll get good, consistent treatment. But I wish they'd stay away unless it's a really significant case on the law."

Dayton left to alert counsel in the new cases she was scheduling for Carruthers. Thirty minutes went by. Carruthers read that week's copy of the Ontario case reports and waited for word from Wigle, Lawson, and Shannon. Would Charlie Gordon, the man from OHIP, waive the government's claim for payment?

Apparently he did.

"We've got a settlement, your lordship," Wendell Wigle said when the three lawyers reassembled in Carruthers' chambers.

"Everybody happy?" Carruthers said.

"It looks good for my client," Shannon said.

None of the lawyers told Carruthers how much money David Shannon would receive for his care over the years, but a few weeks later, the figure turned up in a newspaper story. About one million dollars.

Before Carruthers left his chambers on the day of the Shannon settlement, he had one more visitor. Her name was Lynn Harris, tall, brunette, and beautiful. She was the secretary to the chief justice of the High Court, and she held down a second job as an assistant to Carruthers in his role as president of the Canadian Institute for Advanced Legal Studies. Harris was carrying a cookiegram with birthday greetings spelled across the top, and she'd caught Carruthers by pleasant surprise.

"Hey, great!" he burst out.

It was his fifty-fifth birthday.

On April 19 and 20, seven hundred Ontario litigation lawyers trooped to Roy Thomson Hall, the glitzy auditorium that is home to the Toronto Symphony, for the fourth annual Advocacy Symposium. Leading counsel from Canada, the United States, and England took part in panel discussions that analysed and illuminated the arts of courtroom argument. The tour de force of the two days came during a lengthy simula-

tion of a battle over a witness in a case. According to the fact
situation concocted for the occasion, the plaintiff, a twenty-
nine-year-old Mennonite farmer, had been left paralysed as
a result of a three-vehicle collision that had taken place on a
straight road on a clear, sunny day. The principal defendant,
who happened to be a lawyer, had ingested booze and drugs
shortly before the accident. He had swerved his car in an
unsuccessful attempt to miss a go-kart that had pulled out of
its lane without warning, and in the collision that followed,
the lawyer smashed into the farmer's car, paralysing the
farmer, killing the passenger in his own car, who was none
other than his estranged wife, and leaving himself unscathed.
The paralysed farmer, played by an actor in a wheelchair,
took the witness-box in the centre of the stage in Thomson
Hall while three senior Toronto counsel went at him in
examination-in-chief and cross-examination. The actor was
so convincing in his role that at one poignant moment he
moved the audience of emotion-proof lawyers almost to tears.
By a striking coincidence, one of the counsel in the make-
believe courtroom drama, acting for the tipsy, drugged-up
lawyer, was Wendell Wigle, the man who had been before
Carruthers earlier in the week on the real-life Shannon case
with the young quadriplegic who wasn't play-acting in his
wheelchair. And the judge who presided over the pretend case
in Thomson Hall was Mr. Justice Douglas Carruthers himself.

At the end of the performance, after Wigle had struggled
through a valiant and intelligent but largely fruitless cross-
examination of the actor-plaintiff, Carruthers had his turn
at centre stage. He unloaded for the audience of courtroom
lawyers a view of the cross-examining process that had been
simmering inside his head for a very long time. His tone was
light, but he made it plain that he wasn't kidding.

"For the last eight years," he said, "the thing that has struck
me most about the trials I've been involved in is the absolute
insistence of ninety-nine-point-nine per cent of counsel to

cross-examine in situations where they shouldn't. I have tried in how many ways to tip off counsel that they oughtn't to bother with cross-examination. 'Do you really have to cross-examine?' I say. 'Do you *have* anything in the way of cross-examination?' And they look at me as if I'd come from Mars. 'Of course,' they say, 'that's my job. I always cross-examine. I'm paid to do it.' I think lawyers get up in the morning and say to themselves, 'Who should I cross-examine today?' But it isn't always necessary. In fact, it can work against a lawyer's interests and against his client's best interests. In a situation like the one in front of us today, that witness shouldn't be touched with a ten-foot pole except in a very restricted circumstance. The best advice I can give about cross-examination is this — don't bother unless it's absolutely necessary."

When Carruthers finished, everyone in the hall applauded, even the actor in the wheelchair.

"Man!" Carruthers said afterwards, "It felt good to get *that* off my chest."

By ten-thirty on each morning of the trial, the young black man in the grey suit would lean his head against the glass at the back of the prisoners' box in the courtroom on the fourth floor of the University Avenue Courthouse. He wore his hair in a modified Afro. After thirty minutes of being pressed against the glass, his Afro would make a small oily circle. The circle got thicker as the day's hearing went into the afternoon. But every morning through the weeks of the trial which began in mid-May, the glass would be clean until the young man once again began to tip his head against it. The young man was on trial for armed robbery and attempted murder, and his case was the nasty business that Mary Dayton had lined up for Carruthers to take care of.

The black man's name was Lindel Payne. He was medium

height, muscular, handsome, and sleepy-eyed. He had a co-
accused in the prisoners' box, another black man, scrawny
and street-wise, named Duane Lyons. Payne was twenty-five,
Lyons was twenty, and the cops thought they had a solid case
against the two of them. According to the police version of
events, Payne and Lyons drove to the Rosewood Food Market in the Metro Toronto borough of Scarborough just before
midnight on September 22, 1983. One of the market's family
of proprietors, a twenty-four-year-old Korean-Canadian
named Sun-Gu Kim, packed the day's cash receipts into a
briefcase. The receipts added up to almost ten thousand
dollars. Someone — Payne, the police theory went — entered
the market. He had a gun in his hand. He grabbed the briefcase
from Kim, who turned to run. Payne, if the police were right
in pinning the violence on him, shot at Kim. He missed. He
shot again. The second bullet hit Kim in the back, a quarter
of an inch to the right of his spine. Payne flew out of the store.
He and Lyons sped away in the car. Both men were known to
the police from previous crimes, and it wasn't long before
they were charged with the shooting and robbery at the
Rosewood Food Market.

Three days before their trial began in Carruthers' court,
Payne was sentenced by another judge to twelve years in penitentiary for a crime that he'd committed after the food market holdup. It too involved gun-play, but when Payne pulled
the trigger this time, the person he shot was himself. The
incident grew out of Payne's try at getting even with a drug
dealer for some real or imagined slight. He put the arm on
the dealer, and pistol-whipped and robbed him. In the course
of the mayhem, Payne's gun went off and a bullet caught him
in the hand. Someone else, maybe the dealer, whapped Payne
over the head with an iron bar. He passed out, and when he
came to, he was arrested, charged, tried, convicted, and sentenced. Duane Lyons wasn't along with Payne on the drug-
dealer fiasco, but he had a criminal record of his own. At the
time of the food market trial, he was serving two years for

beating up his girlfriend. His choice of weapon had been a telephone cord.

Carruthers supervised the selection of the jury, Payne leaned his Afro against the glass of the prisoners' box, and the trial got under way. The crown presented its case in orderly fashion. Sun-Gu Kim testified, nervous and whispery-voiced, and so did a variety of policemen, doctors, and employees of the Rosewood Market. The evidence seemed to point to Payne as the shooter, but, despite all the blood and horror of the crime, the trial had a pale and lifeless feel. The principal tension came from the prisoners' box. Something was up between Payne and Lyons, and on a Thursday late in May, when Lyons took the stand, the reason for the strain was revealed to everyone in the courtroom. Lyons had a surprise.

"I was just along for the ride," he testified. "I didn't know nothin' about a gun. I didn't even get out of the car."

Payne leaned forward in the prisoners' box.

"I had no notion there was gonna be a robbery or a shootin'," Lyons went on. "I was out for a ride, that's all I know."

Payne put his hands over his face.

"Lindel done it all on his own," Lyons said. "He shot the man and I didn't know he done it till he came runnin' out of the place."

Sniffle, sniffle. Payne was crying in the prisoners' box.

Lyons' testimony finished the day, and guards escorted him and Payne back to the West End Detention Centre, where they were being held during the trial.

The next day, Friday, Lyons returned to the witness-box. He had another surprise for the court.

"What I said yesterday," he began, "it wasn't right. I been up all night worrying about saying my friend Lindel did it. He didn't do the shooting and robbery. Somebody else did it."

Who?

"Winston Charles, a guy both me and Lindel know, he shot the man and took the money."

Where's Winston Charles now?

"Nobody knows where he's at, but Winston did it all right."

Carruthers adjourned court for the weekend.

"Something very funny must be going on out at the West End Detention Centre," he said.

On Monday morning, Duane Lyons was back in the witness-box.

"What I said Friday, that wasn't the truth," Lyons told the court, now reeling under the changes in story. "What I said Thursday, *that* was the truth."

How about Winston Charles?

"Winston doesn't know nothin' about the robbery," Lyons said. "Lindel done it all on his own, the shooting and everything, like I said Thursday."

Why did Lyons tell another story on Friday?

"I only said what I did 'cause I got scared. I been threatened out there at the West End, and my girlfriend, she got threats same as me. I had to tell the story about Winston, but now I'm speakin' the truth. Lindel is the one."

Over the next couple of days, new and strange witnesses were introduced to the trial. They were prisoners from the West End Detention Centre. Crown and defence counsel called them to testify about events at the jail. Had Payne threatened Lyons? Were there bad feelings between the two men? What sort of guy was Payne? Who was to be believed?

One of the witnesses from the West End was a young white man who had an upper-middle-class air. He also had a dozen convictions on break-and-enter charges.

"Lindel's a real nice guy," the white man testified. "Whenever I see him, he's reading the Bible."

Several members of the jury looked like they might fall out of their chairs in disbelief, and Carruthers steamed with impatience.

"Just a minute," he said to counsel. "If you're planning on emptying Metro West Detention and lining up half of them along one wall of this courtroom and half along the other wall while they debate whether Mr. Payne reads the Bible or not, you'd better rethink the idea. It's a collateral issue, what went on at the jail, and I don't think anybody's doing themselves any good by getting into this brawl."

The witnesses finished their testimony, the counsel made their addresses to the jury, and Carruthers began his jury charge. He had a pair of tricky matters to cover. A judgment in a case from several months earlier had established that, in order to sustain a conviction on a charge of attempted murder, the crown had to prove beyond a reasonable doubt that the alleged perpetrator possessed an intent to kill. Until that judgment was handed down, it had been sufficient for the crown to show that the perpetrator caused bodily harm and that he had been reckless as to whether death ensued. The new law was more narrow and refined, and Carruthers explained the difference to the jury in careful detail. He also dealt with the difficult question of Duane Lyons' involvement in the crime. In order for Lyons to be as guilty as Payne, the jury must conclude that Lyons shared Payne's intent to kill. And in order for the jury to infer such sharing on the part of Lyons, it would have to find proven facts to show that Payne had told Lyons he was going into the food market with the intention of shooting to kill. But there didn't seem to be anything on which to base such an inference, and Carruthers made it clear that, for himself, he couldn't see the necessary sort of evidence in the testimony of the many witnesses. Carruthers was bold in advancing his views, and his charge had a shaping clarity in a case that had ended in a blizzard of semi-comic confusion.

The jury retired, and when it came back with its verdict, it found Duane Lyons innocent of the charges.

Lindel Payne, the jury decided, had intended to kill Sun-

Gu Kim when he fired into Kim's back. He was guilty of attempted murder and armed robbery.

Before Carruthers sentenced Payne, he spent an evening digesting a pre-sentence report on the man. He learned that Payne had been born in Jamaica in 1959. A grandmother raised him and his brothers and sisters after their mother moved to Toronto. Payne followed north in 1975. He put in two months in school in Toronto. Maybe he had a learning disability. Maybe he was discouraged from going to school by his mother. Whatever the reason, he dropped out of classes, and over the following years he worked a total of seventeen months, mostly in restaurants. The rest of the time he was in and out of trouble, in and out of the courts, in and out of the company of lady-friends whom he had no trouble attracting.

On sentencing day, Monday, June 24, Payne was escorted into court with handcuffs on his wrists and leg irons around his ankles.

"This guy's got a temper," one of the attendants told another.

"Lindel Payne is an incorrigible and violent man," the crown attorney said in his address on sentence to Carruthers. The crown, a hefty, assured man named Rob Nuttal, didn't conceal his contempt for Payne. He spoke for thirty minutes and he described Payne's crime more than once as "an extremely cowardly act". He wanted a tough sentence.

Payne leaned his Afro against the glass in the prisoners' box.

His counsel, David Cohn, was a slim, dark, gentle-voiced man in his early thirties.

"Mr. Payne's mother rejected him at an early age," Cohn said.

"So it's the mother's fault?" Carruthers broke in.

"Mr. Payne would like to work," Cohn went on. "He would like a permanent job. He has shown initiative during the time he's been incarcerated. He's teaching himself to read for the first time. He reads slowly. He reads the Bible. He has a girlfriend who wants to marry and support him."

"From the evidence I've heard in this trial," Carruthers said, "all the guys who Payne hangs out with, they have no jobs and they're supported by girlfriends."

"I meant emotional support, my lord," Cohn said.

Payne's Afro rubbed into the glass.

"Stand up, Mr. Payne," Carruthers said.

Carruthers had a few thoughts to let the court in on before he passed sentence. For some of the time over the next several minutes, he spoke directly to Payne. "What possesses a person to take a loaded gun on what was a planned robbery and to shoot a man in the back who has done nothing—absolutely *nothing*—to jeopardize your life or even to preclude you from carrying out the robbery?" And for some of the time, he seemed to be addressing a wider audience beyond the courtroom. "I'm beginning to think we're losing our grip, we're losing control. Hard-working, dedicated people like the man in this case who was shot in his own store wonder whether it is worth it to work so hard when they see how easy it is for others to profit by resorting to violence against them." And then he'd switch back to tearing a strip off Payne. "The only thing I can see that you have ability at is persuading women to support you. If there's a classic person about whom it could be asked, 'How did he get into this country and how did he get to stay in this country?' it's you."

Carruthers reached the moment of sentencing. He levelled a stern look at Payne and said he was giving him twenty-six years in the penitentiary.

The guards steered Payne out of the prisoners' box, the leg irons clanking as he shuffled away, and all that remained behind of Lindel Payne was the oily smudge on the glass at the back of the box.

In his chambers, Carruthers changed from his gown into street clothes. He had a couple of reservations about the last minutes in the courtroom.

"Maybe I should have prepared some written remarks for

the sentencing," he said. "Maybe talking off the top of my head isn't good enough."

The other reservation had to do with the length of the sentence he'd given Payne.

"I was thinking of life," he said. "But, I don't know, the Court of Appeal might have thought that was too much."

He slipped on his natty beige jacket.

"Well, at least I sent out a message to the bad guys," he said. "The public needs reassurance these days that the courts are sticking up for the good guys."

Carruthers walked out of his chambers. His judicial year was almost over.

Sandy MacPherson

In his first year in the blissful community of Saanichton on Vancouver Island, Sandy MacPherson grew camellias and roses and rhododendrons. He bought an Olivetti word processor and made a start at feeding his memoirs into the machine. He and his wife, Dorothy, pitched in to organize the neighbours for a fight against the developer who was planning a marina in the bay behind Saanichton. And British Columbia's Department of the Provincial Secretary recruited him to resolve a falling out among the board members of the Victoria Symphony. It was a good and active time for a man who'd just retired, and it was a long stretch in distance and style from the life he'd led for twenty-one years as Mr. Justice Murdoch Alexander MacPherson, Jr., of the Saskatchewan Court of Queen's Bench.

"I left the bench because I'd been playing God long enough," MacPherson said one sunny spring afternoon in 1985 as he sat in the living-room of the Saanichton house. "The power of a high court judge is the kind of thing that can go to your head, and I was beginning to notice an arrogance in myself that I didn't think was there before. It was time to go."

MacPherson and his wife sold their house in Regina in June 1984 and headed west to Vancouver Island.

55

"I rejoined the human race," MacPherson went on. "In those last years on the bench, my life had got so insulated that I couldn't tell the genuine people from the people who flattered me just because I was a judge. Now it doesn't matter. I hardly ever wear a tie out here, just corduroys and a sweater, and everybody calls me Sandy. I'm a happy guy."

He looks the part. He's a big man with a hearty, carrying voice. He has a trim moustache and an erect bearing that are leftovers from his five and a half years of army service during the Second World War. Bonhomie comes naturally to him. He likes to weave a story, and he doesn't mind calling a spade a spade. There are good guys in the world and bad guys. Mac-Pherson will name both. He's fond of Scotch whisky, trips to Europe, and photography. For the latter, he has an exquisite talent. The Saanichton house is hung with mounted enlargements of MacPherson's haunting black-and-white studies of European villages and the people who live in them. He's a man who is made up of startling combinations of contrasts. Soldier and artist. Gardener and crusader. Outrage and compassion. And it is no doubt this mix that helped to make him probably the most respected trial judge in his generation of Saskatchewan jurists.

"Dief put me on the bench," MacPherson explained in his Saanichton living-room. "I was always a John Diefenbaker man. Backed him at the 1956 leadership convention. That may seem odd when you consider my father was very important in Saskatchewan politics and he got up at the convention and nominated Davie Fulton for leader. But going on the bench was never in the plans I had for my life until the day in May 1961 when Dief was prime minister and he phoned me out of the blue. He asked if I'd accept an appointment to the Saskatchewan Court of Appeal. Hell, I didn't want the Appeal Court!"

The conversation, as MacPherson recalled it, continued with his suggestion to Diefenbaker of an alternative.

"Sir, there's a vacancy on the Queen's Bench," MacPherson told Diefenbaker.

The prime minister was surprised. "You'd prefer the Queen's Bench to the Court of Appeal?"

"You were a trial lawyer all your professional life," MacPherson said. "Would you have wanted to go to the Court of Appeal when you were forty-four?"

"I think not."

"Sir, I'm a forty-four-year-old trial lawyer."

"Very well," Diefenbaker said. "Queen's Bench it is."

"I'm honoured."

MacPherson sat in the Saanichton house and laughed at the memory of the old conversation.

"I liked sweating over a live body," he said. "That's why I couldn't go to the Court of Appeal. Their work comes in on a wheelbarrow, all those pounds of transcripts they have to sit and read and ponder. Not for me. But I don't know where I got the nerve to speak the way I did on the phone to the prime minister of the country."

In fact, nerve was second nature to MacPherson. So were all his other seemingly contradictory characteristics, and he applied each of them to the trials he heard and the judgments he wrote in his long tenure on the bench. He was playful and he was tough-minded. Compassionate and angry. He could be scornful, and sometimes he let loose his romantic streak.

The playful MacPherson: the skinny-dipping case.

In the spring of 1977, three young men appeared before MacPherson by way of stated case on appeal from their convictions for being nude in a public place contrary to section 170(1) (a) of the Criminal Code. The three had been engaging in a little swimming *au naturel* on a sand bar in the South Saskatchewan River on a summer day in 1975 when other citizens arrived for a splash in the same part of the river. The newcomers were equipped with bathing suits, and when their eyes fell on all the exposed genitalia across the way, they were shocked and appalled. Charges were laid and convictions followed in a lower court.

Two thoughts went through MacPherson's mind as he contemplated the facts of the case.

The first had to do with the origins of section 170(1) (a) of the Criminal Code. Parliament had enacted it years earlier specifically as a weapon against the Doukhobors and their penchant for stripping in courtrooms and other places where full-dressed decorum ought to prevail.

"I knew all about that," MacPherson said in Saanichton. "Some Doukhobors used to disrobe in front of our house in Regina back in the early 1930s when my father was the province's attorney general. Mother had a hard time keeping us children away from the windows."

The other thought was even more personal.

"Not long before the 1977 case came up," MacPherson said, "I'd been down in the Maritimes. It was lovely weather and we were in a remote spot by the water and, hell, I did what was natural. I went skinny-dipping."

MacPherson wrote his judgment.

"It cannot be an offence to swim in the nude at a lonely place in Canada in summer," he held. "That is part of the pleasure of summer in Canada, particularly to young males. If somebody comes along unexpectedly or if the swimmer misjudges the loneliness of the place, the act cannot suddenly become criminal."

MacPherson quashed the convictions against the three young men.

The tough-minded, scornful, angry MacPherson: the Thatcher custody case.

In late 1979 and the first half of 1980, after Colin Thatcher and his wife JoAnn separated but before he was convicted of murdering her, the two battled in court over the custody of their three young children. The case was a hot potato and many judges were reluctant to handle it. They were too aware of the history and gossip about Colin Thatcher: son of a former Liberal premier of Saskatchewan, a Conservative member of the provincial legislature, a wealthy rancher and high-profile citizen, an unfaithful husband whose mental and physical violence had driven his wife from the family home, an abrasive man with a long memory for those who crossed him. Some judges disqualified themselves from hearing the custody case. It eventually fell to MacPherson, and he got his fill of it. He heard it once. Then he heard it all over again.

"I heard it," he said in Saanichton, "and it sickened me."

The first time around, the custody trial lasted two days in the autumn of 1979. Compared with what was to follow, it was a relatively calm proceeding. Still, Colin Thatcher and his counsel, Tony Merchant, managed to get MacPherson's wind up with a handful of ploys that the judge regarded as sleazy.

The first ploy surfaced when Thatcher and Merchant announced they would call the elder of the two Thatcher sons as a witness for Colin's side in the case. The boy's name was Greg and he was fourteen years old. "To make the lad a partisan in a contest between his own parents," MacPherson said, "that was a dreadful idea." Greg did not testify. MacPherson forbade it.

MacPherson wasn't any happier with a piece of testimony that emerged during the trial. Colin Thatcher, it seemed, had attached a newspaper clipping to the door of the refrigerator in the house where he was living with the three children. "Man ordered to pay $80,000 for affair with friend's wife," read the headline on the clipping. The story was from Rhode Island, but the implications were clear to everyone in the house since it was already a matter of common gossip that

JoAnn Thatcher had carried on a brief romance with a man named Ron Graham who happened to be Colin Thatcher's best buddy.

"Thatcher wanted to show the kids that their mother was an adulteress, that's why he put it up," MacPherson said of the clipping. "It was most evil."

Nor did Tony Merchant do his client's cause much good in his closing argument at the trial when he evoked a comparison of Thatcher and MacPherson as men who had grown up in Saskatchewan burdened by the responsibilities that came to them, unasked, as the sons of prominent and successful men.

"You don't bring the judge's personality into a case," MacPherson said. "It was disgusting."

MacPherson took a week to compose his judgment, and on November 27, 1979, he produced it. The judgment was lucidly written, sensibly thought out, and bound not to please Colin Thatcher, who expected to receive custody of all three children. He got one, the older boy, Greg, who had indicated to MacPherson's satisfaction that he preferred his father's care. The other two children, Regan and Stephanie, not yet teenagers, were placed with their mother. MacPherson didn't mince any words in explaining the reasons for his decision.

"The wife," he wrote, "is a much warmer, more affectionate and sympathetic person than the husband. I venture the thought that his lack of these qualities, his failure to appreciate the wife, caused the marriage breakdown. Adultery is rarely the cause, it is the result."

With the judgment, MacPherson thought he had forever put the Thatcher case and its unpleasantness out of his life. He was wrong. In the spring of 1980, he and his wife set off on a leisurely trip through Greece, and when he returned home, he took a long trial in Yorkton, near the Manitoba border. The trial stretched through May and June. While he was occupied, so was Colin Thatcher. He was refusing to obey MacPherson's order granting custody of the second son,

Regan, to JoAnn Thatcher, and the dispute eventually wound back into the courts for another trial. MacPherson viewed Thatcher's duplicity from a distance. But one day in late June, over in Yorkton, he received a phone call that dumped the Thatcher mess in his lap once again.

"Sandy, it's your duty to take this second trial," the voice on the other end of the line said to MacPherson. The speaker was Fred Johnson. He was chief justice of the Court of Queen's Bench.

MacPherson protested. He'd had his turn at the case, and that was enough acrimony for him.

"We think you should do it," Johnson said.

Were other Queen's Bench judges shying away from Thatcher for one reason or another? MacPherson thought so.

"Oh hell," he said on the phone, "I'll take it if that's what you want."

The trial, which was to determine once again the custody of twelve-year-old Regan Thatcher, covered eleven hard and terrible days in July 1980. "It was beyond bitterness," MacPherson later said of the hearing. "It was the exercise of force, the feeling of violence." It wasn't difficult to pin down the origins of the force and violence. Colin Thatcher was the man who unleashed the cruel emotions in the courtroom.

As before, Thatcher insisted that his older son, Greg, take the witness stand. Tony Merchant, Thatcher's counsel, put the matter to MacPherson. The judge hit the roof.

"Now this trial is going to go down in the life of that child for his whole life," he said in court to Merchant. "But your instructions are nevertheless to bring him in here to call his mother names in the sense of she's the one who broke up the family."

"Well . . ." was as far as Merchant got.

"If I were acting for Mrs. Thatcher and you put the boy in the box," MacPherson galloped on, "I would be interested to know how much he knows about the peccadillos of his father inasmuch as he is so concerned about the chastity of his mother. If Mrs. Thatcher's council were to ask him, well, 'Who are you talking about, your mother and her boyfriends? What do you know about the girlfriends of your father?' Isn't that nice?"

"Well . . ."

"Isn't that lovely to raise with a fifteen-year-old?" Mac-Pherson thundered. "I think it is absolutely abhorrent for a father to claim to have the best interest of that child at heart to want to bring that child into this dreadful piece of litigation."

Nevertheless, Merchant had his way. Greg Thatcher took the witness stand. He testified for three hours and he told stories about his mother that were devastating. In one, he described a physical encounter with JoAnn Thatcher in which, Greg said, his mother swore at him, stomped on his bare feet, and sank her teeth into his neck. But there was another quality, apart from shock value, to Greg's tales — they were almost wholly unbelievable. "That loving mother doing a thing like that," MacPherson said. "Ridiculous." Mrs. Thatcher's counsel recognized that the boy's testimony rebounded against Colin Thatcher and he felt a sadness for Greg's predicament. On the counsel's cross-examination, he didn't bother to quiz Greg about his father's girlfriends. The boy had been through enough. Besides, earlier witnesses had already had something to say about Colin Thatcher's womanizing.

"My lord," Tony Merchant said to MacPherson after Greg had stepped down from the stand, "I ask that Regan Thatcher be allowed to testify."

"Are you going to destroy this family utterly?" MacPherson was stunned at the audacity of Merchant and Thatcher. "The purpose of the father, as I understand it, is to keep the family together."

"Yes, my lord," Merchant answered.

"It seems to me I'm shocked enough from what I heard from this boy today," MacPherson said. "Now am I going to hear more of it?"

MacPherson heard no more. Not from Regan at any rate. He forced Merchant and Thatcher to back down on calling the younger boy.

But MacPherson sat through much more testimony. Both sides paraded witnesses to the stand. JoAnn Thatcher's witnesses were convincing. Colin Thatcher's came up short in the conviction department. Accusations and recriminations flew around the courtroom, and the atmosphere, as Mac-Pherson later characterized it, was "of hatred, of oppression, of distrust". And he knew in his head and heart who was poisoning the air. Colin Thatcher.

MacPherson made his conclusion clear when the trial finally ended and he turned to the task of writing his judgment.

"I have no doubt," he wrote, "that the cause of the breakdown of the marriage and of the lengthy and expensive litigation was, and is, the personality, actions and attitude of Mr. Thatcher. He is articulate, domineering and intimidating. As the evidence developed in this trial, it became more and more apparent to me, indeed it was overwhelming, that he was determined to win custody of his son Regan by any means at all."

MacPherson was normally a swift writer. But for the Thatcher judgment, he put in three and a half weeks of sweat and time and effort. When he finished, he had produced a strikingly human document. It was a judgment that read like the script for a heart-breaking piece of theatre. It was a judgment that within a year was being studied in Canadian law schools. It was a judgment that blew the whistle on Colin Thatcher.

The judgment's immediate thrust was to order Regan Thatcher into his mother's custody and to forbid both Colin and Greg Thatcher from having any communication with the younger boy for a whole year. But along the way, MacPherson included in the judgment small and vivid vignettes of appraisal of all the feature players in the grim story.

Of Greg Thatcher, MacPherson wrote: "He is a tall, handsome, intelligent boy. He testified for well over a half day. He said nothing at all critical about his father. He rejects the mere suggestion of wrongdoing on his father's part. In many ways, he reflected his father's personality — arrogant, proud, vain, even belligerent. For his mother, he showed scorn, contempt and disrespect."

Of his own role in the saga, MacPherson wrote: "At the time I wrote my earlier judgment, I possessed the hope that this prominent and intelligent and wealthy and well-educated couple would try to find a way to solve their problems. It was for that reason that I did not treat the husband as critically as I felt then justified. So much for the judge as social worker."

Of the breakdown in the Thatcher family, he wrote: "In a normal home with children in our society, it is the mother who is the mainstay, the planner of everything. The mother has always been the object of love because of her devotion and sacrifice to her family. When, therefore, a mother suddenly abandons her home, it is easy for a man such as Mr. Thatcher to destroy her in the minds of her immature and impressionable children. The natural love for the mother evaporates because in their minds, she has become unworthy. She gets no second chance because she presents her case to closed minds.

"This is exactly what happened in the Thatcher family. This foolish man did so much in such a diabolical fashion that it all becomes almost unbelievable. The sons closed ranks and excluded her. It is important to note that Mr. Thatcher left his sons in complete ignorance of his own adultery."

And on the future of Regan, the son who was the subject of

the desperate litigation, MacPherson wrote: "If the child is to be saved from becoming the image of his father, only his mother can do it. She wants to try. She has had no chance. That has been denied her for nearly a year by the actions of her husband. . . ."

MacPherson handed down his judgment on August 11, 1980. At last, he thought, he was done with Colin Thatcher. MacPherson was wrong for a second time.

Not long after the judgment, Thatcher slipped young Regan off to Palm Springs, California, where he owned a condominium. He enrolled the boy in school under another name. JoAnn Thatcher didn't know what had become of Regan. Neither did MacPherson. All he understood was that the boy had vanished and that his order had been flouted. He was concerned and furious.

In England, when a child goes missing, it's a custom of the judiciary to summon the press and ask its help in tracing the lost boy or girl. That practice has never been common in Canada, but MacPherson didn't hesitate to blaze new trails.

"If Mr. Thatcher is the author of this disappearance of Regan," he told the reporters who gathered in his courtroom in early September, "he may be guilty of contempt of court because my order of the eleventh of August provided he would not interfere with his wife's custody for a period of a year."

Still Regan didn't show up. JoAnn Thatcher's lawyer asked MacPherson for an order directing Colin Thatcher to answer questions under oath about Regan's whereabouts. MacPherson granted the order. But Thatcher put up a stone wall at the examination.

"I refuse to answer on the grounds it may incriminate me," he said to all of the key questions from his wife's lawyer.

MacPherson made a move behind the scenes. He asked Chief Justice Fred Johnson to approach the province's attorney general. It was time, MacPherson argued, for the crown to hit Colin Thatcher with charges of criminal contempt. Other

judges made the same pitch, and Johnson didn't need much
persuading. Everyone favoured the tactic — except the attorney general. He was Roy Romanow, a member of Saskatchewan's NDP government, and he apparently backed off for two
reasons. One was legal: he doubted whether there was enough
evidence against Thatcher to get a conviction on criminal contempt. And the other was partly political: he didn't think it
was proper or appropriate for the government to bring criminal action against a member of the sitting Conservative Opposition in the provincial legislature.

MacPherson's custody order, directing that Regan Thatcher
be delivered to his mother, hung in the air. The months passed.
Regan remained in Palm Springs. JoAnn Thatcher remarried,
and, in the end, her son never came to live in her new home.
She lost the boy. And two years later, in the early evening of
January 21, 1983, she lost her life. Someone beat and shot
her in the garage of her house across the street from the Saskatchewan Legislative Buildings in Regina.

On the night of the murder, MacPherson was at his home
in another part of Regina, alone and waiting to drive to the
airport, where he would meet his wife Dorothy, who was arriving back from a visit to Vancouver. His brother Donald, a
leading Saskatchewan lawyer, phoned him with the news of
the killing. Donald was shaken. "Pull the blinds," he told
Sandy MacPherson, "don't go outside." If Colin Thatcher had
killed his ex-wife and if Thatcher had a hit list of enemies,
then Mr. Justice MacPherson had probably moved into the
number one spot. When his brother hung up, MacPherson
put in a call to a Regina police inspector. He wanted a little
professional advice. The inspector was out, and while
MacPherson waited for him to phone back, he considered his
situation.

"My army training came into action," he recalled in the
Saanichton house. "I went upstairs and got out an old shotgun of mine and some ammunition that was just as old. I

hadn't touched the thing in ten years, but I laid it out on the living-room floor and waited. If some crazy bastard was coming after me, I was damned well going to be ready for him."

No one came.

The next night, he and Dorothy went to a symphony concert at Regina's Centre of the Arts. Former Saskatchewan premier Allan Blakeney, moving through the crowd at intermission, came up to MacPherson.

"Are you travelling with a bodyguard?" he asked.

MacPherson thought Blakeney was referring to Dorothy. He thought the ex-premier was making a small joke. Then he realized it was no joke.

MacPherson told him the story of the previous night, about the shotgun on the living-room floor.

"I don't blame you," Blakeney said.

"Isn't that just a delightful state of affairs?" MacPherson said in Saanichton, looking back. "A former premier and a high court judge in a province in Canada in 1983 talking about arming yourself against an invader?"

MacPherson shook himself in disgust.

"Awful," he said. "And the thing is that none of it might have happened, that poor woman might still be alive, if the custody order of mine had been enforced."

The romantic MacPherson: the case of the Little Sparrow.

Courtrooms are too concerned with gritty reality to permit anything as imaginative and exaggerated as romance to enter. But Sandy MacPherson was just unorthodox enough as a judge to keep an appreciative eye out for a case that touched the heart. And, as background and example, he carried with him the precedent of the great romantic adventure of his own life, an episode that was unrivalled outside the most indulgent inventions of the Hollywood studios.

It centred on his meeting with the woman who became Mrs. MacPherson. She was born Dorothy Borutti, and from the age of six she grew up in a jewel of a French resort town called Le Touquet. Her parents ran a hotel in the town which is exquisitely settled on the Canche River where it meets the English Channel. On an especially clear day, a resident of Le Touquet can see the green smudge of England on the horizon. Dorothy's childhood was filled with good times until the day the German invaders arrived in 1940. The war years turned tough for the Borutti family and Dorothy's father died during the German occupation. She vowed that when freedom finally came to Le Touquet, she would kiss the first Allied soldier who reached the town.

It looked as if she'd have a long wait. After D-Day, the British, American, and Canadian troops chased the Germans through Calais and Boulogne. Le Touquet, over on the Channel, was removed from the mainstream of the fighting. Its German troops cleared out on the run, and none of the Allied forces had time or need to detour to Le Touquet for anything in the nature of a formal liberation.

Sandy MacPherson was a staff captain in charge of supplies for the 2nd Canadian Corps. In early September 1944, almost three months after D-Day, he found himself with a couple of days to spare in Normandy. He and his mates were camped outside the ancient town of Montreuil, which was about ten miles inland along the Canche from Le Touquet. It was a gorgeous day of sun and quiet, September 5, and MacPherson and two other men hopped in his jeep for a spin to the Channel.

"We entered Le Touquet down a long avenue bordered by pines," MacPherson has written in a short memoir of the day. "At its end was the principal square which was surrounded by seriously damaged luxury hotels. We stopped, got out and heard not a sound except the banging of shutters and doors. We headed back along the avenue as fast as possible considering the obvious mines. Then we saw an extremely pretty girl with long blond hair jumping up and down and signalling us to stop. As I was on the right side and so was she, I was the first to be kissed."

The extremely pretty girl was of course Dorothy Borutti, and she was carrying out her resolve to kiss the man who liberated Le Touquet. The kiss was enough to attract MacPherson back to Le Touquet the next night. He brought tea for Dorothy's mother. Dorothy presented him with a rose. He wore it back to headquarters, and the girl from Le Touquet was never out of his thoughts. In April 1945, Le Touquet's mayor married Sandy and Dorothy.

"With an experience like that behind you," MacPherson said in Saanichton, "maybe you're a little more open to the romantic things of life than the next judge."

Divorce cases, however, were not usually the stuff of romance. MacPherson heard several hundred of them in his career on the bench, and when they weren't dull and routine, they were more likely to generate a suppressed laugh or two. "I had a divorce in Moose Jaw that was hilarious," he remembered. "The wife was suing on the grounds of the husband's cruelty. She'd come home from the hairdresser one day with a new coiffure. The husband happened to be painting the kitchen. She found something wrong with the job and said so in fairly blunt terms. Well, the husband responded to that by sliding his paint roller over the coiffure. I couldn't blame him. The woman was a tiger. I gave her the divorce anyway and went back to my chambers for a laugh." But on at least one occasion, MacPherson left a divorce trial with the warm feeling that romance had triumphed. It was a case from the mid-1960s that he has characterized and cherished as the divorce of the Little Sparrow.

"That's because she had a French accent and looked like Edith Piaf," MacPherson explained as he thought over the trial in his Saanichton living-room. "Quite tiny, dark hair and all the right clothes, tight skirt, a blouse and a dark jacket. She may even have been wearing a beret, or maybe that's just my imagination."

The woman was seeking an annulment of her marriage on the grounds of her husband's impotence. "Well, *that* didn't fit the Piaf image," MacPherson said. An annulment was difficult to win in court, since the applicant had to establish that the marriage hadn't been consummated and that the reason for the failure lay in the husband's inability or refusal to perform the act of love. The Little Sparrow had been married for ten years. That meant she had an especially tough case to prove. Ten whole years with no sex!

The Little Sparrow told her story in court.

She had grown up, she said, as the daughter of a working-class family in Paris. In her early twenties she travelled to Canada to visit an aunt who had married a French-Canadian soldier from Saskatchewan. The Little Sparrow met an honourable and prosperous Saskatchewan farmer several years older than she. The farmer proposed and she was intrigued. She gave the notion plenty of thought, and after her family approved, she married the man.

On her wedding night, she dressed in a seductive negligee and waited in bed for her new husband. When he joined her, he was wearing his longjohns, and he didn't take them off for the ten years the marriage lasted. She was a chaste and innocent young woman, but with her reluctant husband she teased and tempted and offered her young body in every pose and dance that her imagination could contrive. Alas, she never lured the farmer out of his underwear.

"This girl really tried with the husband," MacPherson said. "She certainly entranced me and the few other people who were in the courtroom. I knew she was irresistible to a normal man. I had to conclude the husband was impotent and I gave her the annulment."

The annulment didn't end MacPherson's worry about the

Little Sparrow. The farmer had plenty of money, but the sum he was settling on her as alimony was a mere twenty-five thousand dollars, not much after ten years of hard work as a farmer's wife.

MacPherson asked the woman in court, "Are you going to be able to look after yourself on that amount for the rest of your life?"

The Little Sparrow smiled up at him.

"It was the first time she'd smiled in court," MacPherson said in Saanichton. "It was an absolutely brilliant beam of a smile and I knew what it meant."

The Little Sparrow had found a new man.

"I could tell it was love this time," MacPherson said. "And I could tell she knew there'd be no more impotence."

The compassionate MacPherson: the case of the Indian girl on the Diefenbaker Bridge.

MacPherson has lost track of the number of murder trials he has conducted. It is more than sixty, maybe as many as one hundred. He became expert at them.

He said in Saanichton, "There's nothing that so concentrates the mind as a murder case." But it was his emotions rather than his mind that were most affected when MacPherson heard a murder case in which an Indian stood trial. He had plenty of them, and each one gave him a wrench.

In a stretch of a few weeks in the early 1970s, he sat on three murder trials back to back to back. The trials took place in Wynford, a town about 120 miles north of Regina, and it was an Indian who waited in the prisoners' box in each case.

"At one of them," MacPherson remembered, "a little Indian girl, twelve years old, testified that she'd seen her father stab her mother to death. She spoke beautifully in court, but oh my God, it was terrible to listen to."

MacPherson thought the rest of Canada should know about

the grievous stories he was listening to in his court. He called a young CBC reporter named Craig Oliver who was covering the west and persuaded him to take a look at the horrors that were unfolding in the Wynford courthouse. Oliver reported the story, and it ran for two nights on the CBC-TV National News. The story included an interview with MacPherson, and, as was his custom, he didn't beat around the bush.

"I told the people on television that all Indian murders had five things in common," MacPherson said. "There were always plenty of eyewitnesses to the killing and there was always an abundance of booze. Invariably the victim was a relative or friend of the accused. Then there was always a confession, one that was given freely and voluntarily. And at the end, the accused would invariably show genuine and overwhelming remorse for what he'd done to the victim."

Of all the Indian murder cases that MacPherson presided over, perhaps the most rending came with the trial in 1972 of a sixteen-year-old Indian girl whose spirit had been pushed to the shattering point. The trial took place in Prince Albert in mid-February when the days were cold and short. The Indian girl's name was Christina Roberts, and as she sat in the prisoners' box, MacPherson thought she resembled a beautiful little doll.

The story of what had happened to Christina over a couple of days in the previous summer had no beauty to it. She lived with her father and mother and several younger children on land outside Prince Albert. One hot day, the parents took Christina and two of her brothers, a three-year-old and a six-year-old, and drove into town in the father's small truck. The parents headed straight for a beer parlour and left Christina to look after the two boys. Christina had no food, no water, no money, and no shelter from the heat except the cab of the truck. The three children waited.

Hours went by before the parents emerged from the beer parlour with another Indian couple. Everyone packed into the truck. Christina's father drove to a liquor store, where he bought a large bottle of gin. Next stop was a woods north of Prince Albert where the adults drank until they passed out. The children went without food or water or care through the night, and when the little boys began to cry in the morning, Christina took them to the highway, and the three children hitch-hiked back to town.

The John Diefenbaker Bridge spans the Saskatchewan River in the middle of Prince Albert. It's a sturdy, graceful piece of work, built of cement, and it is wide enough to accommodate two lanes of traffic each way and pedestrian walkways on either side with railings that are four feet high. In the centre, the bridge sits forty feet over the water, and it was at that point on the bridge where Christina Roberts and her two brothers were last seen together. Their ride into town had dropped them off near the bridge and they had begun to walk across it. The three-year-old boy never reached the other side. He fell to his death from the middle of the Diefenbaker Bridge, and Christina was charged with his murder.

The evidence against her was mostly of a circumstantial variety. No one had seen her push or drop the boy into the Saskatchewan River. But a truck driver who was passing over the bridge at the time testified in court that he had noticed Christina lift the little boy on to the railing of the walkway. And a woman working in a nearby office building told the court that she had seen something fall from the bridge. She saw Christina and the older brother standing on the bridge at the spot from which the object, whatever it was, had fallen, and she'd seen the two of them, Christina and the boy, rush from the bridge to the bank of the river. The woman felt certain the two were searching for the thing that had dropped off the railing of the bridge.

Another witness was well known to MacPherson. He was the caretaker of the courthouse in which the trial was being conducted. He had been on duty on the day in the previous summer when Christina and her six-year-old brother had burst into the building in tears. They'd walked the mile from the Diefenbaker Bridge to the courthouse. They said they needed to talk to the police. In his testimony at the trial, the caretaker repeated the sentence that Christina had spoken to him.

"I pushed my little brother into the river and he is still there," Christina had blurted out between sobs.

Nine days later, the boy's body was found downstream in the Saskatchewan, and Christina began the wait to stand trial for the murder of her three-year-old brother.

In February, MacPherson took steps to comfort the girl. He asked the people at Saskatchewan Social Welfare to care for Christina during the trial. Social Welfare put him on to a Prince Albert woman named Ahenakew, the wife of a local Indian leader. Mrs. Ahenakew took Christina into her home and sat in the courtroom behind the prisoners' box on each day of the trial.

"Very typical of the Indian people," MacPherson said. "They practise the concept of the extended family."

MacPherson was apprehensive about Christina's chances in court. Legally, murder is the killing of another person with intent to kill. In cases where the act of the accused is a killing act — for instance, the dropping of a small child into a deep, swift river — the jury is entitled to infer that the accused intended the natural consequences of the act. The accused intended, that is to say, to kill. If the jury concludes that the act was done carelessly or wrongfully without any intent to kill, it has another option. It can find the accused guilty of manslaughter.

"Or there might be a defence of accident," MacPherson said. "But I couldn't see how that would apply to Christina if she lifted the little boy to the top of the railing. That was a careless act. Or she intended to kill. So, the way I looked at it going into the case, it seemed as if the verdict would have to be murder or manslaughter."

Christina was represented by perhaps Saskatchewan's most talented criminal counsel. His name was Clyne Harradence, a Prince Albert lawyer, and he conducted a wise, soft, low-key defence. In his cross-examination of the crown's witnesses, he brought out a few telling points. He established that Christina had endured a couple of hellish days leading up to her brother's death. He drew testimony that Christina's English was limited at the best of times and that she may not have grasped the difference between "threw" and "pushed" and "dropped" and "fell". And he got witnesses to describe the weather at the time Christina and her brothers were crossing the bridge. A heavy rain storm, it turned out, had hit Prince Albert just as the three children reached the John Diefenbaker Bridge.

Harradence called no witnesses for the defence, not Christina and not anyone else. Instead he relied on his address to the jury. It lasted thirty minutes and it was controlled and gently reasoning. Harradence emphasized the agony of the experience Christina had been through, neglected by her parents, left with the responsibility of two small children, hungry and thirsty, drenched in a deluge of rain. All the circumstances had come together as if deliberately to break the girl's will. More than that, Harradence argued, there was still the question of how the little boy got into the river. Was it proved beyond a reasonable doubt that Christina had pushed him off the bridge? Harradence thought not. The evidence of the witnesses was not enough. Christina must be acquitted.

"I never had more sympathy for an accused in my whole life on the bench than I had for that young girl," MacPherson said in Saanichton. "I wanted the jury to acquit her. So did everyone else in the courtroom."

As a judge, MacPherson could not show the jury a way to acquit Christina that did not accord with the law and the facts. He steered a proper middle course in his jury charge. He outlined the law for them, defining murder and manslaughter, tracing the nature of the defence and commenting on the facts.

He told the jury that the defence of accident would only apply where the accused was doing a lawful act in a lawful manner, and he repeated what Clyne Harradence had argued on the weight of the evidence. It hadn't been shown, MacPherson said, how the three-year-old boy ended up in the water. But it had been shown that Christina was on the bridge with the boy and that she had been seen to lift him to the railing.

The jury retired.

"Maybe I showed in the charge the feeling all of us had for Christina," MacPherson said in Saanichton. "Who can tell about these things?"

The jury returned with its verdict.

Not guilty.

"Juries don't have to give a reason for what they decide," MacPherson said. "In fact they're forbidden by law to discuss a verdict after they've rendered it. But I think the jurors in Prince Albert simply believed Christina was tested beyond human endurance. I think they said to themselves, 'We must acquit this girl.' For myself, I was profoundly relieved."

After MacPherson had discharged Christina, he went back to his chambers in the Prince Albert courthouse. He sent for Mrs. Ahenakew, the woman who cared for Christina during the trial. He thanked her, and while the two sat talking, the sheriff came into the room. Christina's parents were outside, the sheriff said, and they wanted something. They wanted the clothes that had been taken off the drowned three-year-old boy. Their younger children could use the clothes.

"Mrs. Ahenakew left the chambers to hide her tears," Mac-Pherson said in his Saanichton living-room. "I was alone with mine."

CHAPTER TWO

Down and Out in Old City Hall

Toronto's Old City Hall is everybody's blithe and eccentric aunt. It just misses dowdiness, but for quirkiness it's right on target. An architect named E. J. Lennox designed it a century ago when he was twenty-nine years old and in the thrall of the work of an older American architect named H. H. Richardson of Chicago. Richardson borrowed and enlarged on the Romanesque architecture of northern Italy, and by the time the influences had passed from Italy to Chicago to Toronto, Old City Hall got its lovable and crazy look.

The outside of the building is a busy collection of turrets and peaked roofs, elaborate mouldings and gargoyles and carvings in stone of dozens of men's faces. All of the faces but one have in common their homely features. The faces are said to belong to the politicians of Toronto of the 1880s and 1890s. The exception among them, the one face with the normal features, is E. J. Lennox's own. He didn't care for the rotten deal on price and credit that the city fathers of the day gave him for his design and he got his revenge in stone. Still, he poured his soul as well as his bitterness into the city hall job. He selected gorgeous red sandstone for the building, gave it a rugged but unaffected countenance, and topped it off with a tall and stately bell tower and a clock that still tells the correct hour most of the time.

Inside, the entrance hall on the main floor is done in yellows and whites and pinks and tans. Nineteenth-century Ontario heroes and heroines are celebrated in murals on the walls. Tecumseh, Laura Secord, William Lyon Mackenzie. The lower hall, which is roomy and accommodating, gives way to a pair of grand staircases that sweep to the second floor. From the top of the stairs, halls lead east and west down the sides of the building and meet again at the back. There's nothing much to delight the eye away from the entrance, no more murals or carvings or heroes or jokes in stone. Lennox intended it that way. The building was to be a seat of government, the city hall, a place where employees kept their noses to the grindstone of Toronto's business.

So it was for many decades, until everything changed for the building in 1966. That was the year when Toronto's new city hall, huge and sterile and spectacular, opened across the street. The city fathers and administrators moved their work into it, and Old City Hall, as it then became, was thereafter given over entirely to the Provincial Courts and to the wacky and terrible events and the sad and outrageous characters that are their stock in trade.

The Provincial Courts are the most active of all courts at all levels in Canada. As their name implies, they are the creature of the province and they have jurisdiction over a staggering array of criminal offences. They are the courts in which drinking-and-driving offences are heard, in which all minor and some major crimes under the Canadian Criminal Code are adjudicated, in which bail for a wide variety of offences is set, in which preliminary hearings are conducted to determine whether a person accused of murder or rape or milliondollar fraud or of many other heavy crimes should proceed to a higher court for a full-scale trial. Hundreds of accused offenders are processed through Provincial Courts on any day of the week, and they constitute a gamy slice of life from the wrong side of the tracks.

In Old City Hall, the accused and their lawyers begin to gather in E. J. Lennox's halls by nine-thirty each weekday morning. The lawyers are easy to pick out. They're the trim, bright-eyed young men and women in the suits and skirts. The other people in the suits, usually older and always bulkier, are the cops waiting to testify against the lawyers' clients. All the rest of the men and women in the halls are the accused, a motley crew. Sallow faces. Women on welfare. Kids who've grown up on white bread and hot dogs. Men with tattoos. Hangovers. Consumptive coughs. Clothes by K-Mart. There is among these people a higher percentage of smokers than in the city's general population, of *Toronto Sun* readers, of minority groups, blacks and browns and Canadian Indians, a higher percentage of men and women who are overweight or undernourished or both. And there is one other significant statistic that describes the condition of these beleaguered folk: the percentage of the guilty among them. The overwhelming majority of the accused who appear in the Provincial Courts are guilty of some crime, either the crime they're charged with or something lesser or greater. For many of them, though, guilt seems just one more weight in a life that's already burdened to the brink of collapse and surrender.

In Old City Hall's corridors, the accused and their lawyers gravitate in the direction of the particular courtrooms where they'll receive their moments of justice. There are twenty-six numbered courtrooms on the four floors of the building including the basement, and each courtroom is given over to a different crime or activity. Twenty-seven Court at the front on the first floor with a view from the windows down the Bay Street canyon is for hearings on drug charges. Thirty-eight Court up on the third floor at the back is devoted to drinking-and-driving offences. Forty-two Court on the second floor looking toward Eaton Centre on the east is a high-ceilinged, ornately decorated room. It used to be the chamber where mayors and aldermen gathered for council meetings.

Now it's the courtroom set aside for long trials and for preliminary hearings that are likely to be lengthy and nasty.

The judges who sit in Forty-two Court and in Old City Hall's
twenty-five other courtrooms are appointed by Ontario's
attorney general. They may remain in office if they choose
until age seventy-five. Not many stick it out that long. Their
salary is about seventy-five thousand dollars a year. It's prob-
able that they're underpaid. It's certain that they're over-
worked. Cases come at them each day in a swift tumble.
Defence counsel and crown attorneys who work in their
courts tend to be fresh on the job and sometimes slow on the
uptake. Police witnesses talk in jargon. Defence witnesses lie.
Accused people fart and belch and weep. Life in Provincial
Court is hectic. But no matter how wild and woolly events
may become in their courtrooms, no matter how much tragedy and burlesque comes through the doors, the judges of
Old City Hall will tell you they get a kick out of their work.
There's a touch of masochism in that response, a little pre-
varication, but mostly it's a reflection of their dedication to
the job and of the thrill at finding themselves in the centre of
justice's most tumultuous forum.

Judge Tony Charlton was getting fed up. First, one defence
counsel hadn't shown up on the second morning of the preliminary hearing in Thirty-one Court on this day in late
October of 1985. Then a second defence counsel had had the
bad manners to leave his topcoat draped over an empty chair
at the counsel table. And finally a third counsel insisted on
cross-examining a police officer with a stream of questions
that weren't leading in any convincing direction. What next!

Charlton straightened out the matter of the topcoat and
the breach of etiquette it represented.

"Put that where it belongs!" he snapped at the offending
counsel. "Put it beyond the bar of the courtroom!"

Charlton couldn't do much about the missing defence counsel except worry out loud.

"What do you propose I do when time comes for submis-
sions?" he said, aiming the question in the general direction
of the other two defence counsel.

"Oh well," he answered himself wearily, "I suppose we'll
manage."

As for the counsel with the tenacious line of questioning,
Charlton tried to make his impatience clear.

"You know," he said, "you're not going to *make* this officer change his memory."

The counsel nodded but returned a moment later to his
single-minded grilling of the policeman in the witness-box.

Charlton sighed.

Tony Charlton is in his mid-fifties and has a round, earnest
face. He has been on the bench since the late 1970s and comes
from a small legal dynasty. His father was a judge and his
two brothers are prominent lawyers. If that doesn't make him
an establishment person, his wife does. She's a granddaughter of Sir John Aird, the financial wizard who ran the Bank
of Commerce for several decades.

The accused before Charlton on the preliminary hearing
in Thirty-one Court were five young men who looked as if
they were stepping out to a salsa dance. They had copper skin
and lavishly styled black hair and wore billowing beige pants
and loose shirts in flashing colours. They were accompanied
by an entourage of wives and girlfriends who sat bouncing
in the public section of the courtroom. They could hardly wait
for the dance to start. The five young men were Ecuadorean
Indians who had moved to Toronto a few years earlier and
had carried their own festival with them.

According to the crown, they had also packed hot Latin tem-
pers. Police witnesses took the stand and swore to the facts
of the case. One warm night in the previous spring, it seemed,
the five young men had set out to cruise downtown Toronto

in a Honda Civic. They drank from a case of Labatt's Blue in the car and tooled around Church and Wellesley streets, a district of hookers and drug dealers and guys looking for action. A car pulled out suddenly from the curb and cut off their Honda. They chased it, and on Maitland Street in front of the National Ballet School, the five Ecuadoreans rumbled with the men in the other car. Somebody fell to the sidewalk in his own blood. His face and neck had been sliced, probably with a broken beer bottle. The bleeding man was from the other car. The Ecuadoreans scrambled back into the Honda. The driver started the engine and accelerated straight into the side of a police cruiser that was checking out the neighbourhood. The cops took the man with the sliced face to hospital and charged the Ecuadoreans with aggravated assault and a handful of other offences.

Tony Charlton wasn't enjoying the evidence.

"The man on the sidewalk, I thought he was in shock," one of the arresting policemen testified. "He was all over with blood and his feet kept twitching up and down."

Charlton rubbed his forehead.

The defence counsel were trying to establish grounds for arguing that there might not be a causal connection between the Ecuadoreans and the man on the sidewalk.

"Now, officer," one counsel asked the witness, "you say you found blood on a broken beer bottle in the Honda Civic, correct?"

"Yes, blood on a couple of smashed Labatt Blue bottles."

"To your knowledge, was that blood tested as to its type?"

"Not to my knowledge."

"So, for all you know, the blood could have come from one of the accused and not from the man on the sidewalk?"

"Could of, yes."

"My client's hand was bleeding when you pulled him from the Honda, isn't that right?"

"It was, yes."

"I suggest to you that the blood on the beer bottle was his, that it came from the cuts on his hand."

"I couldn't say."

Charlton's head hung down. His hand held a pen and it was poised over his notebook, but he hadn't written anything. His body language signalled that he wasn't buying the defence counsel's line of questioning. He didn't care for the defence's approach and he wasn't keen on all the distasteful testimony about blood. But Charlton has a reputation as a conscientious judge. He'll suffer through almost anything, and he permitted the defence counsel to ramble on in their cross-examinations.

At last the counsel finished. Charlton looked relieved that all the agitation in his courtroom had come to an end, and he wasted no time in committing all five Ecuadoreans to trial on the aggravated-assault charges and in committing the Honda's driver on a charge of dangerous driving.

That left one more matter for Charlton to deal with. It had to do with a breach of bail conditions committed by one of the young Ecuadoreans. At the time of the fight in front of the National Ballet School, he was out on bail while he waited trial on an earlier assault charge. A condition of his bail ordered him to stay away from another of the five Ecuadoreans in the Honda Civic. The other Ecuadorean was the young man's brother.

"You know your bail conditions say you're not supposed to associate with your brother?" one of the arresting officers had said to him at the police station on the night of the fight. "He's a bad influence on you."

"How can I deny my own blood?" the young man had answered.

Charlton asked the young man a few questions in court. His counsel supplied the answers. Yes, the young Ecuadorean was married. The wedding had taken place two weeks earlier. He was twenty years old, had a promise of a job, didn't own a car, and lived with his wife and a couple of relatives in an apartment.

Charlton said he was fining the young man two hundred dollars for the breach of bail.

Charlton tapped his pen and sighed and stared at the papers in front of him.

"Wait just a minute," he said. "Not employed right now and no car, you say? All right, I'll make the fine one hundred dollars."

The pen continued to tap.

Charlton looked down at the Ecuadorean.

"If you keep up this kind of conduct, it'll get you to the penitentiary one day," he said in a voice as stern as he could muster. "One thing I know about the penitentiary, people die in there. They get killed."

Tap, tap, tap.

"Good luck to you," Charlton said brusquely.

He rose from his chair and left through a door in the side of the courtroom. The door opened on to a hall that led into the main corridor on the second floor of Old City Hall. Charlton arrived in the corridor at the moment when the Ecuadoreans and their wives and girlfriends burst out of the courtroom. For them, the dance had only just begun. They bopped and shouted and hugged and shimmied their way toward the stairs.

Charlton turned to his court clerk.

"These people seem to think court is a spectacle," Charlton said.

His earnest expression had turned to worry.

Judge Donnie Graham prefers, in fact insists, that things proceed in his court at a pace somewhere between lickety-split and supersonic. Graham is Old City Hall's champion dash man. Trials before him are no-frills affairs. If the crown and the defence counsel have worked out an agreement on a case, he doesn't care to know the details. He'll go along with the deal. The catchword in his court is "expedite". Keep the cases moving. Graham is a sound and sensible judge, and he's fast. He works a different timetable than other judges. Most courts close down for lunch at 12:45. Judge Graham's court usually ceases operations at a few minutes before twelve. Defence counsel understand. They know that the judge has to get away for his noon exercise — handball in winter, tennis at the Toronto Lawn Tennis Club in the summer.

There's a story around Old City Hall that illustrates Judge Graham's affection for speed. The story concerns the day he slipped off his chair in court. He was hearing bail applications. The clock was edging toward noon and there were still several accused to deal with. In his anxiety to whiz through the applications, Judge Graham leaned forward so far that he fell from his chair and disappeared out of sight behind the desk. With the judge vanished from view, the counsel whose client was before the court stopped talking.

"Keep going!" Graham's voice came from below the desk. "I can still hear you!"

Graham is a short, visibly fit man, about sixty years old. He has a full head of thick hair and a Kennedyesque face, all vigour and rugged charm. He looks like what he is, a judge who doesn't kid around.

He was as usual in no mood for delay on the morning of October 30, 1985, but events were conspiring to frustrate him. He was sitting in Twenty-seven Court, one of the drug courts, and the immediate accused, in court with his counsel, was a young man with blond hair and a pasty Irish face. He was charged with trafficking in amphetamines, and nothing was going right with the crown's case.

The facts, though Graham was destined never to hear them, began with the young man's presence in the St. Charles, a Yonge Street bar with a reputation on the down side of dubious. An undercover policeman allegedly observed the young man in a series of transactions that involved an exchange of cash for pills. The young man handed out the pills and pocketed the cash. The undercover cop approached the young man in the St. Charles washroom.

"Got any beans?" he said to the young man.

"I'm all out," the young man answered.

The cop arrested him anyway and found in the young man's pockets several orange pills which, on later analysis, turned out to be diet pills. But were they amphetamines — or "beans" in street jargon — and therefore illegal? That would be thrashed out in court.

Matters before Judge Graham, however, were far from the thrashing-out stage.

"Your honour," the crown attorney said to Graham, "one of my police witnesses is at present testifying in another court. That's going to hold up this case. The witness is very necessary. He is an expert on the language of drugs as it is used on the streets. He will testify as to the meaning of a key word in this case."

"What's the word?" Graham asked.

"Beans, your honour."

"*Beans?*"

"Beans, yes, your honour."

"I don't know what beans means," Graham said, "and I don't want to wait around all day to find out."

"I'd like to proceed with the case, your honour," the crown attorney persisted.

"If you can get it done before a quarter to twelve or from two to three-thirty, okay," Graham said. "Defence counsel is in court and ready to proceed, and so am I."

"I'll call another witness, your honour, the officer who made the arrest," the crown attorney said.

The crown turned to the courtroom's duty officer, who happened to be Oriental.

"Call Officer Crockett," he said to the duty man. "He's out in the corridor."

The officer left the courtroom. A minute went by and the officer returned alone.

"I called three times," he said in a singsong voice that made it difficult to understand all of his words, "and there was no answer."

"Oh, for heaven's sake!" Judge Graham exploded. "Get *somebody* in the witness-box!"

The crown attorney lifted his shoulders in a gesture of despair.

"I don't understand, your honour," he said. "Officer Crockett was here a minute ago."

He turned to the Oriental duty man and sent him back to the corridor. This time he returned with Officer Crockett, who didn't bother to keep the grin off his face.

"I was standing right beside the guy when he called my name the first time," he whispered to the crown attorney. "Except I didn't know what he was saying."

"You'll have to go in the box," the crown attorney whispered back. "We haven't got the drug man who's going to testify about beans."

"Well, hell."

"Yeah," the crown attorney said. "If we can't call him, we haven't got a hope of getting a conviction on this guy."

"No beans," Officer Crockett said, "no case."

The crown attorney shrugged.

"Let's get on with it," Judge Graham broke in.

"Your honour," the crown said to Graham, "without the officer who'll testify as an expert on drug terminology, I'm not ready to proceed."

The defence counsel for the pasty-faced young man had been watching the proceedings without opening his mouth. Now he spoke up.

"Your honour," he said, "somebody's going to have to prove that the pills in question are illegal no matter what they're called."

"The beans?" Graham said.

"Beans," said the defence counsel.

"Beans," echoed the crown attorney, whose mouth turned down in an unhappy curve.

The crown had to make a snap decision. He needed his police expert on drug language. But he knew Graham wouldn't give him an adjournment, not with the accused's lawyer in court and clearly hot to fight. Graham liked efficiency. He didn't like adjournments.

"Your honour," the crown said after a short silence, "I'm compelled to withdraw the charge against this accused."

"Very well," Graham said briskly. "Charge withdrawn. Next case."

He looked at the clock on the courtroom wall. Ten-twenty. Plenty of time.

Judge George Carter is black and he's massive in the manner of an old football linebacker who has let his weight find its natural limits. But, as with many heavy men, he gives off gentle waves. When he shakes his head or lifts his hands, the motion is delicate. Carter has been on the bench since the late 1970s. He was one of the few black lawyers in Toronto in the days when they were called Negroes. Carter practised by himself and took a shot at everything until he got his appointment to the Provincial Court.

The man before him in Thirty-one Court one morning in the summer of 1985 was Carter's opposite in every physical way. The man was pale and thin and about twenty-five years old. His body and face were described in lines that sagged in the direction of the courtroom floor. His shoulders slumped, his moustache drooped, and his eyes curved down at the edges. He had on weathered jeans and a dirty white dress shirt with the sleeves rolled up.

The thin man was charged with violating his probation. He had been convicted several months earlier of assault and impaired driving, and even though he had a previous record, the judge at the assault and impaired-driving trial had given him a suspended sentence. In the months since his conviction, however, the man had failed to follow the judge's direction that he report regularly to his parole officer and to the John Howard Society.

The crown attorney read to Judge Carter a list of the man's transgressions and asked that Carter put him away for a lengthy prison term. The crown sounded angry and aggressive, and Carter nodded as he spoke, apparently agreeing with the crown.

Carter spoke to the thin man.

"I can't condone this behaviour, ignoring your parole officer, avoiding the John Howard Society," he began. His words seemed a prelude to a stiff sentence.

The thin man spoke up.

He said, "I have trouble relating my personal problems to people outside my way of life."

Carter was surprised that the man had spoken. He was even more surprised that the man seemed articulate.

"Well, you must remember these people are there to help you — the parole officer, the John Howard Society," Carter said. "They understand your problems."

"I was experiencing difficulties with my marriage relationship," the thin man said. "But I was able to maintain employment during this period."

"You held on to your job?"

"I functioned well, your honour."

"Well, I sympathize with your position," Carter said. "But I must take into account that you chose to ignore the previous court's explicit directions. The least sentence I should impose is three months in jail."

The crown attorney started to rise from his chair. Carter motioned him to stay where he was.

"The very least," Carter said.

The crown attorney fidgeted in his seat.

Carter's eyes lingered for a moment on the thin man.

"Three months it will be," Carter said.

The crown attorney scowled.

A duty policeman handcuffed the thin man's wrists behind his back and led him out of the courtroom.

Judge June Bernhard grimaced. For her, a grimace is a rare expression. She's more frequently seen with a smile in her courtroom. She smiles in court more than any other judge in Old City Hall, an appealing smile that springs from neither contempt nor derision. In her late fifties, Judge Bernhard is petite and dark-haired and has a slight overbite that gives her smile an attractive cast. She smiles in an understanding way when she is debating a legal point with counsel. She smiles in encouragement when she's questioning a confused witness. The smile is a reflex, and it's indicative of a judge whom both defence counsel and crown attorneys respect for her generosity and kindness. But on this March 1985 day, in Thirty-three Court, not liking what she was hearing, Judge Bernhard grimaced.

She was conducting a robbery case. The accused man, husky with a gloomy face, had gone into a variety store and told the young woman behind the cash register he was packing a gun and wanted the store's receipts. The girl called for her father, the proprietor of the store, and when he appeared, the man threatened to kill him. The store owner handed over five hundred dollars, and the man vanished down the street. He was arrested nine days later. The police had no difficulty getting a line on the man. He had been released from prison only a few months earlier on mandatory supervision from a nine-year sentence for another robbery. In court, the accused man's defence counsel told Judge Bernhard that his client had no skills, no job prospects, no money. All he had when he came out of prison was a fondness for drink and drugs and a sense of hopelessness. "He slipped back into crime," the defence counsel said. The crown attorney said that the accused man was "part of the revolving-door syndrome," out of prison, into crime, and back to prison. Judge Bernhard grimaced and sentenced the man to another four and a half years in prison.

"It's not the kind of case I enjoy," Bernhard said later, sitting in the living-room of her home. "Nobody gets any pleasure or challenge out of that kind of awful predicament."

Bernhard lives in a house in the upper-middle-class Moore Park section of Toronto with a Doberman pinscher, a mutt of indeterminate breeding, a marmalade cat, a black cat, and a ferret. When she was a child, she had a notion that she might study veterinary medicine. Instead, she went into law and opened a partnership with her husband. She specialized in civil litigation and built a career as a hard-working, astute counsel who didn't miss a legitimate trick in court. In all her years at the bar, she took only a single criminal case. Nevertheless, her husband encouraged her to leave herself open to a chance at an appointment to the Provincial Court. Perhaps he recognized that the court could use a judge with the gentler qualities as well as the brains of his wife and partner.

Bernhard never entirely believed she'd be named to the bench, not even when the big call came at seven o'clock one night in the spring of 1979.

"I'm the Deputy Attorney General," the voice on the phone said.

"And I'm the Shah of Iran," Bernhard answered.

She got the appointment anyway.

"My first day as a judge was a disaster," she says. "I was assigned to Thirty-eight Court where the drinking-and-driving cases are heard. What I didn't know on that subject would fill several hundred volumes. I was scared out of my wits."

She recovered in rapid order and began to carve out a reputation among counsel. She was the judge who liked to apply herself to the law. She was the judge whom you could spot in her office or over in the law library at Osgoode Hall at nine o'clock in the evening.

"I prefer cases that have a little law to them and aren't just a matter of assessing the facts," she says. "The thing is that counsel often don't direct you to the right law, which means you have to look it up for yourself. You have to research the decisions. Find the precedents. And that's all right by me."

Then there's the other part of her reputation, the part that has to do with her generosity and kindness. It appears to be a natural reflection of Bernhard's own feelings about the accused people who appear in her court.

"They've never had a chance," she says. "If somebody has had a chance and blown it and ended up in my court, I don't feel sorry for them. But for the others, yes, I feel compassion. I was lucky to be brought up by loving parents and to have had a loving husband. That gives me a big advantage over the people who appear before me. They've never had love and I can't let myself forget it when I'm sitting up there on the bench with all the power I hold over those people."

In a drawer of the desk in Judge Lorenzo DiCecco's chambers on the third floor of Old City Hall, he keeps a file of letters that fall into two categories — heart-warming and heart-breaking. The letters come to DiCecco from men who have appeared before him in court. Most of the letters thank him for the treatment he gave them, for the chances he offered, the incentive to get themselves out of crime and prison. The letters bring DiCecco up to date on the writers' progress in the straight world. The future, these letters imply, looks bright.

"Here's one from a drug addict," DiCecco was saying one noon hour in the late fall of 1985. He pulled out a letter written in a graceful hand on two pages of lined yellow paper. The letter was dated July 14, 1985.

"He was maybe twenty-six years old, twenty-seven, this drug addict, when I had him in my court a couple of years ago," DiCecco went on. "I thought he would be all right if he got a little supervision, you know, a little *firm* supervision."

The man's letter brimmed with optimism. It talked of starting up a business building backyard patios. He had so much work that he hired an extra man. He was happy. "I think this was the first year in a long time when I was sober on my birthday," he wrote. "I had a lot of fun just dining and dancing."

That was the heart-warming part of the letter.

"One week after that letter, he fell off the drug wagon," DiCecco said in his chambers. "Who knows why? For some reason, he got stupid and he went to another city and did four break-and-enters in three days. A judge in the other city gave the guy three years in prison."

DiCecco placed the two yellow sheets on the top of his desk.

"But I'm an optimist," he said. "This guy was okay for one whole year, no drugs or anything like that. If he did it for one year, who knows, maybe next time he can do it for longer. Maybe for all his life. In my job, I like to think if you try to look after things the right way, the best can happen in the long run."

Lorenzo DiCecco is in his early forties. He has wavy grey hair, an elegant moustache, and an insouciant style that would make him right at home strolling the Via Veneto. He grew up in Rome and emigrated to Toronto as a teenager in 1961. His ambition from an early age was to become a judge. In the very first year after his call to the bar in 1973, he applied for a position on the Provincial Court. He got it in 1979.

"I love my work," he said in his chambers. When he spoke, there was the music of Italy in his accent and his laugh. "It's not for the money. Oh my God, the *money*? I could make more in one day as a lawyer than I make in one week as a judge.

No, no, what it is, if you really like the law, then being a judge is one of the few ways you can work in the law with a clear conscience. You don't have to account to anybody except yourself. That's a fantastic luxury."

On the job, DiCecco has tinkered together his own particular brand of judge's philosophy. It begins with an affectionate curiosity about the accused who appear before him. "They're all different," he said. "I can hardly wait to see what makes them tick." From this starting point, his philosophy takes a turn that is entirely practical.

The way DiCecco figures it, most of the accused who come into his court, no matter how distinctive they may be from one another in personality, share a few key points of autobiography. They're between seventeen and twenty-five years old. They've been kicked out of the house by their parents. They can't find a decent job. And they live in rooms that are dumps and cost fifty dollars a week. They get themselves in trouble and are hauled into Provincial Court.

That's when DiCecco applies his philosophy.

"I use supervision," he explained. "It's what most young people want anyway, direction and supervision. I don't send these kids to jail if I can avoid it. I put them on probation. I tell them, look, now I got you by the throat. I tell them, I'm adopting you for the purposes of discipline. I'm not taking you into my own home, I say, but I'm keeping my eye on you. You're on probation and I'm supervising you. If you get into trouble again, you're not going into some other judge's court. You're coming back in front of me. I tell them, I'm going to be around for another thirty years. You do something wrong, I say, and I'll throttle you."

In the crunch, DiCecco moves from tough to very tough.

"A kid in court thinks he can outsmart me," DiCecco said in his chambers, his voice a cackle of cunning. "The kid says to me, oh no, I don't want probation, I want to do time instead. This kid knows when he comes out of jail he's automatically clear if all I give him is prison time. He's gone from my supervision. So I say to the kid, okay, you got it. I'm giving you six months in jail. Then I say, oh yeah, I'm also putting you on two years' probation after you get out. I still got my hands around your neck."

The message, DiCecco knows, goes out to the other young offenders. They know DiCecco isn't a judge to mess with. He takes to heart the fate of the accused in his court even if his methods are unorthodox.

"They know me, all the accused," DiCecco said. "Just in case they don't, sometimes I go up to their lawyers in the hall. I say to them, hey, look, you better convince your clients that with me they got a crazy madman on the bench."

It pays off, the probation and supervision, the tough talk, the caring. At least DiCecco thinks it pays off. He thinks he sees the results in court. He knows his philosophy works when the young men who've appeared many times before him suddenly stop turning up in his courtroom.

"It happens when these kids get to be about twenty-five years old," he explained. "They meet a young woman, and then they have someone to care for. It's two people struggling together instead of one all by himself. That makes the difference. They don't want to go back to the old way. They don't want the police any more and the jails and the courts. They don't want me looking over their shoulders."

DiCecco gave an elaborate shrug with his arms.

"Except sometimes they write me," he said. "Nice letters."

His hands fell on the two sheets of yellow notepaper, the letter from the drug addict who was back in prison.

"I always expect a happy ending," DiCecco said. "Even for this guy the drug addict."

There wasn't much Judge DiCecco could do for the final accused he dealt with in Twenty-two Court on the last Thursday of November 1985. The accused was a man about thirty with a receding hairline, a handlebar moustache, and an expression of surpassing glumness. He had pleaded guilty to robbery, and he sat hunched in the prisoners' box listening to the nutty and incontrovertible facts of his crime.

He had been paroled from prison the previous summer after serving four years for robbery. He found a job in Peterborough, Ontario, working for a company that installed swimming pools. He studied advanced carpentry at a community college and met a woman who wanted to marry him. Life seemed okay until the day in early October when he travelled to Toronto for a visit with his daughter from an earlier marriage and got into a bad hassle with his ex-wife. He drank several beers to soothe his angst and headed for Union Station to catch the train back to Peterborough. He walked into a Shoppers Drug Mart near the station to buy a pack of cigarettes. As he stood at the store's counter, he looked down a hall and saw four or five Shoppers employees counting the day's receipts in the back room.

A gear shifted in the man's head. He took a knife from his pocket, a plain penknife with a small blade. He walked down the hall, flashing the knife.

"Gimme the cash!" he said.

The store manager looked up.

"You're not getting any of this fucking money!" he shouted.

A woman clerk threw her cup of coffee at the man with the knife.

He reeled back, wiping at his hot and soaked shirt.

The store manager rushed at the man and slammed a door on his arm. The knife flipped in the air, and the man grabbed at his aching wrist.

He turned to leave.

Too late. Another Shoppers employee jumped on his back and pinned him to the floor.

A second woman clerk stood over the fallen man and waved a heavy bottle at his head.

"Make one move," she said, "and I'll brain you!"

The robbery attempt had lasted less than thirty seconds.

As the crown attorney recited the facts, he began to grin. The court clerk got the giggles. The policeman on duty at the prisoners' box put his hand over his face. The defence attorney looked at the ceiling and his body shook silently. The court reporter sputtered into her speaking device. Judge DiCecco developed a small smile.

Only the glum man in the prisoners' box didn't see the joke. DiCecco decided to cheer him up.

"You know, I once had a bank robber in this court," he said to the man. "He was glad to be here because it was worse for him in the bank. An old lady gave him a terrible beating. This wasn't a little old lady. This was a *big* old lady, and she put her boots to the guy who was trying to rob the bank. She kicked the living daylights out of him. The guy was happy to be arrested. He thought the police probably saved his life when they came for him. The lesson is you've got to be wary of big old ladies."

The glum man stared straight ahead.

"Your honour," the crown attorney said, "defence counsel and I have agreed that a two-year sentence would be appropriate in this case."

"That's fair," DiCecco said.

He looked again at the prisoners' box.

"The other moral is," he said, "you also have to be wary of people who count money at Shoppers Drug Mart."

The glum man still wasn't smiling.

The man appearing before Judge Robert Dnieper in the first week of October 1985 didn't give off the feel of a student or a scholar. But, according to the evidence, he had in his possession 236 learned texts dealing with early Christian myths and history. The man's name was George Elia, he was forty-eight years old, and he'd stolen all 236 books from libraries at the

University of Toronto. It wasn't the first time Elia was caught
swiping university books. He'd been nailed with a bag of texts
in 1981, but since then he'd apparently gone in for thievery
in a much more ambitious way. He'd enrolled in one non-
credit course at the university, thereby acquiring a library
card, and before librarians grabbed him in April 1985, he managed to squirrel away the 236 books which were worth about
thirteen thousand dollars. Elia was hardly the only library
thief in the university's experience, just one of the most cagey,
but as he stood before Judge Dnieper, he and the university
knew that the other apprehended thieves had received nothing worse than a slap-on-the-wrist fine for their crimes.

Dnieper changed the old perceptions in a hurry.

"You have done incalculable harm to other students,"
Dnieper said to Elia. "And this is going to be the first time in
Ontario, and possibly all of Canada, that someone is going to
jail for what you've done."

He sentenced Elia to serve seven days in jail, put him on
probation for three years, directed him to perform three hundred hours of community service, and ordered him to pay
restitution for any of the 236 books that weren't returned to
the university.

That was Judge Dnieper on what most lawyers who appear
regularly in his court would call a good day. On Dnieper's
other days, there's no counting on his decisions or his sentences, his attitude to counsel or the quality of his repartee.
Dnieper is the loose cannon among judges at Old City Hall.
He is bright and quick but unpredictable; he has a sound
knowledge of the law but might bypass it on occasions when
he decides justice is best served by making an end run around
the Criminal Code; he is fast with a genuinely witty line, the
Johnny Carson of the courtroom, but his humour sometimes
takes on an edge that may be black or sexist or patronizing.

Many of his qualities went on vintage display one day in
May 1983 in Twenty-three Court when Dnieper had before

him an old-time rounder named Carroll who was pleading guilty to one count of theft under two hundred dollars. Mr. Carroll had light-fingered a couple of bottles of aftershave lotion and been caught in the act.

"How are you feeling?" Dnieper began with Carroll.

"Fine," Carroll answered.

"How long do you want on this one?" Dnieper asked.

"You mean you want me to tell you how much I want?" Carroll said, slightly amazed.

"Yeah," Dnieper said. "How long do you want in jail?"

At that point, the crown attorney, a woman named Goebbels, decided to put in her oar.

"Your honour," she said, "this is his fifty-third conviction on theft. In January he got three months, and in March he got thirty days."

"I don't have time to read his record," Dnieper said. "This court has to quit at five o'clock."

Dnieper turned back to Carroll.

"Give me an answer," he said. "How long do you want?"

"Ten days?" Carroll tried.

"Why not?" Dnieper said. "Sounds fair to me."

Dnieper swung back to Ms. Goebbels.

"You see, crown," he said. "Mr. Carroll is neither a plague of locusts nor a national disaster. He is an irritation much like a mosquito or a black-fly in June. It is a judgment of God upon our society and something with which we have to live. He is neither a danger to society nor a danger to the individual members thereof. He is merely a pain in the neck."

"Yes, your honour," Goebbels said, "but with respect, one usually tries to swat the black-flies or mosquitoes so they don't come back again."

"You and I must be thinking of different black-flies," Dnieper answered. "Black-flies with which I've had anything to do defy swatting, and Carroll defies correction. So let's accept him and forget about it."

"Thank you, your honour," Goebbels said, tossing in the towel.

But Dnieper wasn't finished with Carroll.

"Listen," Dnieper said to the man, "if I get you again, I'm going to throw you on the street without sending you up to the jail at all."

Dnieper looked over to Ms. Goebbels.

"You see, crown," he said, "the great value of the English common law is its ability to adapt to the situation."

Dnieper has been either outraging or delighting his court-room audiences since the day of his appointment to the bench in 1961. He is now in his mid-fifties, an imposing, forceful man who comes on in the style of Broderick Crawford in *All the King's Men*. He has Crawford's heavy face and the same rumble of a voice. His hair is black and slicked back. His eyes are dark and constantly on the move in the courtroom. He checks out counsel, gives the accused a once-over, and scans the audience. He looks restless, like a judge who doesn't mind a little controversy to juice up his day.

He may often be hard to read in his responses in court, but in a couple of areas Dnieper is utterly consistent. Drug offences make up one area. Dnieper is death on drug users and worse on drug pushers. Almost all Provincial Court judges grant a discharge to kids caught with a small amount of marijuana on a first offence, but Dnieper usually hands out a sentence. Defence counsel are aware of this propensity and try to steer clear of him when he's sitting in the drug courts. What they want to avoid, apart from a criminal record for their clients, is the lecture that Dnieper frequently delivers along with the sentence.

It's The Dnieper Lecture to defence counsel. They know it by heart. It explains how the international commerce in drugs is related to the decline of the western world. Defence counsel are said to develop an automatic groan after too many exposures to The Lecture.

"The traffic in narcotics is an organized evil and a conspiratorial evil," Dnieper began in the course of a typical five-minute version of The Lecture during the sentencing in 1979 of a young man charged with possession of marijuana. "In supporting these men who have no heart to our nation, the accused became one of them, an enemy to our people, and I do not view it lightly."

And that wasn't all.

"I won't bore anyone with a recitation of the amount of Canadian dollars that flows outside the country for these drugs," Dnieper went on. "All this, of course, has to be paid for by the sale of our natural resources."

In the end, the young man's penalty was comparatively light in Dnieper's terms—a one-hundred-dollar fine or seven days in jail.

If Dnieper sounds like a patriot, he is. He emigrated to Canada from the Ukraine with his parents when he was a child, and though his early life was harsh—he was compelled to work in a factory as an eleven-year-old—he developed a love affair with his new home.

But his love does not necessarily extend to Canadian society's dissenters and activists. A twenty-eight-year-old man named Scott Marsden discovered that truth when he appeared before Dnieper on June 24, 1985. Marsden had taken part in a sitdown in the driveway at Litton Systems, the Toronto company that makes parts for Cruise missiles. Marsden was arrested and found himself in front of Dnieper, who convicted him of mischief, bringing Marsden's total to four mischief convictions during four demonstrations.

"The accused in the past has broken the law because he seeks to impose his will upon us all," Dnieper rumbled. "The views of Canadian society are represented in the House of Commons, and the accused cannot contravene the will of the people."

Then Dnieper hit Marsden with the toughest sentence for

demonstrating that regulars around Old City Hall could recall.

Five days in jail, two hundred hours of community service, and prohibition from taking part in similar demonstrations for a year.

When something rouses Dnieper's anger, he holds nothing back. He pitches into the case. An unfortunate pornographer came before him on February 22, 1985. The man was sixty-three years old and the proprietor of a hole-in-the-wall store in downtown Toronto where he sold comic books over the counter. Under the counter, he peddled sex magazines which were imported from Europe and the United States. The magazines were long on violence and bondage, and their price tag was hefty, about thirty dollars per magazine. Dnieper studied the man's product, pronounced it "disgusting", and sentenced him to eighteen months in prison. The crown attorney on the case, John Hansbridge, felt his jaw drop in disbelief. "The usual penalty on such a conviction," Hansbridge said later, "is a fine and maybe a day in jail." Not in Judge Dnieper's court.

On the morning of October 16, 1985, sitting in Forty-two Court, Dnieper put on display another of the tendencies that set him apart from other Old City Hall judges — his blunt style of questioning. In a sense, his head-on directness is a reflection of his own quick mind. He can't abide counsel who don't get to the facts. Witnesses who dawdle over the case's point drive him to exasperation. Dnieper has already absorbed the point while everybody else is still circling it. The difference in speed makes Dnieper twitch with impatience, and he was beginning to squirm in Forty-two Court on October 16 during a preliminary hearing on a first-degree-murder charge.

The accused was a Canadian Indian in his late twenties. He was wraith thin and wore a Fu Manchu arrangement of moustache and goatee and long black hair which was parted in the middle and fell around his shoulders. He sat unnervingly still in the prisoners' box and gave off an aura of calm and peace.

According to the testimony of the crown witnesses, calm and peace may not have accurately described the Indian's habitual state of mind. One of his former girlfriends had been murdered in a way that spoke of suffering and violation, and evidence pointed to the Indian as a certain suspect. The woman's body had been found lying face down on the bed in her apartment. She was nude. Her hands were tied behind her back. Each of her buttocks showed a human bite mark. Her anus bore signs that something had been forced into it. And there were seven wounds on the back and sides of her head inflicted by blows from the traditional blunt instrument.

The police officers who investigated the case and the pathologist who performed the autopsy on the dead woman testified to the terrible facts of the killing with enormous restraint. They skirted around their descriptions of the body and its injuries, and the crown attorney needed dozens of questions to draw out their evidence. Each witness shied away from the horror of the events in the woman's bedroom, and Dnieper wasn't happy with the way the hearing was stretching through his morning. He shuffled the papers in front of him, chewed at the edges of his tie, and let out a couple of giant yawns.

The pathologist stood in the witness-box. He was presenting a list of the marks on the woman's body — rope burns on the wrists, bites to the buttocks, injured anus, blows on the head — and he was taking his painful time about it.

Dnieper made his move. He'd accepted the testimony in edgy silence through the morning. Now he spoke up, addressing himself to the pathologist.

"Your observation is that the dead woman was subjected to bondage, sadism, sodomy, and murder?" he said in a swift tumble of words. "Is that about the size of it?"

The pathologist's mouth dropped open. The crown attorney stood rigid at the counsel table. Everyone in the courtroom fell as still and quiet as the Indian in the prisoners' box.

"Yes?" Dnieper said, still looking at the pathologist.

The courtroom turned instantly into a scene of purposeful action. The pathologist allowed that, yes, the judge's description had summed up the situation. The crown attorney picked up the pace of his examinations. Witnesses grew crisp and authoritative. And fifteen minutes later, almost as an anticlimax, Dnieper wound up the hearing by ordering that, pending a decision on committal for trial, the Indian would be dispatched to the proper facilities, in custody, for a lengthy mental examination.

Court stood adjourned.

Judge Robert Dnieper had struck again.

Joe Addison

"Masturbation in public," Joe Addison was saying. "It's the crime of the 1980s in Toronto. I keep getting the cases in my court. A fella goes into a public washroom and stands at a urinal and starts masturbating and hopes the guy in the next urinal is of the same persuasion as him. Cases are all the same. Either these fellas go to the big washroom on the concourse floor down at the Royal York Hotel or they go to the one on the third floor of the Bay department store. No wonder they advertise you should meet me at the Bay. All kinds of guys are doing it. I had a bank manager from out west and I had a guy from over in St. Catharines with five children. Both of them up on masturbating in public and a lot more fellas like them in my court on the same charge. Crime of the 1980s, I tell you."

Joe Addison was, as usual, half kidding. Addison has been a Provincial Court judge since 1958, sitting almost exclusively in Toronto's Old City Hall, and in all his years on the bench, he's taken a sort of bemused attitude toward the bizarre and terrible events that happen in front of him. He's a funny man, and he likes to laugh on the job. But there's nothing condescending or cruel about his wit. He doesn't score points off the people in the prisoners' box. He doesn't take advantage.

"I'm not gonna go out there resenting the guys who appear

105

before me," he said one spring morning in 1985, sitting in his chambers at Old City Hall. "I don't shake my finger at them or give them a lecture. They know what's gonna happen to them anyway. In a lot of cases, most likely they're going to jail."

There are a couple of other points about Addison. One is that he's a gracious man. He isn't known among defence counsel as "Gentleman Joe" for nothing. And the other is that he's got the art of judging down as fine and fair as it will go. Around Old City Hall, they say that Joe Addison has never been reversed on appeal. It's hyperbole, but it's a measure of the man's honestly won reputation.

"Everybody gets a good trial from me," Addison said. "The fella may not like the result, but he can't complain he wasn't treated right. I've always told my associates on the bench, if I was a person who wasn't guilty of something I was charged with, I'd rather appear before me than any of them. I'm like Bill Klem, the old baseball umpire. I don't think I've called one wrong yet."

Addison started calling them when Kelso Roberts, Ontario's attorney general in the late 1950s, went looking for a judge with very specific qualifications.

"Kelso wanted a Jew with a rich wife," Addison said. "Well, I'm Jewish all right, and even though my wife wasn't rich, I'd inherited a little money, and I could afford to give up the bigger income I'd make practising law to go on the bench. Which was the point Kelso was making. I didn't get much kick out of being a lawyer anyway. I took the judge's job and I haven't felt sad about it for one second since that day."

Nor has Addison changed much in looks and attitude in his time on the bench. He reached his seventy-third birthday in 1985 and could pass for ten years younger. He is tall and erect, and his face suggests Charles Bronson on a good day, all flint and virility. As for his court patter, it too has remained fresh and vivid over the years. Addison isn't a particularly gabby judge, but when he talks, people listen, and often they laugh, especially when Addison puts a W. C. Fields spin on his remarks.

"The accused went beyond the bounds of nicety," he pronounced in an assault case in 1959, a year or so after his appointment, "and I don't think that I, in this lowly court, should deprive him of the full conclave of judges sitting in the appeal court."

Then there was the case of dog theft a couple of years later.

"A dog has feelings that can be hurt," Addison said in his judgment, "and it has preferences that can be expressed."

"Courtroom Bibles," he said in a perjury case, "might as well be dictionaries."

During a gambling trial, a witness testified that a policeman had called him a "Macedonian Hebe".

"Jews get into enough trouble on their own without blaming them for what the Greeks do," Addison said.

Sometimes his fast patter has brought him problems. In 1962, a royal commission on crime in Ontario summoned him to advise it about rumours that he'd been offered a fifty-thousand-dollar bribe in a gambling case that was scheduled before him. Addison said the rumours happened to be untrue, but he mentioned that, by the way, on a couple of other occasions a gambler and a gambler's lawyer had phoned him with requests for a broadminded hearing in court. For anyone else it might have been a delicate moment. Addison skated through.

A couple of his throwaway lines in the courtroom brought editorial writers from the Toronto newspapers down on his neck. Once, Addison told lawyers for some gamblers at a preliminary hearing that if he were trying the gamblers rather than merely deciding whether he should commit them to higher court for trial, he would find them guilty. A *Globe and Mail* editorial reprimanded Addison for violating the gamblers' civil rights, and several *Globe* letter-writers demanded

Addison's head from the Attorney General. Again he survived, as he did in another furor stirred up by all three Toronto papers over his advice to a drunk driver that he would have been better off to ignore tips he picked up in the papers about his rights after arrest. "Newspapers," Addison said in court, "impress on readers methods whereby they can evade the penalty for their wrongdoing."

Hot water again.

"Oh yeah," Addison said in his chambers, "there were times when I'd look to see what stupid son of a bitch had his foot in his mouth this time, and I'd look again and it was me. Once I was going to sue a paper for libel over some of the criticism I took, but my lawyer pointed out that, hell, nobody was firing me, were they? And besides I had a lot of people come to my defence."

During his career, in and out of hot water, Addison has presided over plenty of significant trials and preliminary hearings. He took the preliminary hearing in the Windfall case of the mid-1960s, a massive and complex prosecution for stock fraud that lasted for several weeks in Addison's court and demanded much analysis of difficult legal points before he decided to commit the accused for trial. He tried a Mafia enforcer and assorted other hoods who shocked Toronto when they beat up a gambler named Max Bluestein in the lobby of a busy downtown nightclub in March 1961. It was a tough case to handle, since many of the witnesses, terrified of Mafia revenge, developed severe bouts of amnesia, but Addison found enough evidence to send three of the hoods to prison. And he had two of Canada's most accomplished counsel before him, John Robinette and Arthur Martin, in a series of intriguing Chinese gambling cases in the 1960s.

"That's the pleasure, having those great counsel in your court," Addison said. "Robinette, Martin, the late Joe Sedgwick, Dave Humphrey, guys like that, you can't avoid the fact they're gonna get their clients better results than a

Mickey Mouse counsel. Humphrey could come into my court and make a weed smell like a rose."

Alas for Addison, not every case is a Windfall and not every counsel is a Humphrey.

"It's a dirty job sometimes," Addison said. "The cases I like to hear best are the white-collar kind. Crooked bankruptcies. Frauds. Stock-market swindles. But you gotta live with the messy stuff, too, assaults where there's a lot of blood and these poor fellas in the washroom up at the Bay. But no matter what, I like the job. Some years — this is no fooling — I've given up my holidays to spend extra time on the bench. Where else would I have more fun?"

In the catalogue of the thousands of cases he's heard, Addison looks back on the David Winchell hearing as one he got a special laugh out of. Several laughs. Winchell was a stock promoter around Toronto, and in the late 1970s he was peddling an unlisted oil stock to a number of the city's big shooters. Winchell's adviser in the deals was a lawyer named Sam Ciglen, who had had his own troubles with the law over the years. He had made many trips to court to defend himself against charges of stock fraud. But in the Winchell case he was mainly on the sidelines, which isn't to say he didn't reap a few benefits from the association.

"The two of them, Winchell and Ciglen, used to go back and forth to Switzerland like I go downtown," Addison says. "Switzerland must've been where they had a bank account for the money from the issue of this crazy stock."

The money was substantial, about six hundred thousand dollars before the big shooters began to get nervous and called in the fraud squad. Charges were duly laid against Winchell, though not Ciglen, and the preliminary hearing in the case came before Addison.

"The fellas with the important names who lost money testified for the crown," Addison says. "DelZotto. Rudy Bratty. First time I ever saw those fellas look unhappy."

A crown witness named Sherkin, one of the other investors who'd dropped a bundle, took the stand.

Sherkin looked over from the witness-box to Addison.

"Goodie sends his regards," he said.

Winchell's lawyer, an excellent counsel named Mike Moldaver, sprang to his feet and asked to see Addison in his chambers.

"What's the trouble, Mike?" Addison asked when they were alone.

"This witness, Sherkin," Moldaver said, concerned, "he's a close friend of yours?"

"Mike, I never saw the man before in my life."

"But what about this Goodie he's talking about?"

Addison explained.

"He's talking about Goodie Rosen, Sherkin is," he said. "Goodie's a wonderful guy. Used to play baseball for the old Brooklyn Dodgers in the 1940s. I grew up with him down by Bellwoods Park. Sherkin's a friend of Goodie's, I guess, and so am I. I got no control over what the witness says, but there's nothing wrong here."

Moldaver was mollified and returned to court.

Sherkin wasn't through.

"Winchell used to take us investors up to his summer cottage and ride us around in his boat," he testified. "That cottage, the Taj Mahal is smaller even, and his boat, you could float the *Queen Mary* inside it."

Sherkin said he'd invested so much money in Winchell's stock that his wife had worried herself into a heart condition.

Sherkin looked over at Winchell in the prisoners' box.

"So what are you selling today, David?" he said. "Cancer?"

As the preliminary hearing progressed and as the evidence accumulated against Winchell, Moldaver entered into plea-bargaining with the crown. They worked out a deal and took it to Addison for his approval. Winchell would plead guilty and accept a fine of one million dollars and repay the investors to the tune of some six hundred thousand dollars.

"I agree," Addison said to the lawyers. "How would it help these investors get back their money if Winchell went to jail for three or four years? Wouldn't achieve a thing."

The bargain was struck, and a day later, a court official knocked on the door to Addison's chambers.

"You want to look at something amazing?" the official said.

"Show me."

The official held out a cheque.

"It's from Winchell," he said.

"One million bucks," Addison said. "Certified. How d'ya like that? He came back with it overnight."

"Ever seen one like that?" the official asked.

"Don't move in those circles," Addison answered.

On the first morning of summer 1985, the excitement in Twenty-two Court came from the least likely suspect. Twenty-two Court is the remand court, and Addison was sifting through the long list of people accused of crimes and setting a date for trial for each of them. Most of the accused were out on bail and stepped forward from the public seats in the courtroom for the swift and mechanical procedure of date-setting. But seven men sat in the prisoners' box. They weren't on bail. They would wait out the time to their trials in jail.

Two of the prisoners were charged in the same crime, a matter of robbery. Both looked to be in their early twenties and both looked harmless. One was thin and lanky and wore jeans and a simple expression. The other was shorter and wider and had a thick mass of black hair, olive skin, and an effeminate face. Something about the way the two young men leaned against one another and whispered together suggested that their friendship had a sexual connection.

Addison reached their names on his list.

"How would four weeks from today be for these gentlemen?" he said.

The duty counsel, a young woman whose job was to handle matters for any accused who wasn't yet represented by his own lawyer, moved over to talk to the pair. It was Olive Skin who took care of the whispered negotiations with her. The other man, Lanky, looked on placidly.

"Four weeks will be fine, your honour," the young woman said.

Addison, the crown, and the duty counsel bent their heads over their desks and wrote the entry in the sheets of trial dates.

The policeman in charge of the prisoners' box moved forward to lead Olive Skin and Lanky out of the box, through the courtroom's back door, and down to the cells.

As the two men stepped from the box, Olive Skin suddenly turned to his right and lit out in the direction of the door leading to the corridor and freedom. The door was ten yards away, and the only person between it and Olive Skin was a female court official, a slim woman with a clipboard in her hands.

Olive Skin was neither fast nor athletic. His feet made awkward slapping noises as they hit the floor. For the four or five seconds it took him to reach the door, the only sound in the courtroom came from his feet. Everything else — the people and the events — were frozen in silence.

Slap! Slap! Slap!

Olive Skin bowled into the woman with the clipboard. Her back hit the door and her right shoe flipped into the air. She clutched the clipboard to her breast.

A plainclothes detective leaped out of his chair beside the crown attorney. The policeman clumped from his post at the gate of the prisoners' box. Both reached Olive Skin at the moment his hands began to pull at the courtroom door.

The detective got him by the neck and twisted it in a swivel grip. The policeman hoisted Olive Skin by the legs. Another uniformed policeman came through the door and pinned Olive Skin's arms. The three rushed him past the prisoners' box toward the courtroom's back door. They carried Olive Skin as if he were a battering ram. His head just missed smacking the door as the group charged out of sight.

First there was silence in the courtroom, two or three seconds of shock and amazement. Then nerves and laughter. Then a buzz of exclamation.

Hey, the other accused people said to one another, *far fucking out*!

One person in the courtroom remained unflappable.

Joe Addison.

His expression said he'd seen it all before.

"I thought he was going to make a fuss about something," Addison said of Olive Skin a half-hour later as he sat in his chambers. "His eyes kept jerking around the whole time he was waiting his turn, nothing obvious, just something that caught my eye. I thought he was going to get upset about the remand on his case, maybe about the date or the charge. I didn't think he'd make that big of a fuss. Well, you know, some fellas get excited when they're in custody. What that fella doesn't know is next time he comes back to court he'll be in handcuffs and leg irons and manacles and every other damn kind of restraint. Too bad."

Addison's chambers are in a large, gloomy room at the top of Old City Hall. They're furnished in pieces that might have come from a thrift store — a desk, a couple of armchairs, a sofa, and a coffee table. On the coffee table on this day there rested two fat volumes with blue covers, each volume about an inch and a half thick.

"My judgment from the preliminary hearing on the Southam case," Addison said, gesturing at the blue volumes.

The Southam is one of Addison's prides. The hearing

stretched over several months in his court, and he estimates he read "probably twenty thousand pages of cases" before he wrote his long judgment. The case involved important issues and big names in Canada's corporate community, and it arose out of a series of transactions worked out by the country's three leading newspaper publishers. Over a short period of time in the late 1970s and the early 1980s, the three dealt in several big-city newspapers in ways that attracted the alarm of the federal Attorney General's Office. In Montreal, FP Publications closed down the *Star* and left the daily field to the *Gazette*, a Southam paper. In Winnipeg, it was a Southam paper, the *Tribune*, that folded, leaving a Thomson paper, the *Free Press*, all alone. In Ottawa, the *Journal* ceased publication and turned the market over to a Southam paper, the *Citizen*. And in Vancouver, both newspapers continued operations, the *Sun* and the *Province*, but Thomson assigned its half-interest in the company that owned the two, Pacific Press, to Southam. The federal government regarded all of this manoeuvring as a form of hanky-panky and charged Southam, FP, and Thomson with offences under the Anti-Combines Act.

"I didn't know I was taking the preliminary hearing in the case until the morning I walked into Forty-two Court," Addison said in his chambers. "This was in the fall of 1981, and I looked at the counsel table and what I saw was the A-Team. I knew it was gonna be something very large."

Claude Thomson appeared for the crown, Lorne Morphy for the Thomson papers, John Laskin for FP, and Jake Howard for Southam. All are top-drawer Toronto counsel. The witnesses who appeared for crown and defence were of a similar calibre: Conrad Black, John Tory, Lord Thomson. Addison welcomed and enjoyed the presence of each star.

"A charming man, Conrad Black," he said. "Very articulate witness. Made my job easier."

But not all that easier. The evidence was complex, and the

issues were new to Addison. "I'd never been down that road before," he said. The hearing lasted through the winter until Easter of 1982 with a few weeks off from time to time while Addison and the counsel tended to other cases and other trials. Addison did his homework on anti-combines law, and, as the hearing progressed, it seemed to him that there would probably be enough evidence to commit the newspaper chains to trial on the charges.

Jake Howard, Southam's counsel, must have seen the writing on the wall. He elected to put in no defence on behalf of his client.

"Mr. Howard, do you have an argument?" Addison asked him in court.

"Your honour," Howard said, "I didn't have an argument in the beginning."

Addison laughed. It was his kind of answer.

When the hearing ended and Addison retired to write his judgment, he found himself with new problems. Who, for example, was going to type his judgment?

Writing the judgment was challenging enough. "Many a night I'd wake up at four in the morning with something on my mind," he said. "I'd get up, go to the den at home, and write until I got it all down." The writing took up several four-in-the-morning sessions and most of the rest of Addison's time. "I went to our chief judge, Fred Hayes," Addison said, "and I said to him, 'You may be wondering what I'm doing,' and then I said, 'I may be writing a novel.' "

Addison finished the judgment in longhand and went looking for someone to type it.

"The crazy problems you have in my business," he said. "I had a secretary, but she also worked for four other judges. I gave her the judgment and three weeks later it was still sitting in the same place. So I told her to farm out parts of the judgment to other stenographers. That didn't work. Totally disjointed. Do guys in the Supreme Court of Canada have this kind of trouble? Next we brought in a good legal secretary who happened to be on the loose and got her to type it. At first there was a small difficulty. Her desk was beside the kid who delivered the mail. He smoked. That bothered the secretary. I got her a new office. By then I'd already had to postpone the day I said I'd deliver the judgment. It's crazy, but that's life in Provincial Court."

Addison's judgment added up to 477 typed pages and it took him three days in early May of 1982 to read his words to the lawyers and reporters assembled in Forty-two Court. "Regrettably," he began, "I have been unable to condense this judgment to other than gargantuan proportions." Then he proceeded to analyse the evidence and the law on combines in immaculate detail. He concluded that the newspaper chains must face trial on the crown's charges.

Much later, at the trial in the Supreme Court of Ontario, the presiding justice dismissed the charges against Southam, FP, and Thomson. He based his judgment on fact rather than on law. As a finding of fact, the justice held that the newspaper executives had no intent to break the law, that they had arrived at no prior arrangement to give themselves or the others an advantage in the various newspaper markets. Since the finding was based on fact, not law, the crown was not able to take an appeal of the decision to a higher court.

Addison wished that the case could have proceeded to appeal. He would have liked to see his own conclusions thrashed around in the Ontario Court of Appeal and the Supreme Court of Canada. That was one disappointment the case left him with. And there was one other tiny, niggling regret.

"I wish I'd bought some Southam stock," he said in his chambers. "These guys had just created a gold mine. The stock was bound to go up, and after I'd finished my judgment, which of course was contrary to where my money would be going, I thought about investing. But then I figured, no, I better not touch it. The thing about being a judge is you can't do anything that wouldn't look right."

John Kozachenko appeared in Addison's court on June 26, 1985. He was a slim man in his late twenties. He looked pale and not entirely healthy, but he wore a righteous and determined expression on his face. He was charged with causing a disturbance in a McDonald's restaurant on Yonge Street. Kozachenko didn't think of his actions as a disturbance. To him they amounted to a demonstration. It was the sort of thing he went in for. Kozachenko was an activist for homosexual rights, peace, anarchy, and the cause of the Guatemalans. It was the latter that took him and several like-minded friends to McDonald's.

"Don't eat meat!" they chanted. "Don't kill beef!"

At the same time, according to witnesses for the crown, Kozachenko made a mess by tossing around some earth from the restaurant's plants and littering the place with McDonald's serviettes, the ones decorated with golden arches.

When Kozachenko stepped into the witness-box to testify in his own defence, he explained where Guatemala fit into the picture.

"McDonald's are bulldozing rain forests down in Guatemala to make grazing land for their cattle," he said. "The cattle turn into Big Macs and the Guatemalan people starve."

Kozachenko added a few more details about his personal life. He was unemployed. He was gay. And he had a condition related to AIDS called PLS.

"Because of my illness," he said, "I don't want to have to go to jail."

Kozachenko left the witness-box.

"On the evidence," Addison said, "I find you guilty of the charge."

Addison paused.

"But I'm granting you an absolute discharge," he said. "You've got enough problems without jail."

Addison gave Kozachenko that look of his, bemused, as if he were regarding the world from a great distance and thought it was probably an all-right place.

CHAPTER THREE

Two Gentlemen of the Bench

Ken Lysyk is starting out. John Osler is finishing up. The two men arrived on the bench at very different times in provinces that are far apart, Lysyk to the Supreme Court of British Columbia in 1982, Osler to the Supreme Court of Ontario in 1968. Lysyk's heritage is Prairies Ukrainian. Osler comes from one of Ontario's oldest, most prominent Wasp families. Lysyk sits in the lush new courthouse in Vancouver. Osler's judicial headquarters is ancient Osgoode Hall in Toronto. Lysyk is just past fifty. Osler is twenty years older. Lysyk's career could, in the view of many, take him to the Supreme Court of Canada. Osler is a supernumerary justice, a status that makes him a part-time judge one step away from retirement.

Still, for all the contrasts, the two men are different only in the immediate facts of their biographies. In other essential ways, in the ways of the judiciary, they might be mirror reflections of each other. Both are intelligent, caring, clear-thinking men who understand the life of the law. Both are superior judges.

John Osler is a tall, angular, shy, kind man. He comes from the Toronto Oslers. His great-uncle was Sir William Osler,

119

the pioneering and globe-trotting physician who belonged more to Montreal, Philadelphia, Baltimore, and Oxford than to Toronto. John Osler's grandfather, Sir Edmund Osler, was pure old Toronto. He made the family fortune in banking and the stock market. He was the lord of Craigleigh of Rosedale, perhaps the city's most magnificent mansion, and he sat as a Conservative member of Parliament for West Toronto from 1896 to 1917. John Osler may have inherited his reserved nature from Sir Edmund, who was so private as a parliamentarian that a headline in a Toronto newspaper in 1914 announced, "After 17 years in the House, Osler speaks!"

John Osler has lived in or near Toronto almost continuously since he was ten years old, but he came at the city and his role in it from a different angle in more ways than one. His father, a soldier and financier, branched away from the east to start the western division of his own father's brokerage firm in partnership with Sir Augustus Nanton in Winnipeg, and he stayed on in the city to raise his family. In 1925, young John was sent to Appleby College, a private school for boys in Oakville, thirty miles west of Toronto, and, in most senses, he never went home again. At Appleby he made two connections that became basic to the rest of his life. He dated the headmaster's daughter, Betty Guest, and later married her. And he began in a small way to ask questions about Canada's business and governmental institutions. His queries would eventually carry him several steps to the left of the political position traditionally staked out by men whose last name is Osler.

"I was as naive as any high school student," he says of his Appleby days. "I won a prize for an essay I did on the banking system, a subject I still know nothing about. But this was just after the banks had collapsed in the United States, and I took a very superior attitude in my essay."

Osler's excursions into left-of-centre politics grew less naive with the years. He went to Trinity College at the University of Toronto and involved himself in the CCF. Andy Brewin was his mentor. Brewin filled many roles: outstanding litigation lawyer, socialist theoretician, activist, and, years later, NDP member of Parliament. With Brewin's guidance, Osler made his major jump into participatory politics in a federal by-election that still rates a significant footnote in Canadian political history.

The by-election took place in the Toronto riding of York South in 1942, and the only two candidates in the field were an obscure high school teacher named Joseph Noseworthy for the CCF, and, for the Conservatives, no one less than former prime minister Arthur Meighen. It looked a shoo-in for Meighen. But heavy issues were in the air. The CCF was pressing for a policy of conscription in wartime, not merely conscription of men for the armed forces but conscription of wealth. Ted Jolliffe, a young lawyer who would shortly become the CCF's Ontario leader, ran Noseworthy's show as campaign manager, and the candidate's official agent was John Osler. Conscription of wealth and a member of the Osler family? It seemed an unlikely combination. But Noseworthy, Jolliffe, Osler, and company pulled off a heady victory, and on election night, February 9, 1942, the winners gathered for celebratory drinks at the elegant Toronto home that John and Betty Osler had recently bought.

"Things were going great," Osler remembers of the CCF fortunes, so great that he decided to run for office as the party's candidate in the riding of St. Patrick's in the 1943 Ontario election. St. Patrick's was a long, narrow riding that cut north and south through the west central part of Toronto. It took in the wealthy Forest Hill neighbourhood in the north, middle-class streets in the centre, and lower-class immigrant sections in the south. Osler carried the immigrant vote, held his own among the middle class, and suffered miserably in Forest Hill, the very neighbourhood where he and Betty had lived for most of their married life. When the numbers were added up, Osler lost the riding.

But, under Ted Jolliffe's leadership, the CCF carried an

astounding thirty-four ridings in the 1943 election, a mere
four seats back of George Drew's Tories, who formed the government. That happy state of political affairs encouraged
Osler to run again in St. Patrick's in the June 1945 election,
which the CCF charged into with euphoric expectations of victory. The expectations didn't pan out. Osler lost St. Patrick's.
Jolliffe was defeated in his own riding. And the number of
CCF seats dropped through the floor from thirty-four in 1943
to an almost invisible eight in 1945. The reason for the catas-
trophe lay in a speech that Jolliffe delivered two weeks before
voting day. He accused George Drew of maintaining a special branch of the Ontario Provincial Police which had the
single mission of spying on the CCF and labour unions. "A
Gestapo" Jolliffe called the branch, and though his claims
were largely correct, George Drew put on a wonderful display of indignation that convinced the voters of his righteous-
ness. "Gestapo" turned out to be an unfortunate choice of
label in the public perception, and Jolliffe's speech backfired
at the polls.

"Ted attributed too much malice to Drew in the speech,"
Osler says. "He and Drew loathed each other's guts, couldn't
stand to be in the same room, and that led Ted to lay all the
stress on Drew in his speech. It went dreadfully wrong."

Osler ran once more in St. Patrick's in the 1948 election —
and lost again. "I did a little better each time," he says. "But
not enough better." The 1948 contest ended his out-front political activities, but he continued to work for the socialist-labour
cause in another effective role. He devoted himself to the practice of labour law.

In the beginning, after his Appleby days, Osler's family
didn't aim him for law. His father, his older.brother, and a
regiment of other male relatives on his paternal side took
their education at the Royal Military College in Kingston. So
would young John. He was accepted at RMC but, to universal
family chagrin, he backed off. "I didn't appreciate the mili-

tary," he says. "And I was lousy at mathematics." He chose law, a profession for which his distant ancestors provided a pair of precedents: one great-uncle sat on the Ontario Court of Appeal and another had prosecuted Louis Riel.

Osler was called to the Ontario bar in 1940, and after time out to fight two elections and one war — he commanded a sub-chaser in the North Atlantic in the Second World War — he opened a labour-law practice in Toronto in 1946 in partnership with Ted Jolliffe. Four years later they were joined by David Lewis, who had resigned his job as the CCF's executive director in Ottawa. Lewis knew Osler only slightly through occasional political contacts, and he approached Osler as a law partner with mild apprehension. He needn't have worried.

"Osler was patient and co-operative beyond my expectations," Lewis wrote in his 1981 autobiography, *The Good Fight.* "His tall, aristocratic bearing and quiet style of speaking and working made some union representatives feel out of place in his presence, and his comfortable background made it difficult for him to speak the worker's language at first, but he was a conscientious, knowledgeable lawyer of considerable judgment. He was also a social democrat by conviction and thoroughly immersed in the law of labour-manangement relations on labour's side."

In fairly short order, Jolliffe, Lewis and Osler blossomed into the premier labour-law firm in Ontario. Most of the major unions retained its services, and Osler's share of the practice put him in charge of battles before the Ontario Labour Relations Board and before arbitration tribunals on behalf of the Rubber Workers Union, the Electrical Workers, the International Woodworkers, and the Metro Toronto Police Association. He organized the strategy for most of the tense legal in-fighting for the Steelworkers Union in its long, sometimes bitter, and finally successful fight to displace the Mine Mill Workers in Northern Ontario's mills and factories.

Almost the only union that didn't make use of Osler was the Teamsters. It failed to appreciate the style that Osler brought to argument and negotiations, too gentlemanly for the Teamsters, not enough ranting and raving.

John Turner appreciated Osler's style. When Turner was the federal minister of justice in the late 1960s, he attempted in a small way to avoid appointments to the bench that stuck to a rigid party line. He looked for judges beyond the ranks of Liberal membership, and his eye fell on John Osler. Turner's office approached Osler in the late fall of 1968 with the offer of the trial division of the Ontario Supreme Court. Osler needed no extra persuasion. After almost a quarter-century of tough labour practice, he was ready for the new life of the bench, and on December 23, 1968, he moved into it.

There's a natural faultlessness about Ken Lysyk's appearance. He is orderly and precise, and it's clear he doesn't have to get up an hour early in the morning to look that way. He has an attractively arranged set of features and a closely clipped beard that is dark brown shot through with grey. Altogether, he suggests a lead player in a Masterpiece Theatre production of *Anna Karenina*.

He grew up one hundred and thirty miles southeast of Regina in a tiny place called, for a reason no one has ever explained to Lysyk, Khedive. "The population was about one hundred when the bus was in," he says. By the time he was a Khedive high school student, Lysyk had already set his mind on a career in law. He asked people at the University of Saskatchewan Law School which university subject to study in preparation for his legal future. Philosophy, he was advised, and that became his major when he won a scholarship to travel from Khedive to McGill University in Montreal.

"The advice was right," Lysyk says, an observation that may make him one of the few philosophers on the Canadian bench.

After a B.A. at McGill, his legal studies began back at the University of Saskatchewan, a school with a law faculty that, perhaps surprisingly, boasts a lengthy history of excellence. Bud Estey has a theory about the origins of the excellence. Estey came through Saskatchewan's education system, and it was sound enough to carry him to an appointment on the Supreme Court of Canada.

"There were a large number of immigrant educators and professional people who came west," he explains. "They came from eastern Canada, England, the United States, and they thought they were going to take part in populating the great northwest, maybe building another New York. Well, the depression ended that, and they were marooned in Saskatchewan. They couldn't move professionally, so in the 1930s they became our teachers, and they were absolutely first-rate. When, later in life, I went to Harvard Law School, there was nothing they taught me that I hadn't already heard about in Saskatchewan."

The tradition of quality at Saskatchewan's law faculty persisted through the 1950s when Lysyk arrived as a student. Though the school was small, students and staff set themselves lofty and enduring standards. Otto Lang taught at the school and was later its dean. Barry Strayer was a couple of years ahead of Lysyk, and Walter Tarnopolsky was a classmate. Lang became federal minister of justice, Strayer now sits on the Federal Court of Canada, Tarnopolsky is a member of the Ontario Court of Appeal. And there have been others; Saskatchewan professors Jacob Ziegel, Julien Payne, and Donovan Waters are recognized today as arguably the leading Canadian academic experts in, respectively, commercial law, family law, and trusts. Lysyk was in fast company.

He took another law degree at Oxford and accepted a teaching job at the University of British Columbia's law school, where he specialized in two subjects, constitutional law and the law relating to Canada's native peoples. Interest in the first came naturally to him, but his deepest involvement in the second was thrust upon him in the early 1960s when the Department of Indian Affairs commissioned him to study the lot in life of contemporary Canadian native peoples. He came up with the first serious academic paper on the legal position of Indians and Inuit in Canada, and the study produced two results: it gave the native people ammunition in their struggle for justice, and it assured legal academics and government thinkers that, in Lysyk, they had a new scholar in their midst.

In the late 1960s, Lysyk's pal from the Saskatchewan law school, Barry Strayer, was serving as Prime Minister Pierre Trudeau's constitutional adviser. He hired Lysyk on a contract to work alongside him in the Privy Council Office. That was the first of several intriguing career switches that Lysyk went through in the following decade and a half. The moves took him from Vancouver to Ottawa to Toronto, then to Regina and back to Vancouver, with a side trip to the Yukon. Jobs of vastly different scope met him at each stop along the way.

Ronald Macdonald, dean of the University of Toronto Law School in the early 1970s, was responsible for the Toronto chapter in Lysyk's story. "What caught my eye about Ken," Macdonald says, "is that in his articles for the law journals, he wrote in English. There was no legalese, and his pieces had beginnings, middles, and ends. That was really quite amazing." Partly on the strength of Lysyk's refreshing literary talents, Macdonald phoned him in Ottawa and coaxed him to join the Toronto school's faculty. "It was one of the best hirings I ever made," Macdonald says. "He turned out to be a brilliant teacher and extremely popular with the students."

After a year and a half at Macdonald's school, Lysyk and his family worked up enough confidence in a long-term Toronto future to buy a handsome house in a comfortable part of the city. Exactly three months later, a summons came from Roy Romanow in Regina. Romanow was the attorney general in Saskatchewan's NDP government, and he needed a new deputy, someone with the expertise to go up against the federal government in the constitutional confrontations that Romanow saw looming for his province. Barry Strayer had taught Romanow at the Saskatchewan law school, and he nudged his former student to hire his former schoolmate. Romanow's mother may also have pushed for Lysyk. Mrs. Romanow's dear friend, a lady who lived a block and a half away on Saskatoon's west side, had a bright son. A nice boy named Ken. In some ways, Saskatchewan is a very large small town. Romanow made his pitch to Lysyk.

"I dithered," Lysyk says. "After all, with the splendid sense of timing that characterizes many of my decisions, we'd just bought this wonderful house."

He took a leave of absence from the Toronto law school, rented the wonderful house, and went west. The leave of absence eventually became permanent, the house was sold, alas at the bottom of the market, and Lysyk stayed in the Saskatchewan Deputy Attorney General's Office for four exhilarating years.

"The delight and terror in Regina was that the machine of government was small, without any elaborate bureaucracy," Lysyk says. "That meant in things like constitutional advice to my minister and the premier and the whole cabinet, there was only me. And it meant that when I was asked for a draft bill, my minister wanted it tomorrow, not next year, and that very soon after, to my consternation, the draft bill would be the law of the province."

Lysyk's new job took him into the courts as an advocate. Most specifically, it placed him in the Supreme Court of Canada in the late spring of 1976 on the most important constitutional case that had come before the court since the end of the Second World War. The case centred on the validity of the Anti-Inflation Act, a bill the federal government passed in December 1975 to put into effect a system of wage and

price controls. Twenty-six counsel gathered before the
Supreme Court—lawyers for the federal Department of Justice, for five provinces, for the Canadian Labour Congress,
and for a mix of other interests — and they addressed one
crucial question: Was the Anti-Inflation Act a proper exercise of federal authority or was it, under a correct interpretation of the British North America Act, beyond the powers
of the Parliament of Canada?

John Robinette, the dean of Canadian litigation lawyers,
spoke for the federal side. He contended that the legislation
was good on two grounds. One, it fell under the clause of the
BNA Act that gives the federal government authority to pass
laws that are for "the peace, order and good government" of
Canada. And, secondly, it was a statute that dealt with a
national emergency, inflation, a sphere of legislative jurisdiction that belonged exclusively to the Parliament in Ottawa.

In arguing for Saskatchewan, Lysyk had to follow a subtle
course. All of the provinces except Alberta conceded that federal legislation was necessary to combat inflation. But none
wanted the Supreme Court to justify the Anti-Inflation Act
on the grounds of the "peace, order and good government"
clause in the BNA Act. As far as the provinces were concerned,
such a ruling would set a dangerous precedent. It would
enable the federal government to scoop up legislative power
at the expense of provincial authority. When Lysyk rose to
argue in the Supreme Court, the fourth counsel of the twenty-
six to speak, he was performing a high-wire act.

"He was eloquent and elegant," Peter Russell says of Lysyk
that day. Russell is a political scientist at the University of
Toronto, a close observer of the Supreme Court, and a courtroom junkie who sat through the week of argument in the
Anti-Inflation Reference. "Lysyk didn't take more than fifteen minutes of the court's time and he never used a note. He
went at his argument in the fashion of a very seasoned counsel. Which was amazing, because all of us thought of him as
one of us plain old academics."

Lysyk's argument to the court was that, apart from emergency situations, the "peace, order and good government" clause allowed the federal government to pass legislation only in a few narrow and distinct areas which the provinces couldn't touch. The Anti-Inflation Act didn't fit into such a category, since its subject matter, inflation, intruded on matters that normally fell under provincial jurisdiction. Lysyk put the argument to the court, but it wasn't an argument that entirely originated with him. It had been shaped over the years by another man in the courtroom that day. He was Professor William Lederman, the constitutional-law genius from Queen's University who would later present the same pro-province argument on behalf of one of the unions opposing the Anti-Inflation Act.

"There was a lot of irony in the situation," Peter Russell says. "Lysyk was better at arguing the Lederman approach than its developer was. That's because when Lederman had his turn, he spoke in court like a professor. But Lysyk brought the stuff alive, and he had a powerful impact on the nine judges."

The impact was reflected in the judgment the Supreme Court brought down five weeks later. Though the court's views were clouded by opinions that reached the same result by different reasoning, two facts emerged more or less intact. The court stood seven to two in favour of the national-emergency justification for the Anti-Inflation Act, but it was a possible five to four against justification on the "peace, order and good government" grounds.

Lysyk's presentation had prevailed.

Later in 1976, he packed up in Regina and moved two provinces west, having accepted a posting as dean of the law school at the University of British Columbia. But the following April he interrupted his duties as dean in order to look after an intimidating bit of business for the federal government. The job was precipitated by the news that the long inquiry conducted in the Northwest Territories by Thomas Berger was about to conclude that it would be unwise to build a pipeline through the Territories to transport the vast reserves of natural gas from the Mackenzie Delta and Alaska to the south. The report put Ottawa in temporary shock. How could the natural gas be moved out of the Arctic? Maybe through the Yukon? Somebody should make a study. Lysyk got the call, and though Berger had had a couple of years to complete his report, Lysyk was given a scant three months.

"We started in the shadow of Berger," Rob Pritchard says. He was one of Lysyk's two principal assistants on the commission; Steve Goudge, a superb young Toronto litigation lawyer, was the senior man, and he brought in his friend Pritchard, who is today, still well short of his fortieth birthday, dean of the University of Toronto Law School. "Apart from the Berger thing," Pritchard says, "there was a political claim going around that our inquiry was just a way of justifying a pre-ordained government decision. The rumours were that Ken was being used to rubberstamp what Ottawa had already decided about building a Yukon pipeline. People also said we couldn't produce a really meaningful report in such a short time. All of that made us extremely determined."

Lysyk and his staff worked seventeen-hour days for three months. "My only time off was a weekend in Inuvik," Lysyk remembers. He conducted public hearings in seventeen of the eighteen Yukon communities, and he called into play political skills no one suspected he possessed. "Ken had to broker all the various interests up there," Steve Goudge says. "The whites, the native peoples, the territorial government, the conservationists — all wanted something different. But Ken showed this quiet steadiness, so that by the end, I think everybody trusted his judgment."

When the report was published—the last sections written in a propeller plane during an eight-hour flight that took Lysyk, Goudge, Pritchard, and staff from Whitehorse to the printers who were standing by in Ottawa with presses set to roll — it concluded that the pipeline could be built on the strict proviso that several conditions were met. Those included the establishment of a Yukon Heritage Fund based on a payment of two hundred million dollars from the pipeline company, the settlement of native land claims by the federal government with an advance of fifty million dollars, and the creation of a wide corridor through the Yukon that would provide for the least destructive pipeline route. The report ran to 171 pages, and though not everybody was happy with the conclusions, they had the stamp of comprehensive authority.

Lysyk returned to UBC. He ran the law school, served on a committee that advised the B.C. cabinet on constitutional issues, and took busman's holidays to argue constitutional cases for Saskatchewan in the Supreme Court of Canada. His career seemed settled into a groove, but in the fall of 1982, Minister of Justice Mark MacGuigan changed all of that. He asked Lysyk to take an appointment to the British Columbia Supreme Court. Lysyk's immediate response echoed earlier reactions to shifts in his life.

"More dithering," he says. "I wasn't searching for anything new." Still, he conceded that he felt a call to the trial judge's job. "I suppose," he says, "I was interested to see how I'd cope with a different line of work."

And, with that modest sense of adventure, Lysyk took MacGuigan's offer. There has hardly been a justice at the Supreme Court level across the country with more fascinating credentials. Teacher. Scholar. Civil servant. Counsel. Constitutional adviser. Writer on legal subjects in prose that escapes legalese. Conductor of an inquiry into a project that affected environment, industry, and peoples of more than one race. And Canadian of Ukrainian ancestors from a town called Khedive. It was November 6, 1982, and Ken Lysyk went to the bench.

On balance, the move from bar to bench flowed more
smoothly than John Osler expected.

"The great thing I found about the job was that the phone
never rings," he says. That was a plus for Osler. "It worries
some new judges not to have all those calls they were used to
in private practice," he says. "But the quiet suits me just fine."

In his own practice, he hadn't done any negligence litigation, legal fights over the apportioning of fault and damages
in accident claims. That was a minus. "Insurance cases came
hot and heavy in my early years," Osler says. "They were new
to me and sometimes very difficult. But once I realized it was
simply a matter of getting at the facts of each case, I had the
hang of it."

He'd spent plenty of time in motions court during his lawyer days. That was a plus. "Motions court scares hell out of
judges who come in without any experience at it," Osler says.
"It's the variety that terrifies them." In motions court, a judge
is required to hear in the course of a day twenty or thirty
applications — or "motions" — by counsel who are requesting rulings on procedural or other matters that are usually
tangential to a case's main action. In a single day, the motions
may cover the range from a variation of the claim in a multi-
million-dollar civil action to an order affecting the freedom
of an accused person in a criminal action. "I could deal with
it," Osler says.

"I'm a lazy writer," he confesses. That was a minus. "I handle the King's English reasonably well, but I'm not terribly
organized. If I have something difficult to write, I'll sharpen
a lot of pencils and make two or three trips to the bank before I
get down to it. But once I start, I go very slowly, and as a
consequence I hardly ever rewrite. I write short judgments,
and I'm trying to make them shorter. Take out the repetitions.
And take out the adverbs. Adverbs get in the way."

Murder trials turned out to be duller than Osler expected.
That was a minus. "Seventy per cent of them are all about

formal measurements and photographs of murder scenes taken from every conceivable angle and crown attorneys going at facts over and over with a sledgehammer," Osler says. "Not very exciting." On the other hand, some murder cases have come along that turn on esoteric scientific analysis. "Those kinds," Osler says, "are quite engrossing."

Much of Osler's lasting satisfaction on the bench has derived from cases that opened up the chance to say something new about the law. Like most other Supreme Court judges, he gets a kick out of putting a fresh interpretation on an ancient precedent and giving the law a shove in a different and necessary direction. Often enough, the provincial Court of Appeal or the Supreme Court of Canada will come along later to overrule the novel interpretation of the trial judge and restore the law to something like its former state. But trial judges like Osler with inquiring minds remain on the lookout for pieces of law that in their view need re-tinkering.

"Sometimes you get slapped down pretty thoroughly in the appeal courts," he says. "But sometimes they get around to agreeing that you're on to something. That's where the gratification comes in."

In a 1971 case in Brantford, Ontario, home of the Council of the Six Nations Indians, Osler used one case to try to strike a blow for Indian women. A section of the federal Indian Act directed that any Indian woman who married a white man was thereafter barred from registration as a member of her Indian band. Since the Act contained no section that gave similar back-of-the-hand treatment to Indian men who married white women, Osler held that the offending section represented a piece of blatant sex discrimination. The section, he ruled, was in contravention of the Bill of Rights and therefore inoperative. That decision, coming in 1971 before Parliament and the Charter of Rights said something about such sex discrimination, put Osler in the vanguard of feminism.

Two years later, Osler returned to the Brantford court and

another Six Nations case in which he made a run at more new law. This time, after an intensive examination of Indian treaties and other dealings between Indians and white men dating back to the Royal Proclamation of 1763, Osler declared that the Six Nations Band wasn't a "band" within the definition of the Indian Act and that the lands it had been living on for centuries didn't qualify as "reserve" lands. As if those rulings didn't upset the applecart, Osler went on to hold that the Indian Act itself, since its effect was to treat Indians, as Indians, differently from other Canadians, was inoperative in its entirety.

"Well, it may have been a new interpretation of the Act," Osler says of the 1973 case. "But it was one of those times when the Court of Appeal gave me a real slapping down."

The appeal court restored the Indian Act to operation, and the Six Nations Band got back its status and its lands.

Osler didn't mind taking a shot at fresh law in cases that struck most people as frivolous. The G-string case, for example. In 1980, the Metro Toronto Council passed a by-law directing that no performer in a strip club could take off all of her spangles. She had to leave on "opaque clothing fully covering such person's pubic area".

Business went into immediate decline at Toronto's strip clubs. The customers wanted at least a glimpse of "such person's pubic area", and the club owners went to court to satisfy the customers' desires. Among other arguments, the owners' lawyers contended that the Charter of Rights contained guarantees of "freedom of expression" and that the by-law hindered the rights of the strippers to express themselves freely. Osler sat on a panel of three judges who heard the arguments, and while the other two pooh-poohed the freedom-of-expression point, Osler thought it made sense of a wacky sort.

"While the phrase may frequently be abused," he wrote, "nothing is more common in the artistic world than to hear an individual express the desire to 'make a statement', and this may be by means of the written or spoken word, the painted canvas, the etched stone, or a print thereof, a musical composition or an idea conveyed through the medium of dance. While the word burlesque may be thought of by most to describe a form of expression that is perhaps more vulgar than most of the artistic endeavours I have mentioned, it is nevertheless a form of expression, and to insist on a quality or quantity of clothing for persons expressing themselves in that form does, in my view, limit a freedom of expression otherwise guaranteed by the Charter."

In the end, which came in the Supreme Court of Canada in early 1986, Metro Toronto's G-string by-law was overturned on grounds that differed from Osler's stand on freedom of expression, but he'd had his two bits' worth.

The Scientology hearings gave Osler several cracks at making new law. It was a disputatious and highly publicized case, and it first hit the headlines in early March 1983, when about one hundred officers from the Ontario Provincial Police arrived at the Church of Scientology offices in mid-town Toronto with axes, fire extinguishers, and a search warrant. It was the search warrant that would give Osler much of his cause for rethinking the law.

The Scientology movement was founded by a former science fiction writer named L. Ron Hubbard, an American, now deceased. It calls itself a church but appears to many to be a baroque amalgam of religion, cultism, psychological devices, and a dash of quackery. As far as the OPP was concerned, the Scientologists may also have been running a few sophisticated scams, and after a couple of years of investigation, it obtained a search warrant from Provincial Court Judge Fred Hayes to look in the Scientology offices for evidence of tax and consumer fraud and of conspiracy to commit indictable offences. The raid with the axes and fire extinguishers lasted for eighteen hours and resulted in the one hundred policemen carting away boxes holding a grand total, if anyone was really counting, of 250,000 documents.

The OPP needed more than eighteen months to read through the documents and determine whether the Scientologists had committed an offence known to the Canadian Criminal Code. But lawyers for the Scientologists didn't wait quite that long before they bombarded the Supreme Court with objections to the OPP's procedure. John Osler was the judge on the receiving end of the bombardment, and from the beginning of the long series of Scientology motions in June 1984 until the end of Osler's share of the case in July 1985, he devoted seventeen scattered weeks to the hearing of arguments and the writing of judgments.

"The case went in phases," Osler says. "We'd deal with one point and I'd go away and write my judgment on it. Then, after an interval, we'd consider another point and I'd go away again to write. I must have written eight judgments altogether, but it wasn't hard to keep up with the facts and the arguments even though they were spaced over such a long period. That was because the Scientologists seem to have an infinite command of funds, and they arranged to get almost daily transcripts of each day's hearings from the court reporters. That's a luxury, daily transcripts, I'm not used to."

The first objection raised by the lawyers for the Scientogists was based on the priest-penitent privilege. At least six thousand of the documents, according to the argument, contained details of confessions and other personal revelations which members of the Church, hanging on with both hands to a truth-testing device known in Scientology circles as an E-Meter, had divulged to Church ministers. Seizure of these documents, the argument went, constituted a violation of the freedom of religion guaranteed in the Charter of Rights, and the search warrant under which all 250,000 documents were seized was therefore invalid.

Osler didn't bite.

He found that there was no such legal entity in Ontario as a priest-penitent privilege for any religion. "In a pragmatic way," he wrote, it's the practice of the courts "to press counsel not to pursue questions that would result in compelling a priest or minister of religion to breach a confidence or to decline to compel persons claiming such a privilege to answer." But an absolute privilege? No way.

Counsel for the Scientologists attacked the search warrant from another angle. This argument went that the police officers who had applied to Judge Fred Hayes for the warrant misrepresented the facts on which Hayes ultimately issued the warrant. Specifically, OPP Sergeant Al Ciampini had slipped some egregious errors into a 158-page compilation of Scientology sins which he presented to Judge Hayes. Osler thought the Scientologists might have a point, and he allowed their counsel the rare privilege of cross-examining Ciampini during the argument of the motion before him to quash the search warrant. As a rule, witnesses never appear in motions court, but Osler listened as the Scientology counsel went at Ciampini and he conceded that Ciampini might have goofed in some of his facts. Osler dished out reprimands to the OPP, but he couldn't find enough reason to declare the search warrant invalid.

"It must always be remembered," Osler wrote, "that what Ciampini is putting forward in his statements to Judge Hayes is his belief and his reasons therefor. What is being sought is an investigative tool, the search warrant, and by the very fact that it is required by the investigating officers, it is likely that they are not possessed of the whole story or all of the evidence they require."

Next, the Scientologists' lawyers raised the argument that the warrant lost validity because Judge Hayes, in issuing it, couldn't be expected to grasp the contents of many of the Church documents. These were the papers of a complex, even mystical religious order written in terms that could be comprehended only by its adepts.

Osler had no hesitation about that one.

"The argument that the arcane language may well mean something other than what appears on the surface," he wrote, "almost amounts to an assertion that because it speaks in strange tongues, the church must be immune from investigation. Such an argument lacks the element of reality."

As the Scientology hearings moved toward the summer of 1985, Osler was being pressed to refine in his judgment the precise parameters of that delicate and controversial policeman's tool, the search warrant. He responded to the challenge. "The description of what is to be searched for," he said in attempting to nail down the nature of the application for a warrant, "must not be so broad and vague as to give the search officers carte blanche to rummage through the premises of the target." In short, no fishing expeditions permitted. And yet, Osler continued, in the case of the Scientology warrant, "quite obviously no detailed analysis of the search material could be made under the circumstances in such a way as to afford the officers complete certainty that what they were seizing came within the authorized descriptions." In sum, Osler wrote he was "satisfied that the rule of search first, then seize has been followed as well as it reasonably can in the circumstances." After a year of motions and arguments, Osler declared the search warrant to be entirely on the up-and-up.

Then, on July 5, 1985, he dropped a bombshell.

When police officers seize documents under a search warrant, they are required under the Criminal Code to go before a justice of the peace from time to time to obtain a detention order which permits them to hang on to the seized material. The OPP in the Scientology case had followed the usual drill and, as in all such procedures, had appeared in front of the justice of the peace without a notice to the other side, to the counsel for the Scientologists, and without an appearance at the proceedings by the Scientologists' lawyers. It was the way such matters had always been handled, *ex parte*, with only one party present. To the surprise of everyone, especially of the police and the crown attorneys, Osler said that the age-old practice was improper, unfair, and unconstitutional. It may have been going on for years, Osler wrote, but it's wrong, unless the owners of the seized material, the Scientologists in this instance, have a fair shot at opposing the detention order.

Chalk up a piece of new law for John Osler.

While Osler was carrying on his lengthy examination of the search warrant and detention order, the Attorney General's Office was proceeding on another front against the Scientologists. It charged nineteen past or present members of the Church with theft, possession of stolen documents, and breach of trust. The nineteen included employees of the OPP, the Metro Police, the RCMP, and the Attorney General's own office, and the documents they were alleged to have stolen made up a stack of data that the police and other agencies had gathered on the Scientologists.

The long and treacherous story behind the alleged pilfering seemed to reach back to the 1950s when L. Ron Hubbard, from whose vivid imagination Scientology sprang, set out to blow the whistle on such psychiatric practices as electroshock, the use of certain powerful drugs, and mind-altering experiments. His crusade, so the theorizing goes, roused the suspicion and anger of the FBI and the CIA. In retaliation, the two government agencies dug up dirt on the Scientologists and spread it to other law-enforcement groups in the United States and Canada. To pursue this tale of plot and counterplot to its bizarre end, the Scientologists allegedly recruited members who took clerical jobs in organizations like the OPP and the RCMP, raided their employers' files, and discovered the nature of the dirty stuff the FBI, the CIA, and every other agency had managed to uncover about the Church.

A hint at the machinations on all sides emerged on December 13, 1985, when one of the nineteen accused Scientologists appeared in Provincial Court in Toronto's Old City Hall. Her name was Nanna Anderson, and to the shock of the Scientologists, she told the court that she was breaking ranks with the other eighteen accused and was pleading guilty to charges of possession of stolen goods. She told her story, and it was strange and not a little pathetic.

Anderson was thirty-nine years old and had joined the Church of Scientology in her native Denmark when she was seventeen. She stayed with the Church after she moved to Canada in 1976, and in court she testified that the stolen goods that were the subject of the case against her were photocopies of files from the Ontario Medical Association. The Scientologists had pressed her to take a job at the OMA and to hustle out files during her lunch breaks for swift photocopying. Her actions were wrong, she said to the judge hearing her case, and she regretted them.

"Whatever you did," the judge said, "was because of a situation that developed over a number of years. You've been penalized sufficiently."

The judge in Provincial Court that day was none other than Lorenzo DiCecco, the kindly optimist, and, true to his nature, he permitted Nanna Anderson to leave the courtroom with an absolute discharge and with no criminal record.

"Sentence was passed on you much before today," DiCecco said.

In the meantime, the Ontario Court of Appeal knew that a problem was heading its way. The Attorney General launched an appeal of John Osler's finding that the old and established procedure on detention orders was improper. The Attorney General's Office revealed that it would need many days to argue the appeal. Osler smiled at the news and waited to see whether the Appeal Court would slap him down on his latest poking into new law.

In his first year on the bench, Ken Lysyk had problems. For

instance, taking notes of testimony at a trial, that was definitely a problem.

"The difficulty," he says, "is that the testimony doesn't come in a nice sequential order but in the order that the witnesses happen to be called. You get one side's version of the case before you hear a peep out of the other side. I found it hard to know what testimony was top-priority stuff and what was dispensable until we were well into the trial. So I was always looking at the pages of notes I'd taken and saying I didn't need a quarter of what I'd scribbled down. Now what I've learned to do is draw counsel out early on about what the real battle is over and keep at that mainstream stuff as the trial unfolds."

Nor was judgment-writing a piece of cake for Lysyk in the early days. A constitutional case he heard in May 1983 gave him problems not in arriving at his decision but in explaining the decision on paper. In the case, an NDP member of Parliament, Ian Waddell, challenged the power of the Privy Council to amend an Act of Parliament. Lysyk held that Parliament could delegate to a subordinate agency, the Privy Council in this case, the necessary authority to amend or repeal Parliament's own statutes. So far so good. But putting the decision in clear language, that was entirely another matter.

"It ended up a long-winded judgment," Lysyk says in criticism of his own handiwork. "It was tough to get the facts down so that someone who comes to the case cold will find it comprehensible and yet at the same time to leave out the parts that were extraneous to what I was really deciding. Maybe that's the problem in all judgment-writing — boiling down the recital of facts without making the case even more impossible to figure out."

Lysyk also discovered that his past experience in the law, vast as it was in so many areas, still left him short on knowledge in some areas that are essential to a judge's work.

"I had to cover off whole regions of profound ignorance,"
he says. "My time in court as a counsel was all at the appellate level. I knew little about trials and I hadn't touched things
like practice and procedure since my law school days. No
question, I had to really extend myself as a judge. But that
was part of the fun, and now, oddly enough, the cases I enjoy
most are the kind I never before had anything to do with —
jury cases. They keep me engrossed."

It wasn't a jury trial that gave Lysyk his most compelling
taste of the trial process in his early days. But it was a trial
that packed in all the other ingredients of a gripping court
case — drama, pathos, hard decisions, and a plaintiff whose
life seemed in ruins.

The plaintiff's name was Fred Gerak. He was twenty years
old, a feisty, rambunctious kid, on the afternoon of July 26,
1981, when he and some buddies downed a few beers and
went swimming at British Columbia's Cultus Lake Provincial Park. Fred and the guys had never been to Cultus Lake.
It was new territory for them, but everybody'd heard it was
a terrific spot to cool off on a day as hot as July 26. Man, the
temperature was around thirty-five Celsius.

Fred was wearing his swim-suit under his jeans, and when
the car pulled into the Cultus Lake parking lot, he was already
stripping off his clothes and getting rid of his running-shoes.
Fred and Robin Pallos and Ray Hurley hit the beach on the
run. Fred was out front. He turned on to the long dock. It
reached about one hundred and fifty feet into the lake. The
place was jammed, kids and dads and moms and old folks
sitting on the dock and splashing in the water. Fred ripped
down the dock looking for a clear spot to dive into the water.
He kept running till he was about four-fifths of the way to
the end of the dock.

Hey, this looked good for diving. An empty piece of surface
in between all the people messing around in the water.

"Fred!" Robin Pallos called after his buddy. "It looks kinda
shallow!"

Fred didn't hear Robin. It was too noisy. Fred ducked his head and lifted his arms in an arrow in front of his body and arced into the water.

For a few moments, Fred disappeared below the surface. When he came up, he was floating face down in the water. Some of the people near by thought he was kidding around.

Fred Gerak wasn't kidding. He was unconscious. The water he had dived into was three feet deep. He struck his head on the bottom, and when Robin Pallos and Ray Hurley and the others pulled him on to the dock and got him to hospital, Fred Gerak was a quadriplegic.

Gerak's lawyer was John Laxton. He's a handsome Lanca-shireman in his early fifties who moved to Vancouver twenty-five years ago and earned a reputation as one of British Columbia's premier negligence lawyers. He sued the B.C. Department of Lands, Parks and Housing, the people who ran Cultus Lake Park. He alleged that they had breached their duty of care to visitors like Fred Gerak and had thus caused his injuries. The trial came before Lysyk, and it lasted for two weeks, a period of time in the courtroom that Lysyk says was "frequently very sad".

Laxton set about building his case. He brought out many facts, some subtle, some obvious, that helped to give Lysyk a clear notion of the precise circumstances at Cultus Lake on July 26, 1981.

For starters, Cultus Lake was almost unique in British Columbia, since it was one of only two provincial recreational facilities that were used exclusively for swimming. Even though it had a dock, no boats were permitted to tie up at it. In fact, a line of buoys was stretched across the water sixty feet out into the lake beyond the dock to keep boats away from the area.

Next fact: July 26 was the busiest day in the entire history of Cultus Lake. The water around the dock, according to one of Laxton's witnesses, was "wall-to-wall people".

Another telling point: the park authorities had posted no

signs on or around the dock that gave any notice of the dangers of diving into the water. No warning about the water's depth, no prohibition against performing a flip off the dock. Nor were there life-guards or depth-markers.

Then, Irene MacDonald's testimony. She was a former Canadian Olympic diver, and Laxton called her as an expert witness. She had visited Cultus Lake at Laxton's invitation, and she testified in court that, from her view of the water as she stood on the dock, she thought it gave the impression of being deeper than three feet. She might have been tempted to dive in herself.

"That statement of Irene's," Laxton says, "it was one of the key pieces of testimony."

So was the testimony of another expert witness whom Laxton called to the stand. She was Janice Engemoen, the director of the Water Safety Service for the Red Cross. She took a long look at Cultus Lake and didn't like what she saw.

"The most desirable safeguard," she testified, "would be to remove the wharf completely from the swimming area."

"Why do you say that?" Laxton asked.

Engemoen answered, "A wharf or a float anywhere, regardless of the water depth, is an open invitation to dive."

Lysyk got the point. Cultus Lake seemed a temptation for eager young men like Fred Gerak to get themselves into just the desperate sort of trouble that Gerak suffered. But there were factors on the other side, and counsel for the province argued that Gerak might have been responsible for his own grief. Doesn't a reasonably prudent person take precautions before he plunges into a body of water that's strange to him? And what about the fact that people were standing in the water near the area where Gerak made his dive? Standing — and the water came up only to their waists. Shouldn't that have warned him?

Maybe so, Laxton countered, but remember what one witness said: "wall-to-wall people". How could Gerak be sure of the depth when the water was a seething mass of humanity splashing and swimming and floating and tumbling in their own waves?

Lysyk assembled all the evidence and went away to make his decision. Who was at fault in the terrible accident? The province for failing to take measures that would protect citizens in Gerak's position? Or Gerak himself for his carelessness in diving into water he hadn't first checked for safety? Or would blame be apportioned between the province and Gerak?

The latter division seemed more likely, and Laxton's feeling at the end of the case was that Lysyk would come back with an eighty-twenty split. Eighty per cent of the blame to the province and twenty per cent to Gerak.

Laxton was wrong.

Lysyk arrived at a split of sixty-five and thirty-five. Gerak was sixty-five per cent to blame for his own misfortune and the province bore that other thirty-five per cent.

"A cardinal rule of water safety," Lysyk wrote, "is that one ought not to dive into waters of unknown depth. Gerak violated this precept. He had never been to this site before and yet he failed to take steps to ascertain the depths of the water before launching into his dive. He operated on an assumption which, sadly, was unfounded. In my view, the major responsibility for the accident is his."

Lysyk's decision was upheld on appeal by the British Columbia Court of Appeal, and the Supreme Court of Canada declined to hear a further appeal.

Lysyk's division of fault stood.

Since Lysyk also found that Gerak's total damages amounted to slightly under three million dollars, money that would be needed to care for Gerak over the rest of his long life in a wheelchair, the province was required to pay thirty-five per cent of the total, which amounted to almost one million dollars in damages, interest, and costs.

John Laxton might have been disappointed in the result, but his disappointment didn't extend to Lysyk.

"He was really okay," Laxton says. "I knew he hadn't any trial experience as a lawyer. But he showed something else in the courtroom. He showed the human qualities. I never had the feeling he was removed from the hard realities of life, and Lord knows we had plenty of those in Fred Gerak's case."

A three o'clock on the afternoon of March 18, 1982, John Osler entered courtroom four on the second floor of Osgoode Hall to deliver his decision on a motion that had earlier been made before him. Courtroom four is the gem of Osgoode, a tiny courtroom done in mauve, pink, and gold and enlivened with curlicues and sculpted mouldings. The courtroom is not meant for trials but is set aside for motions. Only lawyers appear in it, arguing procedural matters for the most part. Litigants have no reason for showing up in courtroom four, but on this March afternoon, men from both sides of the matter which Osler was to dispose of were scattered over the few rows of benches that slant upwards from the well of the courtroom toward the back wall.

Two groups of Sikhs made up the contending parties. The first represented the incumbent leadership at the Shromani Sikh Society Temple on Pape Avenue in an east-central neighbourhood of Toronto. A challenge to its authority came from the second group, a relatively small faction of more radical Sikhs led by a thirty-five-year-old real estate salesman named Kuldip Singh Samra. He had once been a vice-president of the Shromani Sikh Society but had adopted the stance of a revolutionary in the late 1970s. Samra called for viligante action of an unspecified kind to combat racial discrimination against Sikhs in Canada. He hooked up with a Marxist group and took part in marches on Parliament Hill in Ottawa and on City Hall in Toronto. His militancy got him in legal hassles. After one Sikh demonstration, he laid an assault charge against a Toronto police officer. The policeman was acquitted and sued Samra for malicious prosecution. He won a judgment of fifteen thousand dollars, which Samra couldn't pay. In late 1981, more trouble came Samra's way when he was nailed on charges of impaired driving and leaving the scene of an accident.

Samra's quarrel with the Shromani Temple heated up over an election of temple officers that was scheduled for March 28. A slate of nine men was put forward as official nominees by the temple's board. Samra claimed that the executive had packed the list of voters with phony names and that the election should be postponed. On March 8, he applied before Mr. Justice David Henry of the Ontario Supreme Court for an injunction blocking the March 28 vote. Samra appeared in court without a counsel, and Mr. Justice Henry granted a temporary injunction, putting the election on hold for the moment, and directed that Samra and the temple executive retain lawyers and sort out the matter before another judge. That's when the argument made its way into Osler's hands.

In fact, Osler shouldn't have been sitting on motions in courtroom four that week. His schedule called for him to take a trial in Ottawa. But he had already made several trips to Ottawa through the judicial year and didn't care for yet another jaunt. He arranged a switch of assignments with Mr. Justice Gibson Gray, who happened to be looking for a reason to spend time in Ottawa. Gray would hit the road, and Osler would stay home and hear motions at Osgoode Hall.

In the courtroom on the afternoon of March 18, Samra was represented by a counsel named Michael Smith and the executive by its regular lawyer, Oscar Fonseca. Four or five of the temple officers had taken places in the courtroom as Osler entered, and so had Kuldip Singh Samra. He was a man of medium height, about one hundred and fifty pounds, brown eyes, a black beard, and black hair under a white turban. He was wearing loose white clothes and an open raincoat. He sat alone and very still on a bench at the back of the slanting courtroom, a position that put him several heads higher than the lawyers and other Sikhs who were sitting closer to the front. It also put Samra on the same level as the judge's dais.

Osler was brief in his remarks. He reviewed the facts and the arguments from counsel that had been presented earlier to him, and he announced that he had reached a decision.

"I'm going to dissolve the injunction," he said, which meant the election could proceed on schedule. As Osler spoke, Samra rose out of his seat at the back of the court. His right hand was reaching into his coat.

"Go in peace," Osler said, not noticing Samra.

Bang! Bang! Bang!

The interval between Osler's last word, "peace", and the sound of gunshots was less than a second.

Samra had a gun in his right hand and he was spraying the courtroom with bullets. No one could be sure whether he was taking aim or firing at random. No one had time to look.

"Duck!" screamed the court registrar, who was sitting directly in front of and just below Osler.

Whether Samra was aiming or not, his accuracy was devastating. He hit Oscar Fonseca, the temple's lawyer, in the back and the upper right leg. Fonseca slumped over the counsel table where he had been making his argument. He was dead. Samra hit one of the temple representatives, Bhupinder Pannu, in the back. He died two hours later in an operating room. And Samra caught Amarjit Singh Tatla, another temple officer, in the spine. He survived but his wounds left him paralysed. In all, Samra fired six shots. Only one missed a human target. He threw his gun — it was a .357 magnum hand-gun — on to the burnt-orange carpet and ran from the courtroom.

At the crack of Samra's first bullet, Osler had slid out of

his chair and flattened out on the floor behind his oak desk.

"When the registrar shouted 'Duck!' " he says today, "I was already two-thirds of the way down. From where I was sitting, I was almost in line with the shooter. If he aimed a little higher, he'd get me. So I went down fast."

Osler has an explanation for his exceptionally swift manoeuvre. "In a sense," he says, "I was programmed for it." Nothing so sensational or tragic as a shooting, much less a double killing, had ever before erupted in a Toronto courtroom. And yet long before March 18, 1982, Osler had given the possibility of violence in the courtroom a consideration or two. "You get some rough characters in front of you in criminal trials," he says. "And the thought of those fellows had put the idea in my mind that if anything started to go off in my court, I'd just drop. Go right for the floor. You can't outrun a bullet. Of course, I never thought the shooting would happen in a place as peaceful as motions court."

Neither did the court registrar, the man who yelled "Duck!" He had returned to his duties only that week after leave to recover from a heart attack. He asked for a quiet assignment, something away from the tension of the trial courts in the University Avenue Courthouse next door to Osgoode Hall. He'd been sent to the drowsy motions court, where the only noise above a whisper comes from the mouths of arguing counsel.

As Osler lay flat against the carpeting behind his dais, while Samra blasted away with his .357 magnum, he could see nothing. He heard plenty.

"Gunshots," he remembers. "They made a terrific racket in the small space, and the other sound was people saying, 'Oh my God, oh my God.' "

The shooting ended, and Osler raised his head over the desk. The three men — one dead, one dying, one wounded — lay sprawled in their blood. Samra was gone. He fled down the blue-carpeted stairway to the left of courtroom four, through the front doors of Osgoode Hall on to Queen Street, and off on a journey that, according to Toronto police and Interpol, took him into hiding in Sikh communities in Vancouver, Los Angeles, and Yuba City in Northern California, and finally to the Punjab. Extradition papers requesting Samra's return to Canada were prepared, but no one knew whether they would ever be acted on.

"As far as I'm concerned," Osler says, "they can just leave him where he is. He could be brought back here at enormous expense, but that might just stir up the violence all over again."

After the shooting, there were few changes in security at Osgoode Hall. Guards were put on duty for the first time in Osgoode's history. They patrolled the first floor, amiable men who had a kind word for anyone who needed directions. But no screening system was installed, nothing like the device in operation to check for weapons in the family court building at 145 Queen Street across the road. Osgoode kept its serenity even if there had been two deaths on the second floor.

Meanwhile, at the Shromani Sikh Society Temple on Pape Avenue, the contest over leadership was never entirely resolved, and in the fall of 1985, an argument again spilled into the Supreme Court of Ontario. The judge who presided over the case managed to dispose of it without much acrimony. The judge was Gibson Gray, the man whom John Osler had replaced in courtroom four on the day of the terrible shooting.

Ken Lysyk and his family live in the Kitsilano section of Vancouver. It's close to the water. Lysyk likes that. He likes to walk to his work in the Vancouver Courthouse, a forty-minute stroll through the streets near the water and over the Burrard Street Bridge. He doesn't like the bridge. Too much traffic and exhaust fumes. He has a daughter in law school at UBC. Like her father, she took the advice he'd been given back in his days at Khedive High School. She studied philosophy before she entered law school. Lysyk is enjoying life. Maybe, at last, it really is in a permanent groove.

Some of his friends and admirers don't think so.

"He'd be a terrific judge on the Supreme Court of Canada," Rob Pritchard, the University of Toronto Law School dean who worked with Lysyk in the Yukon, says. "By disposition, training, and inclination, nothing could be more natural."

Steve Goudge, the Toronto lawyer who was also on the Yukon team, shares the same opinion and hope.

"Ken has two dimensions that are important to today's Supreme Court," Goudge says. "He has a broad view of what the judicial process is all about and he has a fundamental understanding of the Canadian constitution. I'd suspect if a vacancy comes up for a Supreme Court justice from Western Canada, he'll be considered right up at the top."

Lysyk would never entertain such ambitions. Not out loud anyway. He's busy enough coping with the job of conducting trials. He's happy where he is.

"I must say it's been kind of fun," he says, looking back over his life so far. "All the career changes, they've been a lot of fun."

In the fall of 1983, after John Osler had been on the bench for fifteen years, his seniority entitled him to become a supernumerary judge of the Ontario Supreme Court. He took the opportunity. Under the Judges Act, a supernumerary judge is placed in a category that's one step away from retirement. In Osler's case, it's a long step. He's supposed to "hold himself in readiness at the will of the Chief Justice". Osler and the Chief Justice have interpreted that to mean he'll sit for half of each judicial year, which in practice has worked out to about twenty-seven weeks per year of trials and motions and other duties.

For the rest of the year, he and his wife Betty have carved out a life that's both comfortable and useful. They sold their house in Forest Hill in 1984 and moved into the top floor of a condominium that provides a spectacular look over the city. They set aside evenings for plenty of opera and ballet — Osler is a former president of the National Ballet School — and Betty does some work as a reader of new manuscripts for book publishers McClelland and Stewart. They travel to France and Italy, and in the summers they drive north to the family compound of cottages at De Grassi Point on Lake Simcoe. The compound was begun at the turn of the century by Betty's grandfather, Sir Edmund Walker, a shrewd businessman who was for years president of the Bank of Commerce. Family is at the centre of most things for the Oslers, and it's no accident that the Osler sense of public responsibility has passed down to their three children. All three make their livings in some field of social service.

In late 1985, the Ontario government moved in on Osler's supernumerary time. The Department of Consumer and Commercial Relations wanted to know what was wrong with some of the wines it was peddling in the province's liquor stores, and Osler got the call to conduct a judicial inquiry. The trouble with the wines seemed to be a potentially cancer-causing ingredient called ethyl carbamate. How did it get there and who was responsible for selling it to wine-drinking Ontarians? Osler's mandate was to come up with the answers, and he expected it would take him three or four months of hearings and report-writing to wrap up the assignment.

But before he went about his new duties, he had another chore to attend to. It was a trial in late November in Barrie, a small city fifty miles up Highway 400 north of Toronto. The charge was murder, and as the story developed in court, it wasn't one of those murder trials that Osler finds unexciting. This one had tantalizing scientific evidence and a couple of twists that Perry Mason would appreciate.

The victim was a pretty twenty-two-year-old housewife

named Catherine Little, and the accused was her twenty-seven-year-old estranged husband, Ian, who was supposed to have strangled her. Jealous rage was the motive. Catherine and Ian had separated only a few weeks before the killing in May 1984, and Catherine had already found a new boyfriend by answering a personal ad in the *Hamilton Spectator*. The fellow who placed the ad was recently divorced and perfectly presentable. He and Catherine hit it off, and Ian didn't like the idea of the new romance, especially when his wife flaunted the boyfriend. According to the crown's case, Ian strangled her in the home where Catherine was living with the couple's two small daughters on the afternoon of May 24. He bundled her nude body into the trunk of his car and dumped it in a ditch along Highway 400 near Barrie. Three days later, mushroom-pickers came across Catherine. The police worked on the investigation for six months before they charged Ian. He denied everything.

The strongest piece of evidence against Ian Little was a flake of paint. It was found on a template — a guide used for cutting stone or metal — which was in turn found on the side of Highway 400 near Catherine Little's body. The police traced the template. It had belonged to the man who sold a car to Ian Little. He'd left the template in the car's trunk. A police laboratory technician studied the template through an electronic microscope. Nothing turned up. He went over the template a second time. Nothing. A third time. Bingo! He found a tiny flake of paint. More testing established that the paint flake matched paint from one of the three coats that had gone on the car that Ian Little had bought from the man who'd left the template in the car trunk. How did the template from Ian Little's car end up at the side of the highway near Catherine Little's body? The crown at Little's trial argued to the jury that there could only be one explanation: Little was on the scene to dispose of his wife's body and had dropped the template, perhaps accidentally, at the same time.

The jury went for it.

Little had been charged with second-degree murder, but in Osler's instructions to the jury, he advised them that if they concluded Little had acted "in the heat of passion caused by sudden provocation", it was open to them to come back with a verdict of manslaughter.

The jury chose the manslaughter option, apparently deciding that Catherine Little's bragging about the new boyfriend had inflamed poor jealous Ian. Osler thanked the jury for their verdict and sentenced Little to eight years in prison.

Then he drove home to think about wine.

Davie Fulton

Davie Fulton looked as if he belonged in an English movie, something directed by Sir Carol Reed. Fulton would play the deferential and enigmatic older gentleman, the character who knows where all the bodies are buried but isn't giving away a thing. He had a long, handsome, patrician face. His eyes looked out as if from behind a mask, and his luxuriant hair showed the even lines of an expert combing. This was in May of 1985, and Fulton was sitting at his desk in a medium-sized office at Swinton & Company, a large law firm on the thirteenth floor of a glass and steel building in downtown Vancouver. Fulton was one of three associate counsel in the firm. He had on a three-piece grey suit, a white shirt with thin blue stripes, and a figured blue tie. His shoes were Wallabees. They seemed just right for the enigmatic fellow from the Carol Reed film.

Fulton was talking about his appointment to the trial division of the British Columbia Supreme Court in 1973.

"In my mind," he said, "it was the culmination, the high point if you will, of a career which included a long period in politics but always with a legal aspect to it." Fulton parcelled out his words with enormous circumspection. "It was the peak of a lawyer's career, an honour that is greatly to be appreciated but that brings with it a very great responsibility to discharge the expectations which you and others see in holding such an office."

That was saying plenty, "the culmination of a career", because from the mid-1940s to the early 1960s, Fulton had had one of the most brilliant streaks in contemporary Canadian public life. He began with the advantage of a collection of accomplished ancestors. One grandfather and a great-uncle were premiers of British Columbia. The great-uncle ended his career as the province's chief justice. An uncle of Fulton's was Speaker of the B.C. legislature in the early 1930s, and his father was both provincial attorney general and federal member of Parliament for the Cariboo riding in the Borden government. Davie Fulton absorbed his elders' example. By 1945 his résumé showed him to be a Rhodes Scholar, a lawyer, a field leader in the Italian campaign during the Second World War, and the Conservative member of Parliament for his home town of Kamloops. He hadn't yet reached his thirtieth birthday.

In Parliament, Fulton proved himself early as a master of procedure and an eloquent, attacking speaker. Two of his speeches, or, more accurately, collections of speeches, are celebrated as classics of the genre: his clobbering of the Liberal government during the pipeline debate in 1956 and his majestic and canny defence several years later of a Tory cabinet minister's involvement with a woman, Gerda Munsinger, whose background, morals, and associates made her a shady customer.

Fulton moved his talents — among them honesty, an aloof, principled dignity, and a dandyism acquired in his Oxford days — from opposition to government after John Diefenbaker led the Tories to power in 1957. Fulton got the Justice portfolio and held it for five years. He accomplished much: he brought non-capital murder into the Criminal Code, revised the anti-combines laws, improved conditions in federal penitentiaries, and established the Parole Board. He also attracted to Justice some of the best and brightest of the young civil servants. They came to him — Marc Lalonde and Michael Pitfield and Lowell Murray and others — because Fulton offered both intellectual stimulation and, as Conservative politicians went in those days, the glamour of a star.

John Diefenbaker saw to it that Fulton's star shone no brighter and not much longer. Perhaps Diefenbaker found reason for resentment in the widely held belief around Ottawa that Fulton possessed most of the brains in the Conservative Party. Certainly he never forgave Fulton for daring to oppose him at the 1956 Tory leadership convention which picked a successor to George Drew. Fulton finished far back in the contest with 117 votes and third place to Diefenbaker, who had 774 votes, and Donald Fleming, who had 393. But the margin of his victory over Fulton may not have been enough satisfaction for Diefenbaker. He put Fulton on his list of people who must pay. He occasionally torpedoed Fulton in cabinet after the Conservatives arrived in power, and following the 1962 election, in a step that seemed calculated to insult, he moved Fulton to the much less authoritative portfolio of Public Works. Fulton recognized that he wouldn't thrive in John Diefenbaker's Ottawa. He decided to try British Columbia politics.

That turned out to be a lousy idea. A group of B.C. businessmen set up Fulton with the "Fraser Trust", an arrangement that would provide him with an income while he restored the provincial Conservative Party in a province where Social Credit ruled. Since the Conservatives lay at zero in organization, cash, and members of the legislature, the job looked formidable. In fact, it was impossible. In the next provincial election, Fulton lost in the Kamloops riding to "Flying Phil" Gagliardi, the cocky Minister of Highways, and none of the other Tory candidates he had recruited did any better. The Conservatives remained at zero.

Then things got worse for Fulton. He took another crack

at the federal Tory leadership in 1967 and was trampled by
Robert Stanfield. The campaign put Fulton into debt. Not long
afterwards, decorating his home in Vancouver with Christmas lights, he slipped off a ladder and broke his leg. Gan-
grene set in. Fulton came close to death. He deserved some
good luck when the offer of an appointment to the B.C. bench
arrived in 1973.

And yet, as he explained in his office at Swinton & Company, he gave the offer much careful thinking before deciding whether to grab it. Fulton doesn't appear to take any steps,
even the steps that turn into pratfalls, without much careful
thinking.

"I asked myself whether I would be able to do justice to
the duties of the position," he said. "This would be a task
that involved making decisions which would affect people,
not just momentarily, but with respect to their futures, their
entire lives. I wondered about that, and then I thought, well,
I ought to be able to handle it, because in politics, particularly in government, I had the reponsibility of making a number of important decisions that had an effect on the welfare
both of individual people and of the whole nation. I thought
that if I felt, as I did, that I discharged those responsibilities
with efficiency and acceptability, then I should be able to meet
the new responsibilities."

That bit of soul-searching out of the way, Fulton took the
appointment, and it must have given him a strange sensation. Here was the man who, a dozen years earlier, had been
the cabinet minister charged with the task of choosing judges.
Now he was himself one of the chosen. It was a curious role-
reversal, and in one aspect Fulton found the bench decidedly
different from the cabinet in a way that caused him a touch
of initial uneasiness. That aspect lay in the impact that the
decision-making process had both on the decision-maker and
on those on the receiving end of the decisions.

"The thing that impressed me quite early," he said, "was

that while one had been making decisions in government that were fraught with serious consequences, two qualities made them different and perhaps easier than judicial decisions. The first is that cabinet decisions are made in the collective, and the responsibility is shared. In judicial decisions, on the other hand, you are alone when you hear the case and, harder still, alone when you decide it. The responsibility never leaves your own shoulders. The second difference is that decision-making in government is carried out at some distance from its effect, and it deals with situations en masse. But, as a judge in court, the people whom your decision most affects are standing in front of you. You can see and hear them. It's terribly personal, and there is no possibility of standing at a distance. I found that most onerous."

Nevertheless, Fulton liked the job. He discovered, this formal, correct, dignified fellow, that he liked mucking about among the common folk. He liked to stew over their problems. He liked the people in his courtroom. He liked working with the ordinary men and women who sat on his juries.

"I never failed to experience happiness and assurance in being associated with a jury," he said in his office.

He also came to like working alone, liked the solitariness of the job. And when he talked about his favourites among the cases he heard during his years as a judge, and on the evidence of the judgments he wrote in those cherished cases, it seemed clear that where Fulton made his mark on the British Columbia court was as a kind of judicial technocrat.

Judges hear many cases that are picky and dull. They're as intricate as the *Sunday Times* crossword puzzle and just as frustrating. Fulton didn't mind such cases. Better still, he came up with solutions to them that, according to the appeal courts that were sometimes called on to check his work, were exactly right. Somewhere along the line, maybe as minister of justice, likely earlier, Fulton developed a knack and a fondness for personal working systems, ways of nailing down facts and opinions with precision. When he reached the bench, the systems helped to make him a wonderful technocrat.

There was, for example, what he called his "notes of evidence" system. He evolved it when he recognized that a judge, working toward a decision, is torn between two tendencies.

"One tendency is to have throughout the trial process an overview of the case," Fulton said. "Or, if I might phrase it another way, to go on gut instinct."

That tendency, Fulton decided, was fallible. It was better, he found, to pursue the second tendency, which had about it a technical exactness.

"I preferred to be analytical," he said. And he proceeded to explain with considerable relish the system he constructed to go after that tendency. It called for plenty of paper work. Every judge makes notes of the testimony of all the witnesses during a trial. Fulton carried the note-making process a large step further.

"I would read over my notes of the evidence given by the first witness," he said, "and, as I did so, I would take a separate sheet of paper and write down the testimony under a series of headings, one heading for each significant area of evidence."

Fulton followed the same laborious drill for each succeeding witness. He placed their evidence under his series of headings. Next he summarized all the evidence under all the headings. Finally, he linked the headings with a series of cross-references, thereby assuring himself that all the evidence was tied together.

"It was time-consuming," Fulton said, an understatement that was typical of the man. "But it told me, beyond any gut instinct, what the case in fact really concerned."

Indeed, Fulton concluded, his devotion to the paper work proved to him that analysis usually got closer to the truth than instinct.

"There were many cases," he said, "where I would end the

trial with one impression, a leaning toward one party in the case, but that impression would be drastically altered when I had finished reviewing the notes of evidence according to my system and I might then find in favour of the other party."

Fulton showed a shade of a smile.

"I was pleased to find in those cases assurance of the value of such a system," he said.

Fulton the technocrat was ideally suited to handle, for example, the perplexing matter of Carlos Diligenti the restaurateur. Diligenti made a deal in 1972 with three businessmen under which the four, as partners and shareholders, formed a company that purchased and operated two franchises in the Keg 'n Cleaver restaurant chain, one in Kelowna and the other in Prince George. At first everything went swimmingly. Diligenti, the brains of the operation in the restaurant department, ran the two Kegs, and all the partners reaped handsome profits.

But in 1975 the four had a falling out, and the three businessmen ganged up on Diligenti. Acting in their capacities as company directors and overriding Diligenti's vote, the three passed a group of resolutions which, among other results, kicked Diligenti out of his post as a company director and out of his job as managing partner of the two restaurants, cut him off from any further remuneration, turned over the running of the restaurants to a new management company of which the three were the only shareholders, and awarded generous management fees to the newly created company. Diligenti was understandably upset and looked to the B.C. courts for relief. His suit came before Mr. Justice Fulton.

Poor Diligenti's situation called into consideration a unique section of the new B.C. Companies Act of 1973. Section 221 provided that any shareholder in a company, as Diligenti was, might apply to the courts where "the powers of the directors of the company are being exercised in a manner oppressive to" the shareholder or where a resolution of the directors of the company is "unfairly prejudicial" to the shareholder. Did Diligenti qualify for help under section 221? Would he be recompensed in dollars for his various losses and hardships? On the face of it, it would seem so, or at any rate one would hope so. But as Fulton delved into the law, tiptoeing behind the new B.C. Companies Act and its wording to the former Act and its quite different phrasing, and beyond the statute law to a mighty load of interpretative Canadian and English case law, it appeared to be a near thing for Diligenti.

His salvation in the end, as Fulton doped it out in a piece of reasoning that was utterly painstaking and compellingly kind, lay in the phrase "unfairly prejudicial" in section 221. The two words did not appear in the previous B.C. Companies Act or in comparable English statutes. Nobody quite knew what they meant. Under both the old B.C. Act and the English Acts, the one and only remedy to someone in Diligenti's dilemma would be an order winding up the company that had been the vehicle for putting the shaft to the unfortunate shareholder. No other remedy and no recompense would be possible. But in Fulton's view — he was speaking as the first judge who was called on to interpret section 221 — the magical phrase "unfairly prejudicial" put a fresh twist on matters.

In strict law, Fulton said, the three businessmen were entitled to strip Diligenti of his chores and cut off his pay in the day-to-day operation of the two Keg restaurants. There was nothing wrong with such a step. A majority of directors could always decide how and by whom their company was managed. But the three businessmen stepped too far when, at the same time as they fired Diligenti, they switched the management fees which Diligenti had once received to their own new company.

"Can it be equitable," Fulton wrote in his judgment, "for three shareholders to say to the fourth: 'You shall not take any further part in management, so you shall not benefit directly in that way,' and then appoint their own creature to manage so that they benefit directly and exclusively? In my opinion, the answer must be 'No' — that such an act is unfairly prejudicial to, if not indeed oppressive to, that fourth member.''

At the conclusion of the case, Diligenti got even — or almost. The company that he and the three businessmen had formed in 1972 was obliged to buy his shares in it at a valuation which Fulton arrived at after he worked out a complicated and generous piece of accounting.

Exit Diligenti, slightly happier.

Fulton took satisfaction of two sorts from the case. The first was entirely of a judicial nature. "I was very glad to find that law and equity agreed in giving relief to the plaintiff,'' he said in his office.

With his second sort of satisfaction, Fulton allowed his ego to peek around the corner of his habitual modesty.

"I am told,'' he said, "that the Diligenti case is referred to in the law schools as a leading case in this area of the law.''

Fulton gave another shadowy smile.

Seat belts engaged him in a second case he was proud of. Seat belts are hardly a subject that rouses much intellectual excitement, but in a trial that took place in the fall of 1976 they mattered desperately to a couple of young men named Gagnon and Beaulieu and, by extension, to Mr. Justice Fulton, the master technocrat. He adjudicated the dispute between the two young men, and, in the process, he clarified and codified the B.C. law on the wearing of seat belts. It was an exacting kind of case, the sort that many judges might be tempted to slough off. Fulton didn't.

Beaulieu was driving the car, a 1972 Vega Hatchback, and his pal Gagnon was sitting in the front passenger seat. Gagnon hadn't bothered to tie himself in with his seat belt. At that time, the summer of 1974, B.C. legislation didn't require anyone to wear a seat belt. But Gagnon no doubt wished he'd buckled up when Beaulieu, the driver, piled into the rear of a pick-up truck that had stopped at a railroad crossing. Gagnon pitched into the windshield and suffered all sorts of bloody injuries—cuts on his forehead and scalp, a broken cheekbone, the loss of his right eye. His face would never be the same, and, as he later pointed out at the trial, his sex life was ruined, since no young woman would ever go for someone as disfigured as he was. Gagnon sued Beaulieu for damages, and there was no question of Beaulieu's liability. But he argued, in mitigation of damages, that Gagnon had also been negligent by failing to strap himself in with the seat belt.

Fulton dived into the case law on seat belts. It was, he found, in a state of confusion. It wasn't in the same state when he finished with the case before him. He sorted through the law in his diligent manner, throwing up an organized flurry of notes and lists and cross-references, and, in the end, he produced a set of definitive propositions.

One: The failure of someone in Gagnon's position to wear a seat belt was a failure to take a step that he should have known was necessary to his own safety.

Two: If that person, Gagnon in this instance, was injured in an accident and if the evidence showed he wouldn't have suffered such serious injuries if he'd worn his seat belt, then he had been guilty of a piece of negligence that contributed to the injuries.

Three: It was up to the defendant, Beaulieu in the immediate case, to prove that the plaintiff's injuries, Gagnon's, would have been prevented or lessened if he'd buckled on the seat belt.

Four: The views of any party on the effectiveness of seat belts, meaning in this case Gagnon, who testified that seat belts were probably useless, didn't have any bearing on the first three propositions.

Applying his precisely calibrated propositions to the Gagnon-Beaulieu case, Fulton concluded that Gagnon, with his banged-up face and wrecked sex life, had partly contributed to his own grief. Beaulieu was seventy-five per cent to blame, and Gagnon's proportion of responsibility made up the other twenty-five per cent. Fulton gave Gagnon forty thousand follars. End of litigation.

"The case," Fulton said, "fits into the category about which one feels a particular satisfaction with both the work that has gone into the decision and with the decision itself. It didn't develop new law, but it cleared up the previous law, which had really been very complicated and somewhat uncertain."

Fulton's face hinted at another smile.

"Again," he said, "I am told this case is referred to frequently in our law schools and it has been applied in several subsequent cases."

Another small triumph for the technocrat.

A bigger triumph, at least as far as a company called Canfor Limited was concerned, emerged from another burdensome trial Fulton conducted in 1975. Canfor was one of several companies grouped under the giant Canadian Forest Products Limited, and, in the normal course of business, Canfor took in goods and services from affiliated companies in the group. In calculating its paid-up capital for tax purposes in 1972, Canfor didn't include trade accounts payable to the affiliated companies in the amount of some four million dollars or secured bank indebtedness in the amount of eight million dollars. The Minister of Finance ruled, on the contrary, that those two substantial items must be placed under paid-up capital and proceeded to whack Canfor with a hefty tax assessment. Canfor cried unfair, and the matter ended up in a trial before Fulton.

"Totally inequitable and unjust," Fulton said of the Minister of Finance's tax assessment. But that conclusion was reached only after the most laborious and detailed dissection of the Corporation Capital Tax Act of British Columbia and of a whole raft of cases that interpreted the Act. Fulton was at his busiest in making the usual notes of evidence and lists and headings and cross-references. His judgment, a solid and lengthy piece of writing, represented a technical tour de force in favour of Canfor Limited. But that didn't stop the Minister of Finance from appealing Fulton's decision to the B.C. Court of Appeal, nor did it stop that court from overruling Fulton on one key finding. Canfor carried the Appeal Court's judgment to the Supreme Court of Canada, and it was there that Fulton received vindication in spectacular fashion.

The Supreme Court's judgment, delivered by Mr. Justice Roland Ritchie, consisted of a mere three sentences. Two concerned costs in the action, and the third was, as Fulton described it, "the delightful sentence".

"I would allow this appeal," Ritchie wrote, "and adopt the reasons for judgment delivered by Mr. Justice Fulton at trial."

Ah, sweet triumph.

"I do not say this form of one-sentence decision by our highest court has never happened before," Fulton said in his office at Swinton & Company. "But it is a rare and uplifting event."

This time, Fulton made no effort at reticence. He allowed his smile to light up the office.

The smile reflected a rare and happy moment, and it served to underline a point about Fulton. There was, as it happened, an explanation for his subdued nature, for the convoluted and achingly-thought-out sentences he used to describe his judicial career, for the efforts to be at such pains to describe his years on the B.C. court. The explanation was that during those years as a judge, part of Fulton's life was going badly askew. He was drinking heavily. He was an alcoholic.

It's tempting to play the amateur psychoanalyst and speculate that his political disappointments of the 1960s had overtaken him, and he had turned to martinis as an antidote. Whatever the reason, booze got Fulton into trouble. He was charged with impaired driving in early 1979, and he was convicted of the offence.

Soon, in an ugly episode that followed, the conviction

seemed the least of his troubles. A Vancouver prostitute named Wendy King published her memoirs, in which she named Fulton as one among many of her prestigious clientele which had earlier included another jurist, B.C. Chief Justice John Farris. In Farris's case, King had apparently been right, and he resigned from the bench. In Fulton's case, King was wrong, and Fulton fought back. He brought a libel suit against King. Before the suit reached trial, King announced that, oops, sorry, the client she had in mind was a lawyer named David from Kamloops and she'd made the mistaken leap to Davie Fulton.

It was all too monstrously unfair, and it was too late. Fulton had resumed drinking, and in April 1981 he was again caught on an impaired-driving charge. He was again convicted, and, since it was a second offence, he was compelled to serve a sentence of fourteen days on weekends at the Marpole Community Correctional Centre. At the same time he resigned from his position as a justice on the B.C. Supreme Court.

Fulton faded from sight.

But, four years later, sitting in the office at Swinton & Company, Fulton was showing that what lay behind the enigmatic, correct exterior was the heart of a very brave man. The terrible events of his life had struck him in his mid-sixties, a time when it would have been easy enough to surrender. Fulton had refused to fold. He had put behind the problems that seemed so overwhelming. His drink of choice was now Bitter Lemon. He moved easily among his friends at the Round Table, a group of Vancouver's leading lights who gathered for lunch and important talk every Tuesday in a private banquet room in the Hotel Vancouver. He was co-operating with a reporter at the provincial press gallery in Victoria who was keen to put together Fulton's biography. And at Swinton & Company he was plunged into work that absorbed him.

Most conspicuously, in the spring and summer of 1985 there

was the one-man government inquiry he was conducting into the claims of the Lubicon Lake Indians of northwest Alberta. There weren't many Indians left in the Lubicon band, a couple of hundred at most, but they had a legitimate beef. The Lubicon people were identified as a separate and distinct band in 1939. But in all the years that followed, as Alberta and the federal government, in a bureaucratic mix-up of breathtaking proportions, batted around the problem of which lands the Lubicon band was entitled to, the Indians themselves had to put up with a grim collection of threats to the traditional life of hunting and fishing which they still maintained. The provincial government came through their territory with oil and gas developments. The moose which they depended on for food were driven away by encroaching white entrepreneurs. And some of their own people were beginning to lose heart. The Lubicon leaders continued to resist the threats, but they were hampered by the failure of Ottawa and Alberta to let them know exactly what lands they could claim and defend as their own. It was at this point that Fulton was brought in to make sense and justice out of the confusion.

Fulton was on familiar ground. This was a problem that called for discussion papers and organization and formal presentation, for analysis and evidence and lists and cross-references. Fulton flew often to the Lubicon Lake area. He stayed in a house that had no running water, and he met with Indian leaders, making notes and recording the facts. He was in his element.

And, in one special way, he was the man for the Lubicon Indians. They were a group of people who'd been through hard times and taken bad breaks. Fulton was an expert on hard times and bad breaks. If any man could show the people of Lubicon Lake a path to better days, one he'd found for himself, it was Davie Fulton.

CHAPTER FOUR

The Thinking Person's Judge

It was what the roly-poly nineteen-year-old boy did to the neighbour's dog that put the capper on his case. The boy was stuffed into his best three-piece navy-blue suit and stood in the prisoners' box on a morning in the summer of 1984. His well-dressed parents sat in the row of public seats immediately behind the box. They looked stricken. It was little wonder. As soon as the boy had pleaded guilty to the charges against him, the crown attorney read to Judge Stephen Borins a policeman's report of the facts in the case. First the boy took the neighbour's small son into the garage and masturbated in front of him. Then he took the neighbour's little daughter into the garage and fondled her vagina. Finally, he took the neighbour's dog into the garage and sodomized it.

This was not the sort of case that most pleases or challenges Steve Borins. But as the pathetic tale unfolded before him, he showed the same understanding and intelligence he brings to every case. Borins is a judge of the District Court of the Judicial District of York sitting in Toronto's University Avenue Courthouse. Many lawyers and academics who have followed Borins's work think he's cut out by brains and temperament for a higher court, for the Ontario Court of Appeal. He's a thinking person's judge.

"If you'll excuse me a few moments," Borins said to the

crown attorney and the nineteen-year-old's counsel, "I see there are reports on the accused from four different psychiatrists. Let me skim them now and I'll read them more carefully later."

Borins gives off an air of being everybody's favourite professor, casual and scholarly and comfortable. He's just past fifty but hardly seems that old in manner or appearance. The female registrars on the District Court have their own secret nickname for him, "Stevie Wonder", leaving no doubt that he possesses the accessible and rather vulnerable looks that many women respond to. Put a moustache and a pair of glasses on actor William Hurt and that's Borins.

"This case is difficult to resolve in the sentencing," he said after he'd spent ten silent minutes turning through the assessments from the psychiatrists. It was open to him to sentence the boy to a term in prison. Both the defence counsel and the crown attorney resisted that alternative. So, it seemed, did Borins.

"I'd like a pre-sentence report on the accused if I may," he said. "Let's put the case over for a few weeks and I'll have time to read it and these other reports."

Time is a commodity in short supply around District Court. The court occupies a curious and overburdened middle ground in the judicial system. It's several cuts above the Provincial Court in jurisdiction and quality of work, but it handles cases that for one reason or other don't make it to trial in the Supreme Court. A grab-bag of matters comes the District Court's way. It has jurisdiction over every sort of criminal offence except murder, piracy, and high treason. On the civil side, it can hear cases in which any amount of money up to twenty-five thousand dollars is at stake, and, if the parties to a case agree, the court can proceed to deal with a dispute involving an unlimited sum. Its jurisdiction also covers a jumble of odd and difficult statutes. The Narcotic Control Act. The Food and Drug Act. The Combines Act. The

Condominium Act ("What that gets us," Borins says, "is a lot of funny arguments over the conduct of tenants' cats and dogs"). The Income Tax Act. The Extradition Act. The Customs and Excise Act. When a District Court judge reports for work, there's no telling what may turn up in his courtroom. It may even be a roly-poly nineteen-year-old who's done something unseemly with a dog.

In his reading and research into the sentencing of the nineteen-year-old, Borins found one case in England with similar facts involving a man, a dog, and sodomy. The English judge likened the offence to molesting a child and sentenced the prisoner to two years in jail. Borins was amused and appalled. "The judge must have been one of those English dog fanatics," he said. He was relieved when he discovered that England's Court of Appeal had set aside the two-year sentence as excessive punishment.

"I gather that the accused has been continuing with his psychiatric counselling?" Borins said many weeks later when all the parties had reassembled in the courtroom, the boy in his three-piece navy suit, the distraught parents, the crown, and defence counsel.

Everybody murmured and nodded that, yes, the treatment was still proceeding. "Fine," Borins said, and he began to talk to the boy and his counsel in a moderate, assuaging tone. He said he was placing the boy on probation and he spelled out the terms of the probation. There was a temperate and concerned mood in the air as he talked, and for several moments the courtroom seemed less like a place of law and more like a consulting room where social workers were addressing themselves to a tangle which they knew that they, as reasonable people, could straighten out.

"You must never ignore the fact you've committed a serious offence and caused a great deal of harm," Borins said to the boy. "But surely this is something that counselling and your own intelligence will overcome."

The roly-poly boy and his parents left the courtroom. The mother had a tiny, encouraging smile for her son. For the first time, she looked hopeful.

When Steve Borins's father, Norman, was called to the Ontario bar in 1930, he had two obstacles in his way. The depression was on and Norman Borins was Jewish. In those days, not every legal door in Toronto was open to Jews, and the hard times made employment in the law even tighter. The elder Borins struggled in practice for a few years before he joined the provincial crown attorney's office. He worked alongside such legendary prosecutors as Henry Bull and Fred Malone, men with panache and wit and the killer instinct who made a life's career out of the crown's work. Borins developed a legend of his own — the guy who was tough but fair — and in 1947 when he returned to private practice, he established himself as one of Toronto's most eminent criminal and civil counsel. His name was mentioned in the same breath as those of legendary lawyers John Robinette and Arthur Maloney and Joe Sedgwick.

In 1963, Prime Minister Lester Pearson went looking for a first — the first Jewish lawyer to be appointed to the Ontario High Court. Norman Borins's name popped up at the top of the list, and the Liberals floated discreet overtures in his direction. Borins appreciated the honour but turned Pearson down largely because he couldn't face the prospect of hiking off on circuit fifteen or sixteen weeks each year to conduct trials around the province. Home and family came first.

It was at the evening dinner table that Steve Borins caught his first whiff of the law from his father. He liked the aroma. That wasn't the case with the other son at the table, Edward, a few years younger than Steve. He was turned off by all the talk about law.

"Right around the time I graduated from university and

was expected to follow Steve to law school," Ed Borins remembers, "my father took me down to the jail while he interviewed a seventeen-year-old kid who was charged with murder. This boy had rolled a drunk in the winter and left him unconscious to freeze to death in the cold. It was a really grisly story."

Ed Borins listened, and when the boy's story ended, Ed threw up.

Ed Borins went into the book business, and today he and his wife, Eva, are proprietors of Edwards Books, a chain of stores around Toronto that are high on quality and profits.

Steve Borins didn't throw up at the tale of the seventeen-year-old and the frozen drunk (though the boy was found guilty, the only defence in a murder trial that Norman Borins ever lost), and he proceeded through law in an arrow-straight path. He took his degree at the University of Toronto Law School in the school's golden era when it was small — only thirty-two graduates in Borins's class — and when the faculty included such matchless teachers as Bora Laskin. After his call to the bar, Borins was singled out for the honour of serving a year as the clerk to the Chief Justice of the Ontario High Court. And at the end of that instructive term, he joined his father's small firm and absorbed the wisdom and hard knocks of litigation practice.

In 1969, Borins indulged another side of his fondness for the law. He left practice to teach at Osgoode Hall Law School. He lectured in civil procedure, criminal procedure, torts. "I always preferred teaching first-year students," he says. "They hadn't had enough exposure to law to become cynical, and there was a chance for me to have input in their development while they were still enthusiastic."

Borins is at home with ideas and books and good talk. Unlike many lawyers and judges, he reads widely outside the law. His wife, Elaine, is a psychiatrist. His oldest and best friends tend to be men who get things done in law and education: Mr. Justice John Morden of the Ontario Court of Appeal, President Harry Arthurs of York University.

Late one Sunday night in the spring of 1975, Borins and his wife arrived home from a wedding reception. The phone was ringing.

"Hi, Steve," the voice on the line said. "It's Ed."

Borins thought it was his brother. But, no, he'd left that Ed at the wedding reception a few minutes earlier.

The last name of the Ed on the phone, an old friend of Borins, was Ratushny. He was working at the time as a special assistant to federal Minister of Justice Otto Lang. Ratushny is another of the Ukrainian-Canadian wizards of the law who, like Ken Lysyk, grew up on the prairies and charged out of the University of Saskatchewan Law School. His job with Lang was a one-of-a-kind affair. He roamed the country checking out lawyers who, regardless of party affiliation, stacked up as prime candidates for the bench. He looked for men and women who knew their way around a courtroom, possessed a sound sense of the law, and didn't have a drinking problem. Ratushny kept a little list, and the only other person who had access to it was Otto Lang.

"Steve," Ratushny said on the phone that Sunday night, "the minister would like you to consider an appointment to the bench."

Borins allowed that, yeah, well, sure, he'd consider it.

"We'd like an answer by noon tomorrow," Ratushny said.

Borins didn't sleep much over the following hours, and early in the morning he telephoned his friend John Morden of the Ontario Appeal Court.

"Take it," Morden said. "They may not ask you again."

Borins took it.

His assignment was to the County Court in Brampton, a bursting exurban community northwest of Toronto. Brampton is the county seat for the county that takes in Lester B. Pearson International Airport, and that geographical fact meant that Borins was called on to preside over many drug trials of enormous complexity. Drug dealers use the airport as a point of import for shipments of heroin and cocaine, and when customs officials and the RCMP sniff out the shipments, the prosecution of the dealers usually takes place in the Brampton court. Many of the accused drug people have access to large bank accounts and can afford the most resourceful counsel. Early in Borins's career on the bench, he grew used to the ingenious defences that high-priced counsel threw at him, and he came to relish the catcher's role.

He sat on the infamous Rowbotham drug trial, involving millions of dollars in drugs and many accused, who were led by a man named Robert Rowbotham, the brains of the outfit. The defence counsel were brilliant and unceasing in raising cute evidentiary points. Some seemed frivolous, but others got at the heart of several delicate rules of evidence. Borins responded. "In the course of the trial," he says, "I believe I read my way through an entire very thick book on evidence." As the case made its mind-stretching progress, Borins handed down a lengthy series of evidentiary rulings and phrased them in such finely tuned prose that they are used today as teaching tools in classes on evidence at many Canadian law schools. At the end of the trial, on the basis of the evidence that made it through Borins's rulings, he found Rowbotham and friends guilty.

But it was his decision in the Shand case that brought Borins the most attention during his Brampton tenure. Shand was a thirty-five-year-old man from Toronto who dealt in pre-Columbian art. He made frequent trips to South America and admitted that he smuggled home art objects which he hid in the false bottom built into his suitcase. On a visit to Peru in the winter of 1974, Shand used the secret compartment for a different illegal cargo — seventeen plastic bags containing twenty-four ounces of cocaine that he bought from an American hippie for the bargain price of eight hundred dollars.

He arranged to have a lady friend carry the hot suitcase home
to Canada, but at the airport in Toronto, a sharp-eyed customs officer spotted the fake bottom. The woman was
arrested while Shand strolled safely through the airport. Seventeen days after his friend's arrest, Shand's conscience took
him to the RCMP, where he confessed all. In court before
Borins many months later, he pleaded guilty to importing
drugs, and the plea gave Borins a dilemma.

Under the Narcotic Control Act, the minimum sentence for a
person guilty of importing a narcotic into Canada is seven
years' imprisonment. No matter how small the amount of
drug, no matter what the circumstances of the case, the sentence is an unvarying seven years. Borins considered the punishment to be too harsh in many cases, Shand's included.
Shand had no previous record. He was not a veteran drug
dealer, and though his flimflam with the South American art
objects may not have qualified him as citizen of the year, he
was far from a seasoned criminal. A prison term of seven
years for Shand made no sense to Borins, and he resorted to
the Bill of Rights as a novel and daring method of circum-
venting the strictures of the Narcotic Control Act. Section
two of the Bill protected Canadians from "cruel and unusual
punishment". Borins invoked the section and held that seven
years in jail was decidedly cruel and unusual punishment
for someone like Shand. Instead, he gave Shand two years
less a day, together with a five-thousand-dollar fine.

A buzz of amazement, admiration, and doubt swept through
the Ontario legal community. In one way or another, ingenious
or ridiculous, Steve Borins had come up with a new twist.
For its part, the Ontario Court of Appeal rejected Borins's
slick piece of reasoning. In a judgment lucidly written by Mr.
Justice John Arnup, the appeal court held that a seven-year
sentence could not be interpreted as "so grossly dispropor-
tionate" as to constitute cruel and unusual punishment. It
was up to Parliament, not individual judges, to determine the
appropriateness of penalties, and Parliament had arrived at

seven years for drug importers. Arnup gave Shand his seven years in jail.

Still, even though Borins was overruled, he found that his judgment had a modifying effect on drug cases in Brampton. "The crown began to use its discretion for laying charges in a more liberal way," he says. "Instead of charging everybody at the airport who had some drugs in their luggage with the crime of importing narcotics, they got selective. They charged the big importers, the real criminals, with the heavy crime, importing narcotics. But they charged the ordinary people, the Shands of the world, with simple possession, which brings a much lighter sentence. That had a very salutary influence on the trial list in Brampton. It enabled people to plead guilty and know they wouldn't go to jail for seven years."

By 1979, Borins had had his fill of the Brampton court. "I didn't want to see another drug case for a long time," he says. "And I knew there was much more variety in Toronto." He arranged for a transfer to the University Avenue Courthouse. That switch brought about a curious conflict.

When Borins accepted the appointment to the Brampton bench, he and his wife and two daughters had moved to a splendid country home that put him in pleasant driving distance of his new job. In preparation for the return to Toronto, he listed the country home for sale. An offer came in that Borins accepted. The offer was in a woman's name. It meant nothing to Borins until he discovered that it was the maiden name of Paul Volpe's wife. Everyone knew Paul Volpe. He was the number one mafioso in Toronto.

Was it advisable for Borins, a member of the judiciary, to sell his house to Volpe, a member of the underworld?

Borins went to the top for advice. He consulted Bora Laskin, his old law school professor and now chief justice of the Supreme Court of Canada.

"Well, did the offer come through a real estate agent in the usual way?" Laskin asked Borins.

Yes.

"Are you taking back a mortgage on the deal?" Laskin asked.
No.

"Nothing wrong with it, Steve," Laskin concluded.

The deal went through, and a few years later, Volpe's body turned up in the trunk of his wife's car at Pearson International Airport, a victim of some underworld nastiness.

Borins revelled in the change to the District Court in Toronto. The work-load could be crippling, but he seized the chance to preside over a much wider spectrum of cases than he'd experienced in Brampton. And he found himself called on to face up to many intricate and original points of law. He didn't back off from the tough stuff.

In one 1984 case, a first of its kind, he dismissed a charge against a man of escaping lawful custody on the ground that the man was not served with a copy of the warrant for his arrest that the justice of the peace had issued. The ruling upset a long-established habit. The police routinely arrested suspects without showing them the warrants from the justice of the peace under which they were acting. In fact, police officers frequently didn't bother to carry the warrants. But Borins decided that the old custom was improper and that henceforth ordinary citizens who were collared by the police had to be shown copies of the arrest warrants at some point prior to or shortly after arrest.

In the Cathy Smith case, Borins performed a series of balancing routines in matching the Extradition Act against a slew of challenges. Cathy Smith was a Toronto singer, rock groupie, and drug addict who spent most of a week in March 1982 hanging out in Hollywood with the comedian and actor John Belushi. At the end of the week, Belushi died of an overdose of heroin and cocaine. Smith admitted to reporters from the *National Enquirer* that she had handled much of the shooting-up for Belushi, who gave the impression of being a relative novice in the hard-drug game. It was Smith who injected Belushi with the heroin and cocaine that may have killed him. The Los Angeles police laid a murder charge against Smith, but before the State of California could bring her to trial, it had first to get its hands on her. Smith had returned to Toronto, and California brought proceedings under the Canadian Extradition Act.

The extradition hearings arrived in Borins's court, and before they were over, they stretched off and on over the best part of two years and required Borins to make a series of taxing decisions.

Smith's counsel, Brian Greenspan, initiated the marathon by asserting that he had the right to cross-examine the proponents to the affidavits from California which purported to spell out the case against Smith and which were at the basis of California's request for Smith's extradition. It looked as if Greenspan had the makings of a nice point. In most courtroom proceedings, witnesses give their evidence viva voce, in court and in person, and opposing counsel have the chance to cross-examine them on their testimony. But the Extradition Act provides that in proceedings under it, the foreign state asking for extradition of a fugitive, as California was asking for Smith, could introduce evidence by way of affidavits taken in the foreign jurisdiction. In such cases, the witnesses who swear the affidavits aren't present in court to be cross-examined, and Canadian judges have traditionally upheld this practice. But Greenspan waved the Charter of Rights at Borins and asked him to overturn the traditional practice.

Greenspan had in mind two particular sections of the Charter. Section seven guarantees that no one will be deprived of his liberty except in accordance with the principles of fundamental justice. And section eleven says that any person charged with an offence is presumed innocent until he's proven guilty in a fair and public hearing.

"Both these notions, a fair hearing and fundamental justice," Greenspan argued, "demand the right to cross-examine on affidavits in an extradition hearing under the situation that Miss Smith faces. How do we know that what's sworn to in these affidavits is true unless I can test them under cross-examination?"

Greenspan argued for four days, and Borins went away to write his judgment. Not a bad argument, he said in effect to Greenspan, but not good enough. Borins pointed out in his twenty-three-page judgment that for one thing the purpose of an extradition hearing isn't to determine anyone's guilt or innocence. It's merely to decide whether there's sufficient evidence to order the person's return to a foreign jurisdiction. Affidavit evidence is good enough for that purpose. And speaking of the Charter of Rights, Borins wrote, what about the Charter's section one? It says that the freedoms guaranteed under sections seven and eleven and all the other sections are subject to such reasonable limits as can be demonstrably justified in a free and democratic society. That was the clincher for Borins, and he held that admitting the affidavits in evidence against Cathy Smith without cross-examination was a reasonable limit on her rights under the Charter.

"I appreciate," he wrote, "that there is always the risk that an innocent citizen might be extradited to face trial in a foreign state on the basis of evidence which, if it had been tested by cross-examination, would have been exposed as false. Such a situation, I am confident, would be extremely rare."

End of round one.

Next, Greenspan brought into court a book which was hot from the publisher's warehouse: *Wired: The Short Life and Hard Times of John Belushi* by Bob Woodward, the writer who won fame as an investigative reporter with his Watergate scoops. The story in *Wired*, Greenspan argued, convicted Smith of the very murder that California was seeking to try her for committing. Didn't the book militate against her chances of a fair trial in Los Angeles? Shouldn't Canada refuse to expose her to a jurisdiction in which the atmosphere might create an injustice to a Canadian citizen? Borins made snappy work of Greenspan's argument. He ruled that *Wired* was a concern for the California court, where the murder charge would be addressed, and not for his court, where extradition was the only concern.

Brian Greenspan tried another angle. The acts that Smith was alleged to have committed — injecting Belushi with drugs that led to his death — constituted murder under the California Penal Code. But the injecting of drugs, even if it resulted in death, wouldn't be considered murder under the Canadian Criminal Code unless Smith, in shooting up Belushi with the heroin and cocaine, *intended* to kill him. In California, simple injection was enough to qualify as murder; the presence or absence of intent didn't matter. So, Greenspan contended, if it was murder in California but not in Canada, then the Extradition Act didn't apply. For the Act to come into operation, the crime would have to be murder under the definitions of both jurisdictions. Ergo, the lady couldn't be extradited.

Ah no, Borins held, after he'd done his hard homework. The offence did not have to be murder as defined in both jurisdictions. The Extradition Act applied if Smith's conduct constituted murder in California and if it constituted *any* offence in Canada. It was clear that what she was alleged to have done to John Belushi — injected him with drugs that killed him — constituted manslaughter under the Canadian Criminal Code. Thus, the Extradition Act applied in her case.

Borins ordered Smith to be extradited to California. Greenspan appealed the decision, but he was running out of arguments, and he negotiated a deal with the Los Angeles district attorney's office under which Cathy Smith returned voluntarily to face the music in Los Angeles. Her trial, it appeared, would reach the courts some time in 1987.

"Those were interesting arguments that Brian raised," Borins said when it was all over. "Kind of exhilarating at times."

He found more exasperation than exhilaration in an obscenity case he tried in the fall of 1984. The proprietor of a video store was charged with peddling obscene material when he made available to his customers three particular films. Two of the movies, *Trashi* and *Demented*, fell vaguely into the pornographic category, and the third was Andy Warhol's version of *Frankenstein*. Borins screened the films. "*Demented*," he said, "may well be the worst movie I have ever watched." He listened to the evidence and argument, and he had no difficulty in holding that none of the films violated contemporary community standards. They weren't obscene, and the accused was innocent.

What exasperated Borins, however, was the unfair position that the Criminal Code had put the video store owner in. Under the ambiguous and probably inept drafting of sections 159 and 160 of the Code, the proprietor couldn't know that he was dealing in obscene films until he had been arrested and brought before a judge who determined whether the films he was dealing in were obscene. Was this Canada or was this Kafka? Borins thought it was Kafka.

"To condemn people to the stigma of a criminal prosecution," he wrote in his judgment, "for violating standards they cannot understand, construe and apply is a serious thing to do in a nation which, by its recent Charter of Rights, has affirmed its dedication to fair trials and due process." He went on to make explicit his belief that until a proceeding under the relevant section of the Criminal Code has first determined that a film or other object is obscene, no criminal prosecution should be sustained. Otherwise, Borins wrote, the law is "a trap".

"Steve's a mild maverick, an innovative person," Ed Ratushny says of Borins's work. Ratushny, now a teacher at the University of Ottawa Law School, is still one of the most astute observers of the Canadian judicial scene. "I think some of the more senior judges feel Steve's moving too fast," Ratushny says. "That's the maverick side of him. But I'd like to see him on the appellate court, because he loves the law. He loves to work with it, and when he has the chance, he produces really valuable stuff."

Through late January to the end of February 1985, Borins was stuck with a string of three awkward and demanding criminal cases. It wasn't his choice. He'd been hearing exclusively criminal trials for many months and he wanted something different, a handful of cases on the civil side. But many York District Court judges refuse to take criminal cases. They find them too chaotic and they can't get the hang of working comfortably with juries. Borins doesn't have trouble with chaos or with juries, and as the backlog of criminal cases piled up in the winter of 1985, he was called on to hear the three tough jury trials.

He brought the first trial to an unexpected and abrupt ending. The accused was a middle-aged woman who was charged with defrauding her employer, a trust company, of "valuable securities" amounting to more than two hundred thousand dollars. The jury was selected, the crown attorney put in his case, and the defence counsel made a start at his presentation. At that point, something occurred to Borins that had escaped everyone else in the courtroom, including the two lawyers. The woman was charged with stealing "valuable securities". But the documents she had allegedly swiped were unissued bearer bonds which didn't acquire a worth in dollars and cents until the trust company formally issued them. Hence, they were not "valuable" within the meaning of the charge, and the woman had committed no offence. Borins directed the jury to acquit her.

"A careful crown or somebody schooled in commercial law would have seen the issue long before I spotted it," Borins said later. "But I discovered that the crown had only been given the case on the day before the trial started, and the defence counsel admitted to me that, because of the options system at the law school, he'd never studied a commercial law subject."

The foul-up moved Borins to a general reflection on the state of Toronto's litigation bar.

"Sometimes when I'm sitting in court and the counsel in front of me are obviously not prepared," he said, "I think to myself, if members of the public walk in here right now and see this exhibition, they're going to be appalled. It's a far cry from what I saw when I was the Chief Justice's clerk twenty-five years ago. Excellence in preparation and presentation seemed to mean something back then. From where I sit now, I don't see the excellence nearly so often. The cases are more difficult today, but the counsel aren't consistently as good."

Martin Bell, the accused in the second of the three trials, looked like a tough customer. He was in his early twenties, short and restless and angry. He was charged with robbery. According to the crown's case, he went into a discount store in downtown Toronto on a September evening and demanded the money in the cash register. The cashier hesitated. Her name was Jihee An, a young Korean woman who was on her very first day of work in the store. Bell pulled back his fist and smashed it in Jihee An's face. The punch broke a bone near her eye socket. She slumped to the floor. Bell yanked open the cash drawer and sped off with two hundred and eighty dollars.

In court, Jihee An was so terrified of Bell that she could barely raise her arm to point him out in the prisoners' box. But her identification of Bell was convincing, and there was also the damaging evidence of a fingerprint on the cash drawer. It belonged to Bell.

His defence was that he'd been out of town at the time of the robbery. *Way* out of town. Up in Algonquin Park. Hundreds of miles from downtown Toronto. But the crown produced witnesses who swore they saw Bell in the city on the night that Jihee An had been robbed.

"It was probably the most hopeless case to defend I think I've ever encountered," Borins said later.

The members of the jury saw it the same way. They needed only ten minutes to arrive at a verdict of guilty.

"That was also the shortest I've ever had a jury out," Borins said.

In the courtroom, Borins was in the act of thanking the jury when he caught a rapid movement out of the corner of his eye.

It was Martin Bell who was making the rapid movement. He was hurtling through the air, flinging himself out of the prisoners' box and across a counsel table, howling four-letter curses as he flew. His arms were outstretched and his legs were flailing. For an instant, Borins thought Bell was in flight for the judge's bench. But Bell was going for the police sergeant who'd been in charge of the case against him. The sergeant was sitting beside the crown attorney, and Bell got him by the neck.

The neck was all he got.

In a flash, five policemen landed on top of Bell. The cops were members of the hold-up squad who were in court on another case.

"I think the hold-up people were winding up to pound the daylights out of Bell," Borins says. "Until they remembered they were in a courtroom."

The policemen cinched Bell in a network of grips and bundled him toward a side door. Bell trailed a stream of curses until the door closed behind the charging little band of cops and prisoner.

"Well," Borins said in the shocked stillness of the courtroom, "in the absence of the accused, I suppose I'll not proceed with the sentencing."

Next day Bell returned to the courtroom. He was draped

in handcuffs, chains, and leg irons. Borins added up Bell's previous convictions, got a total of twelve, called him "a persistent offender", and gave him seven years.

In the last of Borins's three criminal cases, the man on trial faced charges of attempted murder, aggravated assault, and wilfully setting fire to a building. The target of all the mayhem was the man's wife. His name was Wayne Bright, he was thirty years old, and he had a record of activities like assault and burglary and mischief. Bright's wife, Loretta, was twenty-three, and a prostitute, and she testified for the crown. Bright, she told the court, dragged her into an alley in the neighbourhood where she worked her profession and stabbed her in the face, chest, and throat. Then he went to the apartment where the couple lived and set fire to her wedding dress and their marriage certificate. The blood-letting and arson took place one week after Wayne and Loretta had been married.

The trial reached its ninth day. "It was moving along very nicely," Borins says of the case. "Counsel were good. There was no time-wasting or unnecessary witnesses, and I could tell that the jury was very intent on what they were hearing." On the ninth day, Wayne Bright took the stand. He was pleading not guilty to the charges, but as his lawyer led him through his testimony, Bright did something astounding. He broke into tears, and he told a very different story from the tale that his own counsel was expecting.

"I found my wife in bed with the guy who used to be her pimp," Bright said between sobs. "This was a week after we got married. I was embarrassed, stunned, hurt. I felt like a failure."

He went out and drank boilermakers, beer and rye, and washed down tranquillizers.

"I needed to relax," Bright said in the witness-box.

When he'd cooled himself out, he confronted his wife in the alley. Loretta pulled a knife, Bright said. He flashed a knife of his own. He swiped at Loretta.

The words tumbled out of Bright. His counsel couldn't stop the babble. Bright was determined to tell the whole rotten story. He was confessing.

"I was flipping out," Bright said in court. "I used my knife on Loretta."

The confession was complete, and Bright took the final, inevitable step. He changed his plea from not guilty to guilty, and Borins gave him a long prison sentence.

Afterwards, Borins dropped by the Martin Room on the University Avenue Courthouse's fifth floor. The Martin Room, named after former Senior Judge Walter Martin, is the spot where District Court judges gather for lunches, coffee breaks, and loose moments. Borins told the other judges about the bizarre wind-up to the Bright case.

"Ah, I see," one of the judges said. "The accused cracked during cross-examination?"

Borins laughed.

"No," he said, "the accused cracked during examination-in-chief."

With the three consecutive jury trials, Borins felt exhausted.

"It's far more tiring to run a case with a jury than it is to sit alone," he said. "With a jury, you have to take more care that evidence doesn't creep into a case that shouldn't be there. You have to be on guard that the wrong question isn't asked by counsel. When you're sitting by yourself, you know you can put out of your own mind the things that aren't techni- cally correct. But for a jury, it's got to be right down the middle, clean and proper all the way, or the whole trial might be jeopardized."

And there are little things to worry about, the jury's com- fort for example.

"Whenever a *voir dire* comes along, an argument over a legal point that takes place while the jury's excluded, I get edgy. I know the jury isn't having any fun. I know it's stuck out there in one of those windowless rooms where they're always sent. That always concerns me, the discomfort of these people who've come down to the courthouse to do their civic duty."

On the other hand, Borins finds compensations in working with a jury.

"I enjoy dealing with these twelve strangers who've gathered to make a decision about someone's guilt or innocence. They're all different in background and education and personality and they'll never see one another again. It's fascinating. I try to make everything comprehensible to them. It's a little like teaching law school again. Except there's one big difference — with a law class, I might have a week to explain the principles of fraud or *mens rea* or something else, but with a jury, I've got to make them understand the thing in about five minutes. There's an aura of unreality to it."

The unreality of the three consecutive trials had worn at Borins's stamina, and he was feeling fed up with a couple of other matters. There was the staggering backload of 3,500 criminal cases still waiting for trial. There was the stalling in Ottawa over the long-delayed pay raise for District Court judges. And there was the crowded space for his court in the University Avenue Courthouse, where the District Court takes a back seat to the Supreme Court.

Borins and his wife decided to fly to their favourite winter retreat for a few days, the French island of St. Martin in the Caribbean.

"Outside of Paris," Borins says, "it's got the best food in the world."

Even a thinking person's judge needs a break.

Marcel Gaboury

Marcel Gaboury calls himself a pea soup.

"The word they use for us these days is frog, you know?" he says. "But an old guy like me, I prefer pea soup. That's what I am, born in Montreal, lived my whole life in this town. I knew Duplessis personally and he knew me by my first name. *'Hey, Marcel!'* I didn't like his politics. I am a Liberal because my father was a Liberal before me. But Duplessis knew I was an honest man even if I wasn't with him. That's my life, always in Quebec. A hundred per cent pea soup."

Marcel Gaboury was born in 1905. He lives with his wife on the north side of Mount Royal in a stone house in Outremont which he and his father built. He is tall, strong, energetic, and a noisy talker. He shouts and laughs and hectors and rails against the unfairnesses he came across in his days as a lawyer and a judge. He likes sports and politics and long drives in his car. Taking it slow and easy isn't his idea of a good time. When he sits in conversation, he puts on a restless display of tics and signals. When he tells a story, he reaches out his long arms as if to embrace his audience.

"The way I went into law, it was a matter of exchanging one hero for another," he says, his hands flicking in the air. "My first hero was Louis Morel, who coached me in sports at

McGill University. Discus, pole vault, all that. He was a great athlete and a wonderful inspiration. He was also a cop, and then, by jeez, he joined up in a gang that robbed the Bank of Hochelaga. There was this gang, Serafino, Gambino, Tony Frank, a couple of kids, and Louis Morel, and what did they do? Oh my, they killed a bank messenger and the bunch of them go on trial for murder. This was in the early 1920s and me, I was hearing lots of court cases because I had a part-time job reporting for the *Montreal Herald*. At the Bank of Hochelaga case, a lawyer named Bob Calder was the prosecutor. He worked with an adjuster from the insurance company for the bank. This adjuster who investigated the crime, he had two bullet holes in him from the Boxer Rebellion, a tough guy, and he had all the facts on the gang. But Bob Calder was the star in the courtroom. Everybody knew it. The adjuster knew it. Hey, he used to carry Bob Calder's briefcase into court for him every day. I saw it. I was in court for the whole trial. I could not take my eyes off Bob Calder. He was a fantastic lawyer. He was like Clarence Darrow. And he got convictions against all of the gang. Louis Morel stood up in court and said, hang me for the murder but don't hang the two kids. So everybody in the gang was hanged except those kids. I went home and didn't sleep for a couple of nights because my hero Louis Morel was hanged. But I had made a new hero. Bob Calder. And that's how I went into criminal law."

Gaboury practised his criminal law for almost thirty-five years. At first he worked in an office with a couple of partners, but mostly he operated on his own. In the years after the Second World War, some divorce cases came his way. "They were for war brides from overseas," he says. "They had married Montreal guys who painted pictures of living in a castle when all they had was a flat on the fourth floor." And he took a few prosecutions for the RCMP. But his practice stuck mainly to criminal defence work, acting for the accused rounders and thieves who walked through his office door. He pleaded a few murder cases. He had fun. He didn't make a lot of money.

"In law school," he says, "they told us there is nothing less lucrative than the practice of criminal law but there is nothing more exciting. I am here to justify both statements."

Gaboury's other grand passion was for the Liberal Party. His father swore by the Grits. It was under a Liberal government that the senior Gaboury was rewarded for his years of service in the post office with an appointment in 1923 to the job of deputy postmaster general, the first French Canadian to reach the deputy-minister level in Ottawa. Like father, like son; Marcel Gaboury worked as a Liberal money-raiser and organizer, and in 1940 when the party beat Maurice Duplessis and the Union Nationale in the provincial election, he was put in charge of civil defence for the whole of Quebec.

"I didn't get any holidays on that job," Gaboury says. "I couldn't sit around drinking with the guys like I might want to. But it was a job that made me very happy."

Duplessis was voted back into office in August 1944. Gaboury, dismissed with the rest of the Liberals, was about to return to his private practice when Duplessis phoned to invite him to Quebec City for a chat.

"Look, Marcel," Duplessis said, as Gaboury recalls the conversation, "I know you wouldn't pull any dirty tricks if I kept you in my government. What office do you want?"

"Hey, Premier, I'm a Liberal," Gaboury answered. "I can't give you the time of day."

"Okay," Duplessis said. "I hope I find a guy as good as you."

"That'll be hard."

From 1944 to 1960, Gaboury practised law and worked as a bagman for the Liberal Party.

"I was in charge of collecting from all the bars and restaurants in Montreal," he says. "Ruby Foo's gave the most, but no matter what came to me from them and from everybody else, I knew the Duplessis guys were getting five times as much."

A couple of months before each election, Gaboury would

send a discreet notice to the city's tavern-keepers and restaurant proprietors. "Marcel Gaboury will be in his office every day from ten a.m. to noon and from two p.m. to three p.m." The gentlemen came to call and brought their wallets.

"One thing for sure, I gave all of them receipts," Gaboury says. "That kept them honest and kept me the same way."

In 1960, Jean Lesage led the Quebec Liberals to victory, and Gaboury received a prize for his bagman years. He was named a judge of the Court of Sessions (Criminal), a position he held until he retired ten years later. The job and Gaboury made a perfect fit. The Court of Sessions (Criminal) was where Gaboury had conducted most of his practice, the busy court where he defended his thirty-five-year collection of robbers, thieves, and break-and-enter artists. It was Gaboury's home turf.

"The difference on the bench was that now I was looking down on the accused," he says. "But only in a physical sense. A judge in the criminal courts, his work is to know two things, the law and human nature. And something else or he is worse than a useless guy, he must be fair at all times."

Fairness and justice are two constants that run through Gaboury's conversation and reminiscence. When he calls another judge or lawyer "a fair guy", he's handing out the highest praise. And when he rates his own past performances, it's on the scale of just dealing. "I was square with that guy," he'll say of an accused who appeared before him, and he'll laugh and clap his hands. He had passed his personal test.

Two stories — two cases — from Gaboury's history rouse his sense of injustice. They make a pair of touchstones in his talk about the law. He rejoices in spinning out the tales of the two, roaring at the inequities he sees in them. The cases are very different and have in common for Gaboury only their affront to justice. One case came to him when he was a lawyer, the other after he had been appointed to the bench. The first, which reached Gaboury in 1945, began thousands of miles away from Montreal and ended in Ottawa. The second, in 1967, lasted for its entire run in Montreal. One was a loser for Gaboury; the other was a winner, and he says so even if he was the impartial judge who decided which man won.

The first case had its start on Mauritius, an island in the Indian Ocean which was the birthplace in 1910 of Count Marie Alfred Fougereaux de Marigny. Mauritius had been English since Great Britain took it away from the French after the Napoleonic Wars, but the old families of the island were allowed to hang on to their traditional French titles. Freddie de Marigny's father was aristocratic and cold-spirited. His mother was beautiful and warm-hearted, and she ran away with another man when little Freddie was four years old. The father made Freddie's childhood miserable. As soon as he was old enough, he left Mauritius with his title, a small inheritance, and not much else. He was six feet, three inches tall, handsome, charming, clever, and rascally.

Over the following years, in the 1930s, de Marigny worked at jobs that attract rascals. He was a lounge lizard in London, a stockbroker in Manhattan, a real estate dealer in the Bahamas. He married three times. The third marriage, in the spring of 1942, was to Nancy Oakes of Nassau. With her, de Marigny had hit pay dirt. Nancy's father was Harry Oakes, the man who made three hundred million dollars from a gold mine he discovered near Kirkland Lake in Northern Ontario. Oakes, an American turned Canadian, moved to the Bahamas for two reasons: the islands gave titles to its rich citizens and didn't bother to tax them. Sir Harry, as he soon became, hadn't counted on Freddie de Marigny coming into his life. Freddie was thirty-two when he married Nancy Oakes, she was nineteen, and Sir Harry was unhappy.

In the early morning of Thursday, July 8, 1943, someone bashed in the left side of Sir Harry's head, set fire to his body as it lay in bed, and sprinkled it with feathers from a ripped pillow. In later years, the most scurrilous yet plausible explanation for Sir Harry's murder was a complicated business about the Mafia's plans to open a gambling casino in Nassau. Oakes opposed the idea and the Mafia decided to teach him a lesson. The plot involved as participants at various levels Lucky Luciano, the Duke of Windsor, Meyer Lansky, and a Bahamian real estate operator named Harold Christie, who happened to be the person to discover Sir Harry's body. But immediately after the crime, most of the English on the islands pointed their fingers at Freddie de Marigny as the guilty party. He wasn't their sort, too foreign, too flashy. He must have done it. The Duke of Windsor shared the general prejudice against de Marigny. The Duke was the governor of the Bahamas, and within hours of Harold Christie's finding of Sir Harry's body, he sent for a couple of detectives from the Miami police force named Barker and Melchen to get to the bottom of things. As far as the Duke was concerned, that meant pinning the deed on Freddie de Marigny.

Barker and Melchen were more Keystone Kops than *Miami Vice*. If there was a case against de Marigny, they probably botched it. The only piece of damning evidence that Barker and Melchen came up with was a fingerprint of de Marigny's which Barker, who was supposed to be the fingerprint expert of the pair, claimed he found on an ornately scrolled Chinese silk screen in Sir Harry's bedroom. De Marigny was charged with murder, and at the trial, Barker was the chief witness against him.

On Barker's examination-in-chief, he did not produce the crucial fingerprint or a photograph of it; rather, he put in evidence a rubber lift or impression of the print which he said he removed from the Chinese screen by applying Scotch tape. The crown pronounced itself satisfied that Barker's rubber lift clinched the case against de Marigny.

A leading Nassau barrister, Godfrey Higgs, rose on behalf

of de Marigny and conducted a classic piece of cross-examination.

"In testifying in other cases," Higgs began with Barker, "have you ever produced in court the object with the print on it?"

"Yes," Barker answered, "when the objects were movable."

"Why did you not introduce the screen in this court?" Higgs asked. "Is it not movable?"

"It can be moved."

Higgs asked, "What equipment did you bring with you to Nassau on July 8?"

"A small dusting kit, tape, and a speed graphic camera."

Higgs made a display of shock. "Did you not come prepared to look for *fingerprint evidence*?"

"Yes."

"But," Higgs exploded, "you left behind your *fingerprint camera!*"

Baker said, "I thought that the kit I brought was sufficient to take care of a murder case. The fingerprint camera would have been desirable."

"When you examined the Chinese screen on the Thursday afternoon," Higgs said, pushing at Barker, "did you know you were investigating a case of homicide?"

"Yes."

"Could you not have had a camera flown over from Miami by Friday afternoon?"

"I believe I could have."

"And you never made the effort?"

"No."

"I produce to you, sir, exhibit four," Higgs said, weighing in with disdain, "which is a photograph of area five of the panelled Chinese screen. I put it to you, sir, that the camera that took that picture could have been used to photograph the fingerprint on the screen."

Barker conceded that it could have.

"I tell you," Higgs went on, "that the camera which took this photograph belongs to Mr. Stanley Toogood, a commercial photographer here in Nassau. Could you not have borrowed a camera from him to photograph the fingerprint on the screen before you lifted it?"

"Yes," Barker said, cornered, "I suppose I could have."

Under Higgs's questioning, Barker's methods in gathering the evidence of the print were beginning to look fishy. Higgs took another tack which cast even more doubt on Barker's operations.

"How many latent fingerprints that you raised were you able to identify?" he asked.

"Those of the accused," Barker answered, "of the attending physician, Dr. Quackenbush, and of myself."

"*What?*" Higgs demanded. "You did not find a single fingerprint of Harold Christie in that room?"

"No, I did not."

"Although Mr. Christie and Sir Harry often lived there together for several days," Higgs asked again, "you found *no* fingerprints of Mr. Christie?"

"No," Barker said, and then, turning to the presiding judge, in a plaintive voice, "I wonder if I might have a glass of water, please."

Barker was revealed as a bungler. Could he be worse? Perhaps a concocter of evidence? Higgs thought so, and he questioned Barker about an episode in which he and his partner, Melchen, went to great and curious lengths to have de Marigny handle a particular water glass.

"While you were working on the silk screen in the Oakes house on the Friday morning," Higgs asked, "did not Captain Melchen bring the accused upstairs?"

"I understand he did."

"And did Captain Melchen take the accused into the northwest bedroom?"

"I understand he did."

"Did you not go to the door of that room," Higgs asked, "and open it while they were there together?"

"I did not," Barker answered.

"I put it to you that you did," Higgs insisted, "and that you asked Melchen if everything was 'okay'."

"I did not."

"I put it to you that Melchen said 'yes'."

"I didn't even know he was in that room until the next day, I believe," Barker said in a lame tone.

"Wasn't the accused's latent print obtained from some object in that northwest bedroom?" Higgs zeroed in on his point. "From the water glass which the accused touched?"

"Definitely not."

"But," Higgs pushed on, "it was after he left that room that you claimed to have discovered his print, was it not?"

"Yes."

"I suggest to you," Higgs said, his voice rising, "that you and Captain Melchen deliberately planned to get the accused alone in order to get his fingerprints."

"We did not."

"I suggest that exhibit J, the rubber impression of the fingerprint, did not come from the screen," Higgs said, close to a shout.

"It did come from the screen," Barker said.

"Ah," Higgs countered, playing one of his aces, "but you can show us on the impression none of the scroll-work that covers the entire screen. The impression you have produced has a clear background. You cannot show any of the scroll."

"I cannot," Barker admitted without attempting to explain the reason, if any, for the scroll-work's absence.

"I suggest that your desire for personal gain has caused you to sweep aside truth," Higgs wound up. "I put it to you, sir, that you have fabricated evidence."

"I deny that," Barker said.

Higgs was finished. So was Barker.

"I have no further questions, my lord," Higgs said.

The jury needed five minutes less than two hours to reach a verdict.

Not guilty.

De Marigny threw a party of celebration, but he wasn't out of the woods yet. The Duke of Windsor set in motion proceedings to have Freddie deported from the Bahamas on the grounds that he was, as the Duke wrote to the British Colonial Secretary, the leader of "a quite influential, fast and depraved set of the younger generation". Nancy Oakes de Marigny had stood by her husband during the trial, but afterwards she began to listen to her mother, who despised de Marigny even more than Sir Harry had. Perhaps Lady Oakes saw in Freddie an aspect of her own life that she preferred to forget; when she met her much more senior millionaire husband, she was Eunice McIntyre, twenty-four years old and a stenographer in a bank in Sydney, Australia. By 1945, de Marigny had been booted out of the Bahamas, refused a visa to enter the United States where the Duke of Windsor was able to pull a few strings, and separated from his wife. He headed for Montreal.

Canada gave de Marigny a piece of paper that allowed him to stay in the country for thirty days. It became a busy thirty days for de Marigny. Nancy arrived for one last session on their faltering marriage. De Marigny enlisted in the Canadian army, perhaps hoping that his status as a soldier would give him permanent residence in Canada. If that was his motive, it failed, since an immigration board ordered him deported from the country. While he pondered his next move, Freddie became best friends with a woman in Montreal's most chic social circles. The woman told him to take his many problems to Marcel Gaboury.

"He walks into my office, big handsome guy, and my secretary was flabbergasted," Gaboury says. "Fred was as famous as a movie star in those days."

Gaboury liked de Marigny from the start. Maybe it was partly because Gaboury has a touch of the scamp to him. He likes to point out that the first Gaboury mentioned in history books is a horse thief. This Gaboury makes a fleeting appearance in Francis Parkman's history of the Indian chief Pontiac, and he got himself hanged. By one other standard, de Marigny was Gaboury's kind of client — he gave Gaboury a chance to exercise his outrage at injustice.

"Fred was the scapegoat," Gaboury says. "The big shots and the people with the money needed someone to push around, and it was him. I knew I had to help this guy."

Gaboury could do nothing about de Marigny's marital grief. "Nancy Oakes left him flat broke in the Mount Royal Hotel," Gaboury says. But he threw himself into de Marigny's battle against Canada's immigration laws, policies, and bureaucrats. There was, as things developed over the following few weeks, nothing dramatic in Gaboury's struggle. Nor did it represent a major adventure in de Marigny's spectacularly adventurous career. Rather, it turned out to be, at least for Gaboury, a lesson in disillusionment. De Marigny said he was disillusioned, too, but he was getting used to it.

The Immigration Act under which de Marigny had been ordered out of Canada — "a dead copy of the American law", Gaboury says — contained a moral-turpitude clause. "Some lower-level pen pusher in the department thinks you've been a bad guy, he can throw you out," Gaboury says. De Marigny had been summoned before a committee of three immigration officers and questioned about his life in the Bahamas. A week later, he received a terse notice from the Department of Immigration requesting him to leave Canada forthwith. De Marigny told his story to Gaboury, who set about the task of preparing an answer to the deportation notice.

Then Gaboury ran into section 23 of the Immigration Act.

"By jeez, it was the most terrible, undemocratic law I ever read in my life as a lawyer or judge," Gaboury says. "Section

23 said in no uncertain terms and without any ambiguity that
no court of any jurisdiction in Canada had the authority to
reverse or annul a deportation order of the immigration
department. That section made the courts helpless."

Nevertheless, Gaboury put together a twenty-page petition
which marshalled his arguments in de Marigny's favour. He
contended that the deportation order was arbitrary and unjust. He pointed out that de Marigny was a British subject, a
citizen of Mauritius, which had been a British colony for one
hundred and fifty years, that he had violated no laws in
Canada, and that he was willing to serve in the Canadian
armed services. It was a persuasive document, but Gaboury
had no case law on his side in arguing against the infamous
section 23. The courts had annulled a deportation notice in
only a single previous case. That had occurred a year earlier,
in 1944, when Mr. Justice Ivan Rand of the Supreme Court of
Canada overruled the deportation of a Japanese-born woman
on the grounds that her hearing had been conducted by just
one immigration officer rather than the three called for in
the Immigration Act.

"With Fred, they made no errors like that," Gaboury says.
"They went by the book."

Still, Gaboury succeeded in obtaining a court hearing, and
he trotted out his arguments.

"I made speeches to the court," he says. "I said we should
look at the disgusting things we did under the law to our Japanese during the war. These were Canadian citizens that we
pushed around cruelly and illegally, and now the immigration people were giving the same treatment to my client, Fred
de Marigny."

The judge listened to Gaboury's points and shrugged. He
sympathized, but he said section 23 prevented him from dis-
turbing the deportation order.

"It was the same in every court all the way to the Supreme
Court of Canada," Gaboury says. "That's how far I took the

case. I told them the Immigration Act was a disgrace. They said maybe so, but it was still the law. It was a heartbreak to me."

It was also expensive. De Marigny had no money, and though de Marigny's Montreal socialite friend gave Gaboury five hundred dollars, it wasn't enough to cover the smallest fraction of the expenses and fees he'd racked up in the crusade that came to an end with the refusal of the Supreme Court to cancel the deportation order. De Marigny left the country and sailed for Cuba, where he hung out with an old pal, Ernest Hemingway. Later, he was able to obtain a visa that permitted him to enter the United States, and he survived as a minor celebrity in New York City.

Gaboury never saw de Marigny again, but over the following few years he learned a thing or two he hadn't known about de Marigny and the Oakes murder case.

He learned that Barker, the fingerprint man from the Miami police department, had been on the Mafia's payroll for years. He had undoubtedly been operating under instructions from the Mafia, the people who wanted to bring gambling to Nassau, when he testified at de Marigny's trial for the murder of Sir Harry, the man who wanted to keep gambling out of Nassau.

Gaboury learned that, in the weeks before the Canadian immigration officers issued their deportation order against de Marigny, Lady Eunice Oakes had travelled to Ottawa for a private consultation with Prime Minister Mackenzie King. "That's where the plot was hatched," Gaboury says. "Lady Oakes tells the Prime Minister, get this son of a bitch de Marigny out of the country, away from my daughter, send him to that island in the middle of the Indian Ocean. And the Prime Minister passes the word down the line until it gets to the immigration guys." Gaboury believes Lady Oakes later gave the federal government her husband's grand estate at Niagara Falls as a quid pro quo.

"You try to fight fair," Gaboury says, "but money wins in the end."

In the second case that excites Gaboury's sense of justice, the villain was Claude Wagner, the moody, quirky man who was a power in Quebec politics through the 1960s and 1970s. Wagner first attracted wide attention as a hard-nosed, crime-busting crown attorney in Montreal. He transferred his fame and success to politics and served as minister of justice in Jean Lesage's Quebec Liberal government. He moved next to the bench and sat through the mid-1960s as a judge on Gaboury's court, the Court of Sessions (Criminal). In the early 1970s, he left both law and the Liberal Party to return to politics as a Conservative MP in Ottawa. Wagner staked out a strong position on the right wing of the party, and that, together with his style — he was handsome and a slick dresser, and affected an aristocratic manner, peppering his speeches with the royal "we" — made him a strong contender for the Conservative leadership at the party's 1976 convention. He came close, losing to Joe Clark by only sixty-five votes on the fourth ballot. Wagner turned sulky after the defeat, and in 1978 he accepted a Liberal appointment to the Senate, where he sat, brooding, until his death a few years later.

Gaboury knew Wagner in his early days through their mutual association with the provincial Liberals, but their lives came in closest contact when they sat together on the Court of Sessions. Wagner was not a favourite of Gaboury's, either as a judge or as a man.

"He forgot where he came from," Gaboury says of Wagner. "He got to be an important person and he didn't remember the guys who helped put him on high. He was the way Brutus said of Caesar in Shakespeare."

Gaboury knows his Shakespeare.

"Brutus's speech at the beginning of Act Two in *Julius Caesar*," he says and begins to speak the passage.

" 'But 'tis a common proof / That lowliness is young ambition's ladder,' " he recites, his right arm flung in the air, " 'Whereto the climber-upward turns his face; / But when he once attains the upmost round, / He then unto the ladder turns his back, / Looks in the clouds, scorning the base degrees / By which he did ascend.' "

Gaboury finishes on a shout, not a line missed, and he laughs in the air.

"That was Claude Wagner," he says. "Cheap back-lane politician."

The case that brought Gaboury and Wagner into collision centred on a man named Adrien Meunier. He was a prominent Montreal lawyer and included among his clients a businessman named André Poupart. In 1964, the Montreal police were investigating Poupart and some of his associates on suspicion that they had worked a fraudulent bankruptcy. In the course of the investigation, a police captain telephoned Meunier and quizzed him about Poupart's business practices. Meunier told the captain he was wasting his time with Poupart, who was, Meunier said, incapable of pulling a piece of fraud. Unknown to Meunier, the police captain had taped their telephone conversation.

A year and a half later, Wagner, in his capacity as judge of the Court of Sessions, held an inquiry into the allegations of fraudulent bankruptcy against Poupart and his colleagues. Wagner's inquiry took place in his chambers. It was not a trial. The crown attorney was merely asking Wagner to issue a warrant charging Poupart and the others with conducting a fraud. Wagner gave the inquiry the full treatment, and in its course he summoned Adrien Meunier to testify before him. By this time Meunier was no longer a lawyer. He had been appointed to the Quebec Superior Court. He was in effect Wagner's senior, sitting on a higher court, but Wagner showed him little respect at the inquiry, calling him "Mr. Meunier" rather than the proper "Judge Meunier". When Meunier testified, he heard for the first time the secret tape that had

been made months earlier of his conversation with the Montreal police captain. Meunier failed to remember the conversation or even to recognize his own voice on the tape. Wagner
dismissed him, and a few weeks later in his decision he declined to issue a warrant for fraudulent bankruptcy against
André Poupart and friends. But he issued a warrant charging Judge Meunier with perjury on the grounds that Meunier
had testified falsely during the inquiry in Wagner's chambers.

"It caused a hell of a sensation," Gaboury says. "But it didn't
surprise any of us judges on the Sessions Court because
Wagner was always telling us we should be more severe.
Severe? That was Claude Wagner all the way through. He
wanted to be severe with Meunier and get his name in all the
papers as a tough guy."

Meunier was temporarily suspended from the Superior
Court and went to trial on the perjury charges. Though
Wagner didn't preside at the trial, he kept his hand in the
action. "Every day during the trial, Wagner was in and out of
the office of the judge who heard it," Gaboury says. "There
was no doubt in my mind what his influence consisted of."
At the end of the trial, the presiding judge convicted Meunier
and sentenced him to two years in prison. Meunier appealed
and was granted a new trial. The second time around, he
appeared before a judge whom Wagner could not influence
— Marcel Gaboury.

The second trial lasted for several weeks through the late
spring of 1967. "It became clear to me as we went along that
Meunier had not perjured himself," Gaboury says. "He hadn't
said anything with the intention of deceiving the court. He
just didn't recognize his voice on a secret tape that was
months old, and anyway, for perjury, there must be untruths
and there must also be premeditation and a conscious attempt
to speak the untruths. There wasn't in this case." When the
trial ended, Gaboury went away to write his judgment. It
stretched to fifty pages, and at eleven o'clock on August 14,

1967, he returned to court and read in French what he had written.

He began by declaring that Adrien Meunier was "honourably acquitted". But that wasn't the news in Gaboury's judgment. The news came in the vigorous language he used to criticize one of his fellow judges, Claude Wagner.

"It is evident," Gaboury read, "that Judge Wagner, while he was questioning the Honourable Judge Meunier, was looking for — and finding — wrongs and mistakes in the conduct of the accused over a year and a half earlier. He would seem to have purposely forgotten the rules of fair play which are spelled out clearly in the penal code and in our jurisprudence. These rules have evolved as judges who had wisely profited from experience gradually and slowly came to understand human frailty.

"The penal code states it clearly: when you ask an accused to play fair, then at least give the example yourself. And especially in the very tendentious and difficult case of perjury.

"When a witness, testifying under oath, does not recall a fact as precisely as the Court would like, the point is not to try to find out and prove the witness has erred, but rather to discover whether the error was made wilfully and deliberately, and this against the background of details surrounding the case, the intelligence of the witness, the advantages there might be in withholding the truth, and the evidence of full intention to mislead the Court."

The fallout from Gaboury's judgment was predictable.

"Claude Wagner never spoke to me again," Gaboury says. "That was okay with me. I didn't want to hear more of his lectures on severity anyway."

As for Meunier, with the perjury charge lifted, he was free to return to his duties on the Superior Court.

"But his heart wasn't in it," Gaboury says. "His wife died during the proceedings against him. She was overwhelmed by the whole affair, and Meunier himself was a broken man."

Gaboury shakes his head.

"Maybe the lesson in the case," he says, "was that not only must there be justice in our courts but there had better be justice from the first and not just at the last."

As he speaks, Gaboury's voice loses its customary shouting heartiness. It falls away almost to a whisper.

"It came at the last for Meunier," he says, "and that was too late."

CHAPTER FIVE

On Appeal

With a few adjustments here and there — take out the dais, rearrange the seating — room sixty on the sixth floor of the Vancouver Courthouse might pass for a wealthy man's dream of a rumpus room. Its walls are tan panelling, the deep red carpeting has a springy feel to it, and the soft armchairs are done in fabric the colour of Dijon mustard. On the ceiling, two large fans turn in a tantalizing drift, waiting for Sydney Greenstreet to make an entrance. The west wall is glass from top to bottom and from side to side and offers a view that has a hint of mountain in the north corner. Given the decor and style, it's the sort of room our wealthy man wouldn't mind running through barefoot. But if he did, he'd probably get himself arrested, because room sixty is a courtroom. And not just any courtroom, but the place of choice where British Columbia Chief Justice Nathaniel Theodore Nemetz, known to one and all, including his colleagues and many newspaper reporters, as "Sonny", holds forth.

On this particular spring morning in 1985, Nemetz was flanked on the judges' dais — its colour continues the tan motif — by his brothers on the Court of Appeal, Mr. Justices Hinkson and Aikins. The three were listening to an appeal from a drug conviction. The appellant's lawyer, a dark, blocky man in his mid-forties, was battling against the facts and the law. It seemed his client had sold a Baggie of cocaine for one hundred and eighty dollars to two undercover RCMP officers in the lobby of the Bombay Bicycle Club, a night spot in downtown Vancouver a few blocks north of the courthouse. The Mounties had their man red-handed, and the drug seller was convicted at his trial.

But his counsel was putting a desperate argument to the three Court of Appeal judges. Couldn't it be that the RCMP officers slipped up in properly identifying the Baggie of cocaine in question? Was the Baggie exhibited at the trial really the same Baggie that the Mounties had purchased from the appellant? The counsel contended that no one could say for a certainty and that the court should direct an acquittal or order a new trial.

Justices Hinkson and Aikins were having none of it. They were growing testy and impatient, and they peppered the counsel with questions and doubts. The counsel perspired and tried to stand his shaky ground. The atmosphere in the courtroom was escalating to acrimony.

Then Sonny Nemetz stepped in.

Nemetz is a small man with a round face, silver hair, and a generous nose that ends in a cleft at the tip. There's a pugnacious touch to the face. Nemetz more resembles a long-retired welterweight boxer than a chief justice.

Now he leaned forward in his chair, looking across the judges' desk, and he gave the struggling counsel an expression of encompassing understanding and regret.

"You'll find us a little difficult this morning," he said in a soft voice that just reached the counsel table.

Nemetz smiled. The smile was close to beatific, and in the instant that it lasted, the anger and tension in the courtroom dissolved and floated in the direction of the fans on the ceiling.

It was the sort of moment that lawyers, judges, and litigants have come to expect of Nemetz. He's a smoother of ruffled feathers, a negotiator, a pourer of oil on troubled waters.

It hardly seemed to matter, even to the appellant's counsel, that a few minutes later Nemetz dictated in court a brief judgment dismissing the appeal.

People who've been around Vancouver long enough — since the mid-1930s anyway — tell the story that Sonny Nemetz made a declaration of intent when he was a student at the University of British Columbia.

"I'm going to do two things in my life," he's supposed to have said. "Be the first Jewish chancellor of UBC and the first Jewish chief justice of this province."

Odds are that the story is apocryphal. Still, true or not, it gets at the early beginnings of Nemetz's ambition and confidence. He came out of the chute a burning little guy with speed, brains, and bravado. And, oh yes, he *was* the first Jew to occupy the two seats of authority he had his eye on.

Nemetz, an electrician's son, was born in Winnipeg in 1913 but didn't stay long in his birthplace. His parents pushed on to Watrous, a small town in the middle of Saskatchewan, where young Nemetz grew from age four to age ten. Six years was a sufficient duration for Watrous to mark down Sonny's name; decades later, after he got famous, the town invited him back for a day of celebration in his honour. Nemetz remembers that he had a good time at the festivities. He's not the sort of man who ever dredges up bad times or the mean events from his past. Religious putdowns, which haven't been unknown to Nemetz in Vancouver, his home since 1923, seem to have washed over him without leaving a residue of bitterness or resentment.

At the University of British Columbia, Nemetz worked on the *Ubyssey*, the campus newspaper that generated many of Canada's most accomplished journalists, from Stu Keate, Nemetz's lifelong pal who became publisher of the *Vancouver Sun*, to Pierre Berton to Allan Fotheringham. Nemetz also honed his speaking style — gentle voice, hard facts — in four years on the university's McGowan Cup Debating Team, and he paid his tuition by stomping it up at weekend dances with a tootling jazz band.

"Every Jewish mother expects her son to be the next Heifetz," Nemetz says. "It's part of the heritage. I just varied it a little. I played violin, doubled on banjo, and earned a pretty good dollar."

His university major was in history, and he came under the wing of Professor Fred Soward, UBC's distinguished historical scholar who died on New Year's Day, 1985. Soward remembered that each week Nemetz would challenge him to a duel of knowledge based on a current-events quiz published in *Time* magazine. Who could get the most right answers to a long list of questions? "Nathan won as often as I did," Soward said. "Maybe more often. He was very very eager."

Nemetz graduated in 1934 with first-class honours, and Soward offered him a job as a beginning lecturer in the school's history department.

"The pay is six hundred dollars," Soward said.

"That's incredible," Nemetz said. "Six hundred dollars a month."

"Six hundred a year," Soward said.

Nemetz enrolled in law school.

He was called to the bar in 1937 and found his way fairly quickly into labour law. It became a specialty that was the backbone of his practice for twenty-five years. He eventually formed his own firm and appeared for unions in court and around the arbitration table. He earned a reputation as perhaps B.C.'s most astute labour negotiator, and he was summoned frequently by the provincial government to mediate the fieriest quarrels between unions and corporations. Nemetz smiled, spoke softly, wielded his expertise, and made peace.

"As B.C. politicians have long known," an editorial in the *Sun* said in Nemetz's heyday, "nothing succeeds like Sonny Nemetz."

At the same time, Nemetz was bustling through the worlds of community service. B'nai Brith, Council of Christians and Jews, Community Chest, Canadian Jewish Congress. Nemetz was a senior man in all of them. For UBC he took on the proper and responsible jobs: president of the Alumni Association in 1956, elected to the University Senate the following year, then a member of the Board of Governors and its chairman in 1965, until in 1972, the electrician's kid, the labour lawyer, the first Jew among all those gentiles, he reached the peak, Chancellor of the University of British Columbia. The role fit like a glove.

Nemetz was also a natural for the bench. He accepted an appointment to the High Court of the B.C. Supreme Court in 1963, switched to the Court of Appeal five years later, and returned to the High Court to become its chief justice in 1973. On December 21, 1978, Nemetz moved once again to the Court of Appeal as its chief justice and therefore as chief justice of the province, and his arrival came as a relief and salvation for the British Columbia bench.

Nemetz's predecessor, John Farris, had resigned in less than dignified circumstances after his name turned up on the appointment calendar of Wendy King, the lady of the night who so sadly wronged Davie Fulton. Farris's predicament hadn't done much for the B.C. court's image. Though much learned in the law, Farris was also an autocratic fellow, often rude to counsel and aloof with the press. Public relations wasn't his long suit. Nemetz stepped in as the refreshing opposite in every department. He was squeaky clean in morals, generous with counsel, and open to newspaper and television reporters. "I couldn't get over the sudden new accessibility," Larry Still, the *Sun*'s long-time court reporter, says. "From the beginning, Sonny has invited me into his chambers to go over obscure parts of his judgments point by point. He has this revolutionary idea that the public should know what the courts are doing."

As for the judgments which Nemetz has led his court in

bringing down, he is perceived as a liberal jurist. The British Columbia Court of Appeal, as with all provincial appellate courts, is the forum that lawyers who feel that the lower courts have erred in their decisions look to for relief from the errors. And there's plenty of justification for concluding that Nemetz, in setting the tone for the B.C. Appeal Court, has taken a generally open-minded and progressive approach in correcting the judgments of the lower courts and in offering them the guidance of his own court.

During his tenure, for example, he has written a decision that upheld the right of a penitentiary inmate to seek release from solitary confinement under a writ of habeas corpus. And, in another judgment, he quashed a lower court's conviction of a couple of actors for appearing in an obscene performance when they presented an avant-garde play called *The Beard* in a Vancouver theatre. The play offered 132 utterings of the familiar four-letter words and culminated in a simulated version of the equally familiar act of love. Nemetz wrote of the play: "I do not understand the consideration of average community thinking to mean that writers are limited to the average person's conception of what should be published or performed or to limit a minority of theatre-goers to the kind of performance that a majority would think good for them."

In yet another judgment, Nemetz reached out a hand to a man who wanted to vote in a provincial election. The man's problem was that he was still on probation after serving six months on a conviction for assault causing bodily harm, and the B.C. Elections Act refused the vote to a person who had been convicted of an indictable offence and hadn't served out full probation. Nemetz didn't think much of the relevant section of the Elections Act. "It is manifest in a democratic society," he wrote, "that participating in the electoral process is one of the paths leading to a return to full integration in the community." The man got his right to vote.

To be sure, there's another side to Nemetz's decisions. "You get the feeling," Larry Still points out, "that sometimes Sonny wets his finger and puts it up in the air to see which way the wind of public opinion is blowing and trims his judgments accordingly." Call Nemetz a pragmatic liberal at least part of the time.

His tougher, more conservative inclinations surfaced in a series of judgments that emerged from the Court of Appeal in the early 1980s. They centred on crimes of violence, and their starting point appeared to be Nemetz's stated observation that the people of British Columbia were manifestly fed up with offenders who assaulted, raped, and otherwise abused their fellow citizens.

The key case came along in 1982. It concerned a twenty-five-year-old man who was a newcomer to the armed-robbery business. He equipped himself with a rifle and seven rounds of ammunition and stuck up the cashier at a movie theatre. The robber was caught and convicted. But before the trial judge handed out his punishment, he made note of two factors: it was the robber's first conviction, and the Court of Appeal had held in an earlier case that general deterrence — a sentence that would deter other potential robbers — was *not* something to be taken into account in arriving at a sentence. The trial judge decided he was therefore bound to let the robber off with two years' probation and no jail time.

The crown appealed the sentence, and Nemetz gave the case what he called "anxious reflection". The difficulty, he said, was with the appeal court's earlier ruling against general deterrence as an element in sentencing. That ruling needed rethinking.

"In this case," Nemetz wrote of the robber's sentence, "the respondent committed the crime of armed robbery with a loaded rifle. In view of the seriousness of the crime, general deterrence should have been the prime consideration. That would have necessitated a term of punishment which would not only punish the offender but warn others of society's abhorrence of crimes of violence which usually result in injuries or death to innocent victims."

The immediate effect of Nemetz's judgment was to change the twenty-five-year-old robber's punishment. Nemetz put him behind bars for a year. But what was more significant was that, in the matter of sentencing and general deterrence, the Chief Justice had overturned an earlier liberal principle in favour of a more up-to-date conservative principle and justified the reversal on the grounds of community feeling. In a sense, old law gave way to new and practical emotion.

In subsequent appeals of cases involving acts of violence, Nemetz and his fellow justices stuck to a similarly harder line. They upheld long sentences for two rapists, and they tacked on two more years to the trial judge's four-year sentence of another rapist. Then there was the child abuser whose appeal came before Nemetz. The case disgusted and disturbed Nemetz and drove him to some of his strongest language.

The appellant was sixty-three years old. The evidence showed that he had committed acts of gross indecency with his three children. Two were boys. The acts, anal and oral sex, often involving two kids at once, took place as frequently as five times a week. They went on, unbelievably, for nineteen years. The father was convicted and sentenced to nine years in prison. He appealed the sentence. Too tough, he argued. Nemetz came as close as he gets to blowing his top.

"What sort of moral upbringing could this man have had — some place in outer space?" he said in court during argument, uncharacteristically baring his anger. "This case is absolutely appalling. I've been on the bench for twenty years, and I've never heard a worse example of incest and child abuse."

Nemetz was certain everyone in the province shared his reaction to the case and its sordid facts.

"There are cases where the punishment should reflect the revulsion of the community," he said. "And this is one of them.

The courts are going to give a clear signal that we won't condone the type of conduct we've heard described in the case before us today."

He dismissed the appeal and left the sixty-three-year-old child abuser to serve out his nine-year sentence.

Aside from such crimes of violation — a category in which Nemetz included pornography after his March 1985 judgment dismissing an appeal from the conviction of the Red Hot Video store on a charge of distributing obscene material when it peddled three tapes that, in Nemetz's words, "portrayed dehumanizing and degrading sexual behaviour accompanied by violence" — the Chief Justice has stuck consistently to a liberal line. Of all the cases he's heard in recent years, perhaps *Vander Zalm* v. *Bierman* most felicitously demonstrates his dominant side as a tolerant and generous judge. It was a delicious case on the facts, and for Nemetz it resonated with echoes of his own brief life as a member of the press. The case from the early 1980s took him back to the *Ubyssey* of the early 1930s.

William N. Vander Zalm was the Minister of Human Resources in the B.C. government from 1976 to 1979. He plunged into his job with a hard-nosed style. A few hours after his appointment in December 1975, he announced that he had ways of dealing with folks on welfare who wouldn't "pick up their shovels". Vander Zalm was a politician who, when it came to welfare and relief payments, which were under his ministry, went in for cutting back, tightening up, and getting tough. He also went in for off-the-cuff cracks. In one of them, in June of 1978, he suggested that any Indians who were hanging around Vancouver just to sample its heady delights ought to head back to their reserves, where they might have a better chance of qualifying for welfare. That remark inspired Robert Bierman to a piece of artwork.

Bierman belonged to the long and distinguished line of Canadian political cartoonists. From John Wilson Bengough of the weekly *Grip* in the late nineteenth century to Duncan Macpherson of the *Toronto Star* in the mid-twentieth century, from Norris to Aislin to Roy Peterson, Canada has a tradition of corrosive cartoonists. Bierman fit honestly into the tradition, and he used Vander Zalm's advice to B.C.'s Indians as the basis for a bitter little drawing that appeared in the Victoria *Times* on June 22, 1978. The cartoon, a model of simplicity, showed a man seated at a table, smiling and plucking the wings from a fly. Other flies were waiting for similar treatment, and the man with the smile was clearly Vander Zalm. He took a look at the cartoon and instituted an action for defamation of character.

At the trial, Bierman's counsel called the cartoonist to the witness-box and asked what he was trying to show in the Vander Zalm drawing.

Bierman answered, "I attempted to say with it that the Minister of Human Resources had a cruel attitude to the defenceless people under his ministry."

"Now," the counsel asked further, "could you describe the significance of the various components of the cartoon?"

"The flies depict the helpless Indians that were in Mr. Vander Zalm's words 'attracted to the big lights'," Bierman said. "And what he is doing there, he is more or less clipping their wings so they can't roam around any longer or fly around to the bright lights, not realizing the pain he causes."

The trial judge decided that Bierman had gone too far. He held that the cartoon falsely showed Vander Zalm as a mean-spirited man and thereby defamed him. He ordered Bierman to pay Vander Zalm $3,500 in damages.

The decision delivered a jolt to all Canadian political cartoonists. To them, it smacked of censorship by lawsuit. How could they be free to take a critical run at fumbling politicians if the courts were going to set limits on their cartooning? The artists rallied round Bierman and rushed to support him in his appeal of the trial judge's decision.

As it developed, it was Sonny Nemetz who saved the day for Bierman and the rest of the country's political cartoonists. It was he who wrote the majority judgment in the appeal and it was he who laid down some law that redeemed the privileges of cartooning.

Bierman's lawyer based his appeal on two grounds: that the cartoon in question was not defamatory and that in any event it was protected by the journalistic prerogative of "fair comment". Nemetz wrote in his judgment that he had no need to decide whether or not Bierman's cartoon defamed Vander Zalm. The defence of fair comment was enough to decide the issue.

Nemetz began his judgment with a few remarks about the nature of political cartooning and its targets. "Most political cartoons have inherent in their satire a tendency to lower their subject in the estimation of the public," he wrote. "Nevertheless, it has been said that persons accepting public office can expect attack and criticism on the grounds that the public interest requires that a man's public conduct shall be open to the most searching criticism."

That background established, Nemetz pitched into a definition of "fair comment" as a defence in libel actions. "The three elements of fair comment are well known," he wrote. "First, the matter must be recognizable to the ordinary reasonable man as a comment upon true facts and not as a bare statement of fact. Secondly, the matter commented upon must be one of public interest. And finally, the comment must be 'fair' in that it must, to quote Mr. Justice Martland in the Supreme Court of Canada in the 1979 case of *Cherneskey* v. *Armadale Publishers*, 'represent an honest expression of the real view of the person making the statement.' "

Nemetz checked the three elements against the facts established in the trial of *Vander Zalm* v. *Bierman*. Recognizable as a comment on true facts? A matter of public interest? And representative of Bierman's honest beliefs?

There was no difficulty in accepting the third element. Bierman's cartoon clearly represented his honest feelings about Vander Zalm. And there wasn't any doubt of the presence of public interest, since Vander Zalm was a prominent minister in the provincial government of the day.

But what about the third element? Was Bierman's cartoon recognizable to reasonable readers of the Victoria *Times* as a comment on the true facts of the Vander Zalm ministry?

Nemetz wrote that the evidence produced at trial portrayed Vander Zalm as a politician who spoke his mind. "Sixteen instances of controversial statements and acts attributed to the minister," Nemetz said, "were pleaded by the defendant as particulars of the facts upon which the cartoon was said to comment." Vander Zalm had been the Minister of Human Resources who tightened up the regulations that classified handicapped people, thus making many of them no longer eligible for provincial benefits. He directed all welfare cut off from people in areas where the picking of hallucinogenic mushrooms was common, and he advised Indians in Vancouver to beat it back to their reservations. It was the style of the man to issue such statements and orders.

"Now," Nemetz wrote, "one can approve or disapprove of these ministerial concerns, but there is little doubt that these statements were provocative. It should not therefore have come to the minister as a surprise that these statements would become well known to the public and that someone would respond to them. One such person was the defendant cartoonist."

Nemetz was inching toward an inevitable conclusion.

"In my view," he wrote, "these statements and actions of the minister, including the statement concerning Indians which was publicized only a few days before the publication of the cartoon, provided the necessary substratum of sufficiently publicized facts to enable the ordinary reader to recognize the nexus of the cartoon and the statements. Ordinary and reasonable people in this country are well acquainted with the allegorical nature of political cartoons and, in my opinion, would have little difficulty in recognizing this cartoon as a comment on such facts, a comment indeed of the very sort which Mr. Bierman testified he intended to make."

Nemetz wound up by holding that the defence of fair comment had been established in the case. Bierman, he said, acted in the honest tradition of critical cartooning and of responsible journalism.

Nemetz allowed the appeal, overturned the trial judge's decision, dismissed the action, sent Bierman back to his drawing-board, and set at peace the minds of the rest of the country's political cartoonists.

"I always order the same thing," Nemetz said. He was speaking of dinner at the Vancouver Club. Perrier water and roast beef, papaya and Sanka.

"Best food in town," he said.

It had taken Nemetz many years to sample the best food in town. The Vancouver Club, incorporated in May 1981, is the city at its most establishment — "that varicose-veined reservoir of tasteful tweed dignity" Allan Fotheringham once described it — and Nemetz was the first Jew admitted to its membership. John Farris and Walter Owen brought forward his name in November 1977. The club could hardly turn Nemetz down. At the time, Farris was still chief justice of the province and Owen was its lieutenant-governor.

"That narcotics hearing the other day," Nemetz said, "it's an example of the sort of case that should never reach us at the Court of Appeal."

He was referring to the appeal brought by the man who sold the Baggie of cocaine to the undercover Mounties in the lobby of the Bombay Bicycle Club, and the point Nemetz was working around to was a complaint that all Canadian provincial appellate courts have been raising in recent years: they've got too much business.

"The fellow's counsel was using the continuity argument," Nemetz went on. "The Baggie wasn't marked properly and it got lost along the way and nobody can say it was the one that the accused had in his possession at the time of his arrest. It's a very old argument. I've been hearing it for years, and I don't think I should have to hear it again. That case was too routine for the Court of Appeal. We should only be listening to cases of significance, public interest cases, constitutional cases, cases that raise fine points of law."

The dining-room of the Vancouver Club is enormous, a place of lofty ceilings, thick pillars, and dozens of tables set far enough apart that diners can safely carry on a private conversation at a semi-shout. Privacy wasn't a worry at this evening's dinner. Apart from Nemetz's table, there were only four other people scattered around the room. The scene had the feel of the moment in *Citizen Kane* when Charles Foster Kane is taking dinner with his second wife at Xanadu. Huge room, many servants, fine food presented in elegance that was mute and isolated.

"Last year, 1984," Nemetz was saying, "we handled about a thousand cases at the Court of Appeal. And do you know how many of those thousand were granted leave to appeal to the Supreme Court of Canada? Twelve. Just twelve, no more. That means in all the rest of the cases we were the final court of decision. We made the law in 990 cases. Well, with that sort of responsibility, we can't be spending our time on cases like the Baggie appeal that don't raise new or important issues."

The history of the sittings of the courts of appeal in B.C. and the other provinces, as Nemetz explained it, has undergone a radical and troubling transformation in the last forty years. Before the Second World War, the appeal courts would sit en banc for the most part. That is, at least five and often seven judges would hear each appeal and then retire to work out the court's group decision. Such a situation made for many probing divisions in judgments, much valuable dissenting, and plenty of decisions in which the justices would split four to three or three to two. But in recent years, with the steadily increasing work-load at the appeal court level, too many cases are coming before the courts to permit the luxury of sittings of seven and five judges. The court must gather in smaller groups. Today the practice is almost universal that, except on very important cases, a mere three judges hear each appeal, and that state of affairs, according to Nemetz, is fraught with grief.

"In a way, an appeal becomes a roll of the dice," he said at the Vancouver Club. "A counsel is going to get varying decisions as he moves from one trio of judges to the next trio. On a criminal appeal, for instance, maybe there are three hawks sitting in one court and three doves in another. The two courts hear cases with similar facts and give the opposite decisions. It happens. What rarely happens, as the lawyers keep complaining to me, is that they get the views of the *entire* court. That's become impossible with all the appeals we're expected to hear."

Nemetz looked out from the large windows in the dining-room across the waters of the city's harbour. The Vancouver Club's quarters are in a prim and gloomy mansion on the northern edge of the city's business district. It has survived long enough to see the former brick and stone buildings that were its former neighbours give way to towering skyscrapers. Even the restful view from the dining-room windows is threatened by a new hotel-apartment complex. But on this clear evening, Nemetz could still watch the tugboats chug through the harbour and look beyond to the mountains that loom over North Vancouver.

"There's a way to rectify our problems at the appeal court," he said. "I want us to set up an intermediate court of appeal.

Down in the United States, they've brought these courts into operation in four-fifths of the states, and I think we should too. This intermediate court would have its own separate judges and they could sit in divisions of three. They'd hear the more routine appeals, and if it was really necessary, an appeal could be taken from their court to the higher court of appeal. But what the upper body would concentrate on is cases about institutional policy matters."

Nemetz paused to tell the young Oriental waiter he was ready for his papaya.

"The higher court would sit en banc," he went on, "and it would produce carefully thought-out judgments that'd show the way to the lawyers and the lower courts on important legal points and on policy."

The waiter returned.

"Enjoy the papaya, your honour," he said.

Nemetz let the error go by. It wasn't from lack of ego that he failed to correct the waiter — "your *lordship*", not "your honour" — but out of a nicely calibrated sense of courtesy. Why embarrass a waiter who's trying to please?

"I'm pushing as hard as I can for this intermediate appeal court," Nemetz said. "So are Quebec and Ontario. It's a race to see which of us gets it first. I hope it's us. It's the logical step to the future, and I'd like British Columbia to be the first province to take the court of appeal into the twenty-first century."

He took a bite of his papaya.

"You know," he said proudly, "they fly this in for us fresh from Hawaii."

Nemetz's mark — and face — are all over the Vancouver Courthouse. The building is downtown Vancouver's architectural glory. Arthur Erickson designed it, and it is a long, low structure of glass and steel and concrete that manages to seem at once tranquil and majestic. A plaque on the fourth-floor level facing into the Great Hall celebrates the courthouse's opening on September 6, 1979. Nemetz's name appears third on the plaque, behind Lieutenant-Governor Bell-Irving's and Premier Bill Bennett's and ahead of four cabinet ministers'. He turns up on another plaque near the entrance at the south end, and outside the library on the third floor a splendid portrait of Nemetz hangs on a choice wall location.

There's a solid reason for honouring Nemetz in the courthouse. "That building and the way it was designed," John Laxton says, "has the personal stamp of Sonny Nemetz on it." Laxton is a prominent Vancouver counsel, and back in the early 1970s when the courthouse was beginning to take shape under the provincial New Democratic government, he was active in the NDP's inner circles. "I wouldn't say the building never would have been built without Nemetz," Laxton says, "but the fact is he's the one man who was around on a daily basis from its conception to its opening."

A committee was formed to look into the planning of a new courthouse in 1959, and Nemetz, still a lawyer at the time, joined it as a keen member and became its equally keen chairman in 1965. Like most other lawyers and judges, he had grown impatient with the old courthouse, which was cramped and stuffy and never quite clean. But dreaming of a new courthouse and realizing it were two matters that were separated by exhausting problems of logistics and personalities.

"W. A. C. Bennett wanted a skyscraper," Nemetz explained one afternoon in the spring of 1985, sitting in his chambers on the courthouse's sixth floor. "He was the premier when we started with the committee, and his idea was to put up a tall building with the courtrooms at the top. I pointed out to him it'd cost a lot of money for the extra elevators we'd need to transport prisoners up to their trials. The Premier got the point, but it took time."

More years were frittered away in the search for the right architect to handle the courthouse's design.

"We went through three of them before we ended up with Arthur Erickson," Nemetz said. "It was one disappointment after another. We'd think we had it right and then the architect would be gone from the job. One fellow's marriage broke up and he left the city for Toronto. If it wasn't one thing, it was another."

Erickson's hiring assured a quality design. He had already earned an international reputation for his graceful and original work — Simon Fraser University inside the province, the Canadian embassy in Washington, and a brilliant collection of Expo pavilions, hotels, and civic buildings around the world — but his first meeting with Nemetz wasn't reassuring for either man.

"Some of my more conservative brethren on the courts wanted something in the familiar Greco-Roman motif," Nemetz remembered in his chambers. "Just about every courthouse in North America is done in Greco-Roman. I don't know why, because Greco-Roman has no historical connection with the common law. But, anyway, I mentioned these desires to Arthur."

Erickson wasn't impressed. "Look, Nathan," Nemetz recalled him as saying, "the way you're talking now, it makes me think that if you and your people had been around at the time of Christopher Wren, you wouldn't have let him build St. Paul's Cathedral the way he wanted."

"Touché," Nemetz answered.

The two men sawed off with the judges having a say on the look of their courtrooms and offices and Erickson taking charge of the building's overall design.

Still there remained one more major drawback — the lack of a friend in government who would assume political control of the project and champion it at the cabinet level.

"A man named Bob Williams stepped in to handle that for

us," Nemetz said. "When the NDP formed the government, Dave Barrett was the premier, but Bob Williams was the cabinet minister who was effective at getting things done. He'd been a student of Erickson's at UBC and he came to care deeply about the courthouse. Of course, that was still the early 1970s. It took seven more years to put the building up."

Nemetz's face broke into his beatific smile.

"Seven years," he said. "But it was worth waiting that much longer."

Nemetz's pride is justified. He isn't a man who seeks out monuments, but if this building is his, as many Vancouver lawyers say, then it's a gorgeous way to be remembered. It stretches seven storeys high, and in length, from north to south, it covers the equivalent of a city block. It boasts all sorts of discreet touches and gimmicks that make it work more effortlessly than other Canadian courthouses — the invisible security, the acoustics that were adjusted to perfection by the American firm that set things right for New York City's Avery Fisher Hall and that make microphones superfluous in most of the courtrooms, the thirty-two elevators artfully located to provide efficient access to the thirty-five courtrooms — but what most distinguishes the Vancouver Courthouse is its stunning beauty.

A building designed in lines that flow, its look from the outside is smooth and uncluttered. The courtrooms and offices are stacked along the east side, while the west is given over to glass and air and calm. The Great Hall takes up the largest public portion of the building, an area that faces to the west through an acre of windows angled at a gracious slope. Inside, the Great Hall, which can accommodate a thousand guests for grand occasions that range from special convocations to performances by the Vancouver Symphony, has a hushed and unhurried atmosphere. It takes the form of a concourse that climbs four or five storeys in tiers of grey concrete relieved by a screen of trailing green plants. None of the surroundings suggest the angst and trouble of the traditional court-house. This courthouse seems built for peace and settlement. Come on in, it says, and don't be afraid. In the dining-room, the napkins are made of cloth, the waiters are polite, and over in the corner there's a white piano. Welcome.

Nemetz's own chambers are hardly overwhelming in size, but they have a few perks that reflect the status of their occupant. The patio is one of them. A sliding-glass door, the only door in the building apart from the entrances that opens to the outside, leads to a companionable little area, complete with shallow reflecting pool, where Nemetz entertains guests against the backdrop of Vancouver's skyline. Inside the chambers, the walls are hung with photographs and drawings that matter to Nemetz. A picture of his wife Bel, of his son Peter, who teaches at UBC, of Lord Denning, the great English jurist. Cartoons by Norris and Peterson. Framed scrolls and certificates.

And there's one other item in the room that matters to Nemetz, an entirely indispensable item for him.

The telephone.

When Nemetz isn't on the bench, he's on the phone. He works the telephone. He checks in with his contacts in Ottawa and Toronto. London. Across the United States. The world.

He loves to gossip. That's one reason for the plethora of calls. "He's a wonderful fellow to hear on the other end of the line," John Robinette says. Robinette of Toronto, the most accomplished and famous of all Canadian courtroom lawyers, has been a frequent receiver of Nemetz's long-distance rings. "He knows more people than anybody I've ever met in my life. In Ottawa, for example, in the government, he's got pals in every nook and cranny."

Which brings up the second reason for Nemetz's fondness for the telephone. There's a purpose in most of his calls, and the purpose is to push for the rights of the Canadian judiciary. The country's judges are collected in several organizations

— the Canadian Judicial Council, the Canadian Conference of Judges, the Canadian Conference of Chief Judges — and Nemetz occupies a leading role in most of them. "The judges' shop steward," the late Bora Laskin once called him. Nemetz constantly lobbies for better salaries and pension benefits for the men and women who sit on the bench, and he is an outspoken opponent of any government measures that might threaten the independence of the judiciary.

"He's an excellent committee man," Robinette says of Nemetz. Robinette knows, since he is the counsel Nemetz retained in the mid-1980s to argue the cause of a committee of judges in asking for higher pay from the federal government. "He likes to keep things moving," Robinette says. "He's speedy but very controlled. That seems to be his nature, and he knows everybody a chairman should know and then a few more. That makes him such a good problem-solver."

Back at the Vancouver Courthouse, problems have continued to turn up for Nemetz to tinker with. When the building opened, some judges registered immediate unhappiness. They complained that its layout made for awfully long hikes from their chambers to the courtrooms. And the air-conditioning gave them fits. The courtrooms were hot, the corridors were cool, and the combination meant that a few judges kept catching colds. They grumbled, and Nemetz went obligingly to the rescue. There wasn't much he could do about the distances from chambers to courtrooms — "the fellows got used to the walking," he says — "but he devoted months to the distress over the air-conditioning.

"We finally got it right," he said in his chambers. "The difficulty was that our building has long, low contours, and air-conditioning runs up and down. That meant it was hard to get into sync."

Nemetz shrugged.

"The building isn't perfect," he said. "Now it's the seagulls that are my major problem."

He looked through the window to the pool and to the building's roof.

"They keep eating the caulking out there," he said.

Nemetz's voice had a trace of impatience.

"They can't be very bright birds," he said.

He pulled himself together.

"We'll soon solve that one."

Nemetz took care of one other annoyance for the courthouse in his own courtroom on June 27, 1985. That was the day when the appeal in the case of *Re British Columbia Government Employees' Union* came before him and two fellow justices on the Court of Appeal.

The case had its start in the fall of 1983 when the BCGEU reached an impasse in negotiations with its employer, which happened to be the provincial government. The angry union put up picket lines at various government offices. One of the lines went around the Vancouver Courthouse, where the members of the BCGEU did their best to restrict the access of lawyers, litigants, and others to the building where they had business to attend to in the courtrooms.

Chief Justice Alan McEachern of the High Court encountered the picket line on his way to work. He was more than a trifle peeved, and he swung into instant action. On his own motion, he issued an injunction that restricted the union from further picketing. The union applied on appeal to Chief Justice McEachern to rethink the matter and dissolve his injunction. He refused, and the union took a further appeal to Sonny Nemetz's Court of Appeal.

Nemetz had spent twenty-five years of his working life sticking up for unions. He was a labour lawyer. But he also cared passionately about the independence of the courts. They must be allowed to function without outside interference. Thus, with the appeal in *Re British Columbia Government Employees' Union*, two of Nemetz's fundamental principles came into direct collision.

How would he decide? On which principle would he make his stand? Would it be a tough choice?

The answer to the last question, as Nemetz revealed it in his judgment, was no. Resoundingly no. Not tough at all.

Nemetz began the judgment by noting two essential facts.

One, "the dispute was between the BCGEU and its employer, the executive branch of government. No dispute existed between the union and the judicial branch of government."

Two, "it is obvious that access to the courts would be inhibited by the presence of the BCGEU pickets. . . . a picket line in British Columbia triggers in its citizens an almost universal and automatic response not to cross it. Whether caused by trade union ethic or fear of reprisal for crossing a picket line, the response of not crossing the line has been described as Pavlovian in nature."

Those points having been made, Nemetz said that for him the case turned on something more basic than disputes between employer and employee and Pavlovian responses to picket lines. The job of the courts, he said, was to adjudicate on citizens' rights and to work out remedies for their infringement. In order to carry out such duties, it followed that the citizens needed to have free and unimpeded entry to those courts.

Nemetz didn't have any doubt that the purpose of the pickets was to keep ordinary citizens from pursuing legitimate business in the courthouse. "The best evidence," he said, "can be gleaned from the fact that the union issued 'picket passes' to those persons whom the union considered eligible to enter the Vancouver Courthouse. Manifestly, the issuance of such passes constituted direct evidence of the union's intention to impede entry to the courts of those persons not given passes."

That was enough for Nemetz.

"We have no doubt," he concluded, speaking for the whole court, "that the right to access to the courts is under the rule

of law one of the foundational pillars protecting the rights
and freedoms of our citizens. It is the preservation of that
right with which we are concerned in this case. Any action
that interferes with such access by any persons or groups
will rally the court's powers to ensure the citizen of his or
her day in court. Here, the action causing interference happens to be picketing. Interference from whatever source falls
into the same category. Accordingly we affirm McEachern
C.J.S.C.'s order and dismiss this appeal."

Sonny Nemetz had solved another problem for his courthouse.

John Arnup

John Arnup was getting ready to move out. There were four packing-cases on the floor of his chambers in the judges section at the rear of Osgoode Hall. It was the early summer of 1985, and after fifteen years on the Ontario Court of Appeal and not too far off his seventy-fifth birthday, Arnup had set October of that year as his retirement date.

Arnup is a slight, fastidious, correct, confident man. He was called to the Ontario bar in 1935 and spent all of his career as a litigation lawyer in the Mason, Foulds firm in Toronto. "We weren't a large group," he says. "But the spirit that pervaded the place was the main reason the firm has never had a bust-up in one hundred and twenty-four years of unbroken practice." Arnup learned much of the art of the counsel from a man a couple of years ahead of him in the firm, Bill Gale, an excellent lawyer whose career culminated with his appointment as chief justice of Ontario in 1967. Arnup put his own spin on Gale's lessons, and by the 1950s, in the field of civil litigation in Ontario, John Robinette stood first and Arnup pressed him from close behind. Often it was a dead heat. In one climactic case, *Leitch Gold Mines* v. *Texas Gulf Sulphur*, the longest civil trial in Canadian legal history, eighteen months of courtroom battle from Halloween 1966 to the spring of 1968, Arnup came out on top. In 1983, when Osgoode

231

Hall Law School instituted the Robinette Medal as an annual
Award of Excellence among its graduates, the first medal went
to its namesake, Robinette. The second winner, in 1984, was
John Arnup.

His move to the Court of Appeal in 1970 proceeded effortlessly. "As a counsel, I'd been doing more appellate work than
any other kind," Arnup says. "The result was I switched from
one side of the bench to the other with hardly a long breath
in between." Robinette couldn't spot any change in his old
friend and adversary as he changed roles. "John's habits and
attitudes stayed the same on the bench as they'd been at the
bar," he says of Arnup. "You can't say that about all judges.
Some lawyers do terrible things after they get to be judges.
John didn't. He was as he'd always been, very thorough, very
meticulous, very precise. As long as I've known him, he's
never got himself so jammed up that you could catch him
unprepared."

From all the signs, Arnup's transition from bench to retirement ought to run off just as smoothly. He's a master at com-
partmentalizing his life. He makes room for each of his interests in their own turn and in his own good time. The interests cover a lot of territory, both expected and unexpected:
curling, the United Church (his father, a minister, served a
term as the church's moderator), clear prose, baseball, the
cottage in Ontario's Kawartha Lakes district where Arnup
has been settling in each summer for the past thirty years,
family, friends, the law. And one more interest — talk. Arnup
has a knack for the humorous aside and the blunt opinion.
He can make audiences laugh and he can put their backs up.
Each, of course, on the appropriate occasion.

Here he is, sitting in his chambers on the 1985 June day,
surrounded by boxes packed with books, talking on the subject of his reaction to his own early days on the Court of
Appeal:

"As a fellow who'd spent the previous thirty-five years doing nothing but counsel work, I missed from that first minute at the court the joy of a counsel's combat. As a judge, the intellectual challenge is still there. That comes from watching two good counsel go at the battle in front of you, though I might say parenthetically that two good counsel in the same courtroom at the same time are getting harder to come by these days. You watch the battle and your brain churns away and you enjoy the intellectual fray. But the fun of me against Robinette, me against other wonderful counsel like the late Walter Williston, rest his soul, that's what I missed with an ache.

"The point is that on the Court of Appeal you must listen without allowing yourself to become too talkative. A question when you don't understand something is only fair to the lawyer making the argument. Some enlargement on the question is okay too. But the so-called Socratic method of conversation back and forth between judge and lawyer only throws the lawyer off his path and annoys your fellow judges. I don't have much trouble holding myself from speaking because I had bitter experience as a counsel with judges who became too gabby. But just in case, I carry a little card about the size of a place card at a banquet. I tuck it in the back of my notebook, and whenever I'm conscious of saying too much in court, I pull out the card and stand it up in front of me. The printing on the card reads, 'Shut up, Arnup'."

When Arnup speaks his recollections and assessments, he is a cross between a lecturer and a stand-up comedian. The words emerge in steady sequence complete with text, subtext, lesson, and punchline. He talks in sentences and paragraphs, and on any subject within his immediate experience he can be counted on to keep the mix rational and witty.

On writing judgments:

"By secondary trade, I'm a writer. When I was starting high school, my father was recovering from a near-fatal illness and he sat beside me at night when we did my homework. He was one of the great Canadian preachers, and he taught me the beauty and power of words, written and spoken. Later, at the University of Toronto, I was sports editor of the student paper, the *Varsity*, and over at my college, Victoria, I was the features editor of our magazine. A fellow named Northrop Frye was the assistant features editor. To say I like writing is to say I like strawberry shortcake. I can't get enough of it.

"Within a year or two of going to the bench, I took a course in writing judgments that was given in Washington, D.C. I was the only Canadian judge in the group. It lasted about a week, and afterwards, each of us was instructed to send our judgments to our tutors at the course for criticism. My tutor was a Washington lawyer who'd worked in the Department of Justice with Bobby Kennedy. He was a very fine writer. He wrote a book on bail, but more to the point, as far as I was concerned, he wrote a wonderful piece for the *Washington Post* about Willie Mays' last game. I mailed a couple of judgments I was fond of to my Washington tutor and he proceeded to tear them to shreds. The tutor's name was Goldfarb, and it became thereafter known around our court that a strict and ruthless revision of another judge's decision was 'doing a Goldfarb'.

"I've encouraged everyone on our court to criticize the writing in the other people's judgments when they're circulated among the rest of us for opinion. We shouldn't have inhibitions about going to a guy and saying, 'Look, I hate to tell you but you've got a non-sentence in your judgment' or 'you've got a dangling participle.' Some guys who are wonderful judges don't know what a dangling participle is.

"Once I sent a judgment to my tutor friend Goldfarb, and he wrote back that the judgment showed merit but it had signs of the WGAS syndrome. I pondered that one for a serious length of time and finally surrendered.

"What, I inquired of Goldfarb, was the WGAS syndrome?

"He let me know what WGAS stood for and I've not forgotten the point of his lesson.

" 'Who Gives A Shit?' "

Arnup's eyes don't roam when he speaks. He fixes his gaze on a point in front of him, an object on his desk perhaps or something in the middle distance, and he concentrates until he's thoroughly vacuumed the subject at hand.

On the hearing of inmate appeals by the Court of Appeal:

"Until very recently, they were called prisoners' appeals. But apparently there is a connotation about the word 'prisoner' that people who are confined in prisons don't like. So 'inmate' it is, and inmate appeals are those appeals that are brought before our court by people in penitentiaries and reformatories. We hear upwards of two hundred and sixty of them every year, and it's the inmates themselves who prepare them with help where needed from law students. We lean over backwards to look for points in these appeals. I'm in breach of my long-standing admonition to beware the man who quotes himself, but I wrote a manual for the Court of Appeal on inmate appeals and one of the things I emphasized was the care with which they had to be read, because I said somewhere in that haystack there's a needle. Sure enough, two or three times we've latched on to points of law that an inmate would never tumble to in a thousand years.

"The most articulate inmates are those who are doing time for fraud. They're very serious fellows when they come before us. They carry on the ancient tradition of the jail-house lawyers and they're pretty quick with the legal terms. Every pen has a library that contains copies of an annotated Criminal Code and other textbooks. That supplies the ammunition, and then we turn up to hear what the inmates have to say. Three of us from the Court of Appeal sit in Osgoode Hall on appeals from the reformatories on the last Monday of each month. Then we take the afternoon train to Kingston and sit on the penitentiary appeals in the Kingston Courthouse on Tuesday

morning. The guards bring in the fellows one by one and
show them where to sit and stand. A crown counsel is present from the Attorney General's Office and he's very helpful
to the inmate. If the court says something the inmate doesn't
grasp — many of these fellows have a grade seven education
and a low I.Q. — he'll walk over and explain the point. Don't
back off, he'll say, the judges are here to help you. Understandably, the inmates are a little suspicious as to whether
our aim is to see that justice is done or to see that they remain
in custody.

"I can assure them that justice is our only interest. It always
has been."

Pride comes through as Arnup talks, pride in the law, pride
in the court he's sat on for fifteen years, pride in his own
accomplishments, justifiable pride. But the pride doesn't get
in the way of a clear-eyed view when he moves the conversation to the history and workings and manners of the Ontario
Court of Appeal:

"In the 1930s, our court was still split into the First Appellate Division and the Second Appellate Division, and the latter was notorious, particularly on the part of three or four of
its members, as being extremely rude, abrasive, and at times
cruel to counsel. I witnessed this behaviour myself in scenes
that, being naive, I wouldn't have believed possible. I remember a Chief Justice in Appeal, a title which died with its holder
in the late 1930s, saying in a strident voice to my immediate
senior in our law firm, Bill Gale, who was one hell of a gentleman, 'If I told you to sit down, would you understand?' This
was supposed to be rational discussion between a member
of the bench and a counsel appearing before him? I thought
my ears had betrayed me, but it was the order of the day for
some judges in the Court of Appeal. No wonder counsel often
had difficulty making their points of law.

"The situation began to change for the better — anything
was for the better — in the 1940s, and I'm confident the Court

of Appeal now has the approval of the bar so far as giving a courteous and careful hearing is concerned. Still, we judges are human, and a long-drawn-out argument, particularly when it becomes repetitious, gives rise to irritation which we try to express in reasonably guarded tones.

"The problem is that cases on appeal are taking longer to argue all the time. One reason is that the world and the law are steadily getting more complex. A second reason is that we now have a wider spread between the best counsel and the worst counsel. We have counsel today who are as talented as counsel were fifteen years ago, and we have counsel who are no worse than the worst counsel of fifteen years ago. Unfortunately, there are now more of the latter, and they take up an agonizing lot of our time.

"We're hearing almost five hundred appeals in civil cases each year and just under one thousand criminal appeals. That's a very heavy case-load by anybody's standards. It calls for a great deal of evening work at home and it explains how you can always identify a judge from the Court of Appeal among the group that leaves Osgoode Hall at a quarter to five each afternoon. He's the guy with the briefcase that's twelve inches wide.

"Criminal appeals especially are growing more complicated because counsel keep raising arguments based on the Charter of Rights. Sometimes three appeals a day raise Charter issues. Or alleged issues. I describe the attitude of some defence lawyers to the Charter as being like a smorgasbord. They walk along the table and say, I'll have one of those and a sample of that and some of the other. They choose from the Charter whatever looks like it might make an argument.

"Some of the Charter arguments are pretty far out. But some raise points that nobody ever thought of. Not even the people who drafted the Charter, which is interesting, because one of those people who drafted the Charter is now on our court. I don't say it's a bad thing that the Charter arguments

are novel. Indeed, it's a good thing, because we're really
infants in the constitutional-law field. Constitutional law used
to mean fights between the provinces or between a province
and the federal government. Now, each John Jones of the
country has something called Charter rights, and that changes
the ball game in constitutional law. It's having severe reper-
cussions on the sort of decisions we make on the Court of
Appeal, and I wouldn't be honest if I didn't say I have no idea
where it's all going to end.

"The only thing I do know is that, having served fifteen
years on this court, I'm going to quit and let other people
worry about it."

In Osgoode Hall's courtroom number one on the morning of
Wednesday, October 30, 1985, John Arnup's three-year-old
granddaughter was the only person with a concern. She had
the idea that if her grandfather was going to be out of a job
after that day, then he'd turn into one of those men she saw
on downtown streets, wearing raggedy clothes and begging
for quarters. Grandpa'd be a tramp. Arnup reassured her that,
no, his future wouldn't be as bleak as that.

October 30 was retirement day, and family, old lawyer
friends, and most of the members of the Court of Appeal
gathered in courtroom one to say goodbye to Arnup. The
ceremony was informal and brief, not more than twenty
minutes, and it focussed more on laughs than on regrets. Bill
Howland, Ontario's chief justice, said some words of farewell.
Bunny Austin, a partner from the law firm where Arnup had
practised for thirty-five years, cracked jokes at Arnup's expense. And Arnup got up and said he'd miss the collegiality
of the Court of Appeal, the work with fellows whom he liked
and respected. He spoke for only a few minutes, and he had
some playful fun with the nature of that morning's occasion.
If the ceremony he'd gone through fifteen years ago was a

swearing-in, he asked, then what was today's ceremony? A swearing-out?

Afterwards, Arnup, his wife, and his daughter Jane went to the Barristers' Lounge for coffee. It was a day of mixed feelings for Jane Arnup. She's a criminal counsel in her early thirties with a bright future. She had never, of course, argued before Arnup — no counsel appears in front of a family member — and this day, Arnup's retirement, marked the first and only time when Jane Arnup had worn her gown in the same courtroom with her gowned father.

Arnup finished his coffee and went home to the house in the Lawrence Park section of the city where he has lived for many years. He had a large project to make a start at. He was going to write a book. Earlier in 1985 he'd finished another book, a dandy little history of one of his favourite institutions, the Toronto Curling Club. Now he'd taken on something more ambitious. It was a biography of the late William Middleton, a judge who sat on the Ontario Supreme Court, both trial and appeal divisions, for thirty-three years before his retirement in 1943. Middleton was noted for many things, apart from his longevity on the bench — for his immense knowledge of civil procedure, for his literacy in many fields, for his gentlemanliness in court. He was a man not unlike his biographer.

Arnup looked forward to work on the book, but for that Wednesday evening he had something more immediate to occupy him. The fourth game of the World Series was on television, St. Louis Cardinals versus Kansas City Royals. Everything in its own time and place.

CHAPTER SIX

Liechtenstein's Man from Canada

Strasbourg has put up with more than any city should be asked to bear. It sits at the juncture of the Ill and the Breusch rivers, two miles into France west of the Rhine, and from its very beginning it's been trampled by successions of conquering hordes. The Celts settled in first, but the Romans soon heaved them out. In A.D. 357, the Emperor Julian whipped the Alamanni, a conglomeration of early German tribes who attacked the town, but fifty years later the Alamanni returned to overrun Strasbourg and the surrounding neighbourhood. The Franks marched through next and stuck around until the Germans under Henry I took over in 842. They stayed for seven centuries. Louis XIV grabbed the city for France during a lull after the Thirty Years War, and it remained French property until the War of 1870, when the Strasbourg garrison surrendered to the Germans. This time, the German visit was relatively short, and they gave the city back to France at the settling of scores in 1918.

Despite the history of carnage and shifting masters, Strasbourg has held on to a distinctive look and personality. It developed some long-established industries, making beer and fattening up the local geese for its *pâté de foie gras*. Strasbourg's old town on an island in the middle of the city is a maze of abrupt streets that are graced with lovely buildings, mostly dating from the Renaissance and the eighteenth century. The Münster towers over all of them. It's the ancient cathedral, parts of it going back to 1015, and it is as complicated and delicious and ornate as the tiered cakes on display in the pastry shops that dot the old town. The politics of the people who live and work in these rich surroundings are surprisingly liberal. "Strasbourg," one of its residents, the mystery novelist Nicolas Freeling, writes, "has the open flavour of medieval times." Its history is marked by intellectual excellence and religious tolerance, and that background makes it easier to understand the presence in Strasbourg of the European Court of Human Rights.

As its name explains, the European Court of Human Rights is in the special business of sticking up for the rights and freedoms of any European man, woman, organization, or state who comes asking for its protection. It was established in 1959 by the Convention for the Protection of Human Rights and Fundamental Freedoms, which was subscribed to by twenty-one countries. The purpose of the convention is to create an environment in which the rise of another Hitler will be preventable, and it has assigned to the court the task of monitoring the environment through legal processes. When a citizen from one of the twenty-one member countries brings to the court a claim of violation of rights or freedoms, the court adjudicates and sends back its decision to the country in question. In the majority of the twenty-one countries, the judgment becomes automatically the law of the land. In a minority, including the United Kingdom, the judgment is binding on the country in the slightly different sense that it is left to the country to implement the judgment in its own more flexible way.

The Court of Human Rights was slow getting off the ground, and for its first fifteen years, people were reluctant to carry their complaints to Strasbourg. But, as the possibilities that the court offered became clearer, cases began to pour in through the late 1970s. Now the twenty-one judges who sit on the court, one from each of the member countries, receive about five hundred petitions a year, though not nearly that many reach the final-hearing stage, and, as of the autumn of 1985, the court had found eleven member governments guilty of fifty-one rights violations.

Britons have been especially active in pursuing remedies through the Strasbourg court. The reason is easily explained, since the British, unlike most of the other subscribers to the convention, have no guaranteed liberties at home. There's nothing to shield citizens from acts of Parliament, and in the search for protection, many Britons with a gripe have turned to the Court of Human Rights. They've objected to everything from brutal interrogations in Northern Ireland to corporal punishment in Scottish schools, from the use of plastic bullets against demonstrators to curbs on the press in attempting to report the scandal over the use of thalidomide. And the court has not shied away from the job of speaking out on such controversial matters.

Three employees of British Rail got a typical sample of the court's demanding standards and intellectual integrity in the early 1980s. The three refused to join a rail union on the reasonable grounds that they objected to the union's policies. They exercised their right to opt out. Their employer, which operated a closed shop, told them they had no such right. British Rail fired the three, and the dismissed employees proceeded to the Court of Human Rights, where they challenged that heretofore sacred English institution, the closed shop.

"Democracy," the court held, "does not simply mean that the views of the majority must always prevail. A balance must be achieved which ensures the fair and proper treatment of minorities and avoids any abuse of a dominant position."

The three rail men got their jobs back, and, not long after, the British Parliament passed new legislation which banished the closed shop.

The English take their beefs to Strasbourg, and so do the nationals of the other twenty member nations, which include all the European countries together with a few off-shore ringers. The twenty are Norway, Belgium, Portugal, Turkey, Sweden, Denmark, Italy, Luxembourg, Switzerland, the Federal Republic of Germany, Spain, Malta, Austria, Cyprus, France, Iceland, the Netherlands, Greece, Ireland.

And Liechtenstein.

One afternoon in the autumn of 1980, Ronald St. John Macdonald was going about his business as professor of international law at Dalhousie Law School in Halifax. His telephone rang. The man on the other end of the line, speaking English in a thick accent, said he was calling from Liechtenstein. He seemed unaware of who Macdonald was or where he lived, but he was certain of one thing. Three days from that date, Prince Nicholas of Liechtenstein wished to have lunch with Macdonald at Claridge's in London. "I'd be delighted," Macdonald said, as if European princes routinely requested his company at luncheon.

Macdonald is a man who is always game for adventure. He's in his mid-fifties and an intellectual of the law. But his learning and erudition lie under the cover of his quicksilver manner. He's all smiles and easy wit and good company.

Macdonald paid six hundred and fifty dollars for a round-trip plane ticket and landed in London on the appointed day. He spent the morning visiting with Paul Martin, who was then Canada's High Commissioner to Great Britain. At noon in Claridge's, two very tall men approached him. One was a bodyguard, the other was Prince Nicholas of Liechtenstein. Macdonald needed a moment to sort them out. Over lunch, the Prince introduced the topics for discussion. The Red Cross. Soccer. Travel in North America. Macdonald held his own in the first, was at sea in the second, and sparkled in the third.

The conversation was amiable but had nothing to do with international law. Lunch ended, and the Prince left with his bodyguard. The bill seemed to have been taken care of. Macdonald shrugged and flew home.

Four days after his return to Halifax, Macdonald received another phone call from Liechtenstein. This time, the man on the line spoke impeccable English and knew precisely who and where Macdonald was. "Prince Nicholas wishes you to be Liechtenstein's representative on the European Court of Human Rights," the man said. "You have forty-eight hours to make your decision."

Liechtenstein is a wiggly-shaped little kingdom, sixty-two square miles in size, tucked in between the eastern folds of Switzerland and the west bank of the Rhine. It is the fourth-smallest country in Europe with 26,500 citizens who enjoy one of the highest per-capita incomes in the world. It owes its beginning to a land purchase. At the turn of the eighteenth century, a wealthy prince named Johann Adam of Liechtenstein was on the look for a country which he could call his own and which would enable him to become a voting member of the Holy Roman Empire. He bought a couple of large blocks of property next door to Switzerland in 1719, lumped them together, and created the principality of Liechtenstein, making it the only country in Europe named after a family. The principality got Prince Johann Adam into the Holy Roman Empire, but neither he nor his immediate descendants did much for the new country. For its first 250 years, ignored by its founding family, which lived in Vienna, Liechtenstein laboured under hard economic times. Since 1945, however, when Franz Josef II took over and became the first ruler to make his home inside the country, things have looked smartly up. Industries and banks moved in, tourism thrived, the country took on a Swiss-like efficiency, and the royal family displayed its world-class art collection, which includes the largest and most significant group of the works of Peter

Paul Rubens still in private hands. Liechtenstein had put itself on the map, even if it occupied only a tiny portion of any map.

Macdonald knew nothing of Liechtenstein's history, nothing of the Rubens collection, of the name of the country's only city (Vaduz), of its official language (German), or of its cuisine (French-Swiss). But he knew much about the European Court of Human Rights and he admired it.

He accepted Prince Nicholas's appointment, and six weeks later he was in Strasbourg for his first session on the court.

Liechtenstein's choice of Macdonald was a daring and enlightened departure. The representatives on the court from the other countries are nationals of those countries; most are judges who, at home, sit on their nations' highest courts, some are leading lawyers in their countries, and a couple are legal academics. None comes from a country other than his own and certainly none comes from North America. Liechtenstein, in looking for a new man to take the customary nine-year term on the court, decided to search out a citizen from a country that had a federal structure, thus making him compatible with the judges from most of the other member countries. Canada qualified. And so, eminently, did Ron Macdonald.

He has made a career out of distinguishing himself in international law. He has served on United Nations committees, co-drafted the constitution of the Republic of Cyprus, taught international law in places as exotic as Peking. For much of the time, he's shoe-horned those jobs in among his duties as dean at various Canadian law schools. He is probably more visible than any other Canadian in the world community of legal scholars, and as soon as someone pointed him out to Nicholas of Liechtenstein, the Prince couldn't miss Ron Macdonald.

The curious part is that at the beginning of his career,

Macdonald didn't intend to pursue a life in any kind of law. He had External Affairs in mind. As a matter of training and background, he took a law degree at Dalhousie, another at the University of London, passed some time at Harvard, and in 1955, wrote the examinations for Canadian government service. All that remained was The Interview.

"That was with Norman Robertson, the great old savant of External Affairs," Macdonald says, clearly relishing one more telling of a funny story where the laughs are mostly on himself. "It took place in a room at the old Canada House on Trafalgar Square in London, just an enormous room about the size of a football field. The walk from the door to Robertson's desk seemed to last forever, and on the way, my mouth went dry, my knees were buckling, my hands trembled. I sat in front of Robertson and he looked remote and cadaverous. He asked me dozens of questions about Canadian politics and foreign relations, about current events, and even about Canadian sports. Who won the Stanley Cup that year? I didn't know. In fact, I couldn't answer a single question properly. Which was why I was very astonished to receive a letter some time later saying I was all right for the Department of External Affairs."

But between the day of the interview and the receipt of the letter, despairing of anything very good coming out of his encounter with Norman Robertson, Macdonald had accepted an offer that appeared from the blue to teach some law at Osgoode Hall. He told External Affairs he'd get back to them. External is still waiting.

Macdonald taught at Osgoode for three years, industrious and content, until a new offer came his way. This opportunity turned on another of the oddball interviews that decorate Macdonald's working life. It was with Mr. Justice Ivan Rand of the Supreme Court of Canada. Macdonald had been contacted by the president of the University of Western Ontario in London in the late fall of 1958 with the news that the university was starting up a law school the following year and that Mr. Justice Rand, seventy-five years old and about to retire from the Supreme Court, had agreed to come along as the law school's first dean. Rand had expressed to the president his respect for some articles written by Macdonald for the *Canadian Bar Review* and, though he'd not met the young Osgoode fellow, suggested him as a member of the new school's faculty. All Macdonald had to do was travel to Ottawa for a sizing-up chat with Rand.

"The railway car I took from Toronto was unheated and got shunted on to a siding in Kingston in the dead of winter and I happened to be reading *Ethan Frome*, which is a very chilly book," Macdonald says, off and running on another saga. "Finally, frozen to the very bone, I reached Ottawa and went to Ivan Rand's chambers in the Supreme Court Building. He was an enormously tall man and a great talker. He started to talk and never stopped for the two and a half hours it took us to walk over to the Rideau Club, have lunch, and walk back to the Supreme Court. He talked about Mackenzie King and Chief Justice Lyman Duff and the Minister of Justice, about Senate reform and the Privy Council and the United States Supreme Court. It was highfalutin gossip and I hung on every word. When it was over, he shook my hand and turned to go into his chambers. In all the marvellous talk, he hadn't said a single word about the new law school or whether I was hired or anything that touched on Western."

As Rand was at the instant of entering his chambers, he suddenly whirled around.

"Macdonald!" he said from his great height. "Are you coming with me to the new school?"

"Yes, sir!" Macdonald snapped back.

"He still didn't mention anything about my role or my salary," Macdonald remembers. "But Rand was such a remarkable man, I would have followed him through fire."

Macdonald got to Western long before Rand. It was Prime

Minister John Diefenbaker who made the difference. When Rand retired from the Supreme Court on April 27, 1959, Dief insisted that he conduct a one-man royal commission into the coal-mining industry. Rand didn't reach Western until the spring of 1960 at the tail end of the law school's first year, and in the interim Macdonald covered such essentials as recruiting a staff, building a library, organizing a curriculum, and shepherding through the first batch of students. It was invaluable experience for him, barely thirty years old and functioning as the temporary, substitute, hard-pressed, and enthusiastic dean of a law school. Indeed, the experience set up much of his future career, because in the next couple of decades, Macdonald became the full-time, in-charge, capable, and still enthusiastic dean of two more Canadian law schools.

From 1967 to 1972 he was dean of the Faculty of Law at the University of Toronto, and from 1972 to 1979, he filled the same capacity at his alma mater, Dalhousie Law School. His times at both schools coincided with periods of immense change and turmoil and expansion. Macdonald took the upheavals in his usual loping stride.

At Toronto in the late 1960s, the agitation had to do with ideals and radicalism. Law students, until then a grinding lot who concentrated on preparing themselves for lucrative jobs in large downtown firms, began to ask noisy questions about their role in shaping a better society. Macdonald adjusted the school and its curriculum to the new student mood. But at the same time he maintained his own sense of perspective about the worth and meaning of the attitudes among the questioning generation.

"These students are more aware of injustices than my contemporaries at law school ever dreamed of being," he said in 1971. "But occasionally their impatience to right things prevents them from realizing the importance of hard work and the need to execute. Some of them are involved in a flight from systematic case analysis. They're more in favour of a visceral response, and they tend to think an off-the-top-of-the-head opinion is more valuable than something thought out. Their concern with social issues is excellent, but the point is that if you don't know where the courthouse is and how to perform when you get there, what does it matter how much you care about pollution?"

At Dalhousie, he arrived as the law school was leaping ahead in size, scope, and ambition. That suited Macdonald just fine. "I appreciate the romantic notions down here," he said near the beginning of his tenure. "They have such wonderful aspirations. You know, it's said of the Latin Americans that they may not be democrats, but by God, they *want* to be. Well, Dalhousie may not be Harvard, but by God, it *wants* to be. There's a driving ambition to be first-class." Macdonald helped along the process by expanding the graduate program, hiring bright young lecturers from all around the common-law world, starting up the *Dalhousie Law Journal*, instituting courses on marine law, and putting together the most impressive international-law department at any Canadian university. Dalhousie prospered.

For his part, Macdonald rejoiced in the work of running law faculties.

"In the time since I started teaching at Osgoode Hall," he says, "we've seen the rise to the challenge in Canadian law schools, and now we've got a genuinely sophisticated system of legal education in the country."

But Macdonald always had other irons in the fire. He lectured in China and in Mexico, at the Hague Academy of International Law, and at the Max Planck Institute in Heidelberg. He argued international-law cases for the Canadian government. He took terms as vice-chairman of the International Committee on Racial Discrimination and as president of the World Academy of Art and Science in Geneva. He popped up all over the world. He talked and wrote and advised and adjudicated.

And he accepted Prince Nicholas's appointment as Liechtenstein's man on the European Court of Human Rights.

The Court of Human Rights sits through the last week of each
of nine months of the year, and on Saturday, September 21,
1985, Macdonald gathered two fat bags stuffed with court
documents and headed out the door of his Halifax home for
Strasbourg. It's an arduous trek. A plane from Halifax to
Dorval Airport in Montreal. Bus from Dorval to Mirabel Airport. Overnight flight to Charles de Gaulle Airport in Paris.
Four-hour wait for the plane to Strasbourg. Taxi to the
Sofitel, an elegant and up-to-date hotel tucked across a shel-
tered little square from a fifteenth-century church at the north
end of the city's old town.

"Bloody rooms are too small," Macdonald said, his only
regret about the Sofitel. "Like most French hotels. It's hard
to get your elbows moving at the miniature desk they give
you."

Most of the documents that Macdonald stacked on every
empty space in his unspacious room had the same name at
the top. The Duke of Westminster. He was the complainant
in the major case that Macdonald and the other twenty judges
were scheduled to hear over the following week. It was a
curious and rather comic case, not least because Earl
Grosvenor, the Duke of Westminster, happened to be the rich-
est man in England.

The complaining Duke was the sixth in line of Westminsters,
and his great fortune reached back to his ancestor, Sir Thomas
Grosvenor, who had lived on the family estate in Cheshire.
On October 10, 1677, Sir Thomas married Mary Davies, a
London girl whose father bestowed on the groom as a dowry
three hundred acres of land which he owned to the west of
London. Mary Davies's father was apologetic about his gift;
the land, he was sorry to say, was entirely empty and soggy

in sections. But, over the following centuries, the three hundred acres became Belgravia and Mayfair, Park Lane, Eaton Square, Belgrave Square, and the south side of Oxford Street. It is among the most expensive real estate in the world, and none of the successive Dukes of Westminster have sold so much as a square foot of it. They kept it and leased it to Claridge's and the Grosvenor Hotel, to the American government for its embassy, and to hundreds of upper-class Britons, Arabs on holiday from their emirates, and assorted jet-setters, rock stars, and industrialists who could afford the very steep rents for Mayfair's flats and Belgravia's houses. The Westminsters accumulated other assets around the world: one thousand acres of prime land in Scotland, an industrial park in British Columbia, a hotel in Hawaii, a ten-thousand-acre sheep farm near Wagga Wagga in Australia. The family grew so staggeringly wealthy that Noel Coward teased and immortalized it.

"Whose yacht is that?" a character asks in *Private Lives*.

"The Duke of Westminster's, I expect," another character answers. "It always is."

The present Duke of Westminster succeeded to the title at age twenty-seven in 1979. He is a tall, slim, handsome man and a hard-nosed business dealer. In 1985, he raised the rent so sharply on the quarters of the Canadian High Commissioner in Mayfair that Canada moved its Commissioner to a cheaper neighbourhood. The Duke has another slight connection with Canada — in his teenage years, he worked as a cowboy in Alberta — and he has a gorgeous wife named Natalie who is the great-granddaughter of Grand Duke Michael of Russia.

As of the early 1980s, the Duke also had a business problem. It came at him from an unexpected direction when the British Parliament passed a statute called the Leasehold Reform Act. The statute was principally aimed at correcting a social injustice that had traditionally afflicted Welsh coal miners.

For centuries, those men and their families had lived on rented land under long-term leases, and though they made improvements to the properties and passed the leases down the line from father to son, they were closed off for eternity from buying the freehold. The effect of the Leasehold Reform Act was to shorten eternity and open the possibility of purchase for the plucky Welshmen.

To the chagrin of the Duke of Westminster, some of his tenants in Belgravia and Mayfair wised up to the opportunities for them in the Leasehold Reform Act. They made moves to buy their expensive pied-à-terres from the Duke. He screamed foul. His lawyers went before the courts in England and argued that surely Westminster's properties were exempt from the operations of the statute. They were unsuccessful and exhausted their appeals to the highest English court. All of the judgments affirmed the right of the tenants to purchase the properties which hadn't been out of the Westminster family name since Mary Davies's dowry put them there in the seventeenth century. In a last resort, the Duke shuffled off to Strasbourg.

As with all applications to the Court of Human Rights, the Duke of Westminster's case went first to the European Commission of Human Rights, which also sits in Strasbourg. The commission's job is to vet the cases, weed out those that are frivolous, and make extensive reports to the court on those with merit. Plenty of applications fall into the frivolous category. There was the Ethiopian gentleman who wanted compensation from the Swedish government for his sexual services to the ladies of Sweden, not to mention the Dutch soldier who disputed the right of his country's army to restrain him from wearing female undergarments. But the commission thought the Duke of Westminster's complaint rated a listening by the full Court of Human Rights and passed it up the line.

Reviewing the fat file on Westminster in his room at the

Sofitel, Ron Macdonald was of two minds. He thought the case offered a certain intrigue. At the very least, it demonstrated that there was room in the Court of Human Rights for the rich as well as for the oppressed. On the other hand, it might lack the potential for expressing a fresh opinion on the large matter of rights and freedoms. Perhaps it didn't measure up to some of the other cases the court had recently ruled on. The immigration case from England, for example, the one in which some British women complained that immigration officers made it far tougher for them to bring their foreign husbands into the country than it did for British men to bring in their foreign wives. The Strasbourg court called the situation sexual discrimination and found in the women's favour. And Macdonald thought there might be far more adventurous cases than the Duke of Westminster's complaint lying ahead. He had in mind, among others, the serious allegation against the president of Austria that he had hired a person with Nazi connections for government service.

Early on the morning of Monday, September 24, the concierge at the Sofitel summoned a taxi to drive Macdonald to the building that houses the court. The taxi skirted around the back of the Münster, where tourists were already gathering to inspect the immense cathedral, and took a route over the Ill River and out a couple of broad boulevards, lined with handsome stone houses and dense leafy parks, to the eastern edges of the city. The courthouse sits in the shadow of the huge, modern, and pompous palace where the European Parliament holds it sessions. The parliament's role is to debate on a political level the matters of rights and freedoms that the court adjudicates on a legal level. In the last half-dozen years, the parliament has been huffing and puffing to no influential effect while the court has gathered attention and respect with its rulings. Still, the court's quarters are humble and bursting at the seams. It occupies a functional three-storey building which is so short on accommodation that the judges have no private chambers. They handle their paper work at the miniature desks of hotels like the Sofitel.

Macdonald slipped into a silk collar and black gown and paraded with his fellow judges into the hearing room. The twenty-one judges sat around a long desk shaped in an arc. At tables at a proper remove from the arc, three different sets of advocates took their places. One group represented the Commission of Human Rights, the body that had passed the Westminster case to the court for hearing. The other two groups were headed by counsel for the Duke and for the British government, which was present to defend its passage of the Leasehold Reform Act. Both counsel — Michael Beloff for Westminster, Robert Alexander for the government — were leading English barristers. They were without the gowns and wigs that they wear in England's courts, but in their beauti- fully tailored Savile Row suits, they conveyed a sense of worldly style. Both seemed the very sort of men who might rent Belgravia town houses from the Duke of Westminster.

Behind the desk, each of the judges had a look that was just about exactly appropriate to his country. The man in the middle, Rolf Ryssdal, a Norwegian who is head of his own nation's Supreme Court and is president of the Court of Human Rights, was tall and white and wintry. The judge from Iceland was so large and substantial that an Arctic wind wouldn't budge him. The Irish judge, a man named Walsh, might have stepped from *The Dubliners* with his roguish face and his sly habit of whispering behind his hand to the judge beside him, who happened to be Macdonald. Only Macdonald might not pass as recognizably a native of the country he represented, not unless Liechtenstein's citizens have lean, fair, friendly looks. Macdonald can't be sure. He's never been to Liechtenstein.

The Norwegian president called the court to order, and the lawyer from the Commission of Human Rights spoke first. He outlined the facts of the case, which the judges who had done their homework were already intimately familiar with, and presented a balanced view that came down finally on neither the Duke's nor the government's side.

Michael Beloff rose to address the court on behalf of the Duke and scored an immediate coup. He read in French the section from a Michelin guide that described Belgravia and environs. In one stroke he established his own urbanity and put in perspective the properties that were at the centre of the case. The judges nodded their appreciation, and, smiling, Beloff proceeded with his argument. It was straightforward. Parliament, he said, had passed a law to help poor tenants, but in the result it hurt rich landlords in such a way that it violated the landlords' property rights, and no English court would listen to their legitimate complaints.

"It is indeed in this court alone that such a question can be raised," Beloff said, speaking in English, which meant that some judges who were at home with his French had to adjust their earphones for translation. "In Britain, any such rights always remain at the mercy of a sovereign Parliament."

Though his argument was plain and direct, Beloff decorated it with nice touches. He sang the praises of private property, spoke of fundamental freedoms, quoted from the Old Testament, and ended with a line from *Hamlet*. He needed no reference to notes for his arguments or his quotations. All flowed smoothly from his lips.

Robert Alexander, speaking for the government, tried his hand at the Old Testament. Beloff corrected him. It was good gentlemanly fun. Alexander went to *Hamlet*. "Good night, sweet prince / And flights of angels sing thee to thy rest." Everyone chuckled, though the reference may have escaped some. In among the quotations, Alexander put forward in forceful fashion his argument that the Leasehold Reform Act was a necessary piece of legislation which had the purpose to set right past injustices. Such a statute, no matter what the impact on the Duke of Westminster, could in no way be

construed as abrogating any articles of the Convention of
Human Rights and Fundamental Freedoms.

The argument of counsel wound through Monday, adjourned late in the day, and continued into Tuesday morning. As it appeared to be approaching an end, the judge from
Britain, Sir Vincent Evans, a dry man with spectacles, suddenly spoke up with a few questions of nitty-gritty details.

"Who puts in the plumbing in these Belgravia houses?" he
asked. "Who repairs the dry rot and all that sort of thing?"

Beloff and Alexander pitched in with remarks about dilap-
idations and the Duke's responsibilities. The Greek judge
leaned back in his chair and closed his eyes. The president of
the court decided he had heard enough and declared the hearing finished.

The twenty-one judges and the registrar adjourned to a
committee room, where they took off their gowns and settled
into a discussion of the case that lasted until almost seven
o'clock in the evening. Unlike the common-law courts of the
United States and the Commonwealth countries but more like
the civil-law courts of European countries, discussion among
judges at the Court of Human Rights is lengthy — even inter-
minable — and basic to the decision-making process. And over
the next couple of days, the judges devoted many hours to an-
alysing among themselves the merits of the Duke of Westminster's application. The discussion drew a structure from
questions that the court's registrar and his staff had prepared.
The questions were designed to focus the court's attention
on key issues, and, as the talk went on, it became clear that
there was a sharp division of opinion among the twenty-one
judges on the Westminster case. Majorities formed and dissolved. If there was a consensus, it was in a state of constant
flux. But the lack of initial agreement didn't bother the judges.
They knew that deliberations on the Westminster case, as with
most of the court's cases, would stretch over many meetings
and several months before the point of decision arrived.

On one of the evenings after a long day of talk, Macdonald

arrived back at the Sofitel to discover that a Vivaldi concert was to take place in an hour at the church across the street.

"I don't suppose tickets are still available?" he asked the concierge.

"Ah, monsieur, sold out."

"If you're keen," a man behind Macdonald said, "I can arrange a ticket."

The man was the violinist from the touring chamber-music group that was performing the Vivaldi.

Macdonald took up the offer, and after the concert — "absolutely lovely music" — he asked the violinist if he might reciprocate in some way.

"Buy me a drink," the violinist said.

They walked across the square to the cosy bar in the Sofitel.

"Triple Scotch and a beer chaser," the violinist ordered.

When the drinks came, he gave them his single-minded attention. Macdonald, in his generous, peppy, interested way, asked questions about music and touring. The violinist drank swiftly, mumbled short answers, and ordered another round.

"Triple Scotch and beer chaser."

He downed the drinks in a few practised swallows and hurried out of the bar to join his fellow musicians for the drive to their next stop across the Rhine and north to Mannheim.

"It was a trifle awkward," Macdonald said later of the encounter, still enthusiastic and laughing and looking on the bright side. "But, you know, it was quite fascinating to see another view of the life of people who make such wonderful music."

On Thursday and Friday, Macdonald and the rest of the court turned their attention to other cases that hadn't yet been resolved. They discussed a complaint from Sweden by a man who claimed he had been refused a job at a naval station because of information kept on him in a secret police register, and they reviewed a Belgium case that concerned objections to the manner in which representatives were nominated to the Flemish regional assembly. The weekend break

for Macdonald was given over to more study of reports in his
hotel room and to a round of social and ceremonial obliga-
tions. But on Monday, the last day of the court's sittings, he
and the other judges returned once again to several more
hours of analysis of the Duke of Westminster's appeal.

It would hardly be the last that Macdonald heard of the
case. At the court's October sittings, the judges would devote
three full days of deliberations to Westminster. In November, the president of the court would appoint a committee
composed of seven judges and the court registrar, directing
them to meet in Paris in January and prepare a draft report
on the case. Macdonald would not be on the committee, but,
later in the winter, he and the rest of the court, still not arrived
at a majority on the case, would begin another round of discussions. In the meantime, the Duke of Westminster would
wonder how much longer he could collect his rents in
Belgravia.

On Monday, October 1, Macdonald's final night in Strasbourg before he made his complicated way back to Halifax,
he ate dinner in a small restaurant around the corner from
the Sofitel. The place reflected Strasbourg's ancient and continuing German connection. It had dark panelling and heavy
furniture, a Teutonic waitress, and a menu that was long
on dishes with sauerkraut. Macdonald, weary from several
days of talk and feeling the torpor of all the rich food and
fine wines he'd consumed over his stay in the city, settled for
an omelette and a few glasses of the local Riesling. And, as
he ate, he reflected on the operation of the Court of Human
Rights.

He began with a reservation and a hope for the court.

"Perhaps we judges could have more discussion about when
the court feels it should take a very strong stand on issues,"
he said. "There are some cases that come to us where we might
cast a beacon of light. Develop a doctrine, give direction to
lawyers and scholars and courts throughout Europe, become
an illuminator of the way down the road in the next years.

Those are the cases we should concentrate on rather than the cases that have no particular potential for future guidance. The American and Canadian supreme courts know about this, about holding off until they recognize a case where they can provide a modicum of light in the legal gloom. I would like to see our court go that route in the sessions ahead."

But Macdonald has found plenty of reason for dedication at the court in the years since he began travelling to Strasbourg.

"All of us in the Western world have to pull together," he said. "We're in a terrible minority. Think of one billion Chinese, all those millions of Indians, and millions more of Pakistanis. Wonderful cultures, each of them, but by comparison there aren't many of us left in Western culture. If we want our values to survive, the values that a court like this one champions, shouldn't we know one another in Europe and in North America?"

And Macdonald had one more small specific point about the court and its role.

"There's a feeling of historic mission among the judges and everyone else who works at the court," he said. "So much of the origins of human-rights doctrine came out of the Judeo-Christian tradition, and what we're doing in Strasbourg is continuing that tradition. It's very necessary work."

Macdonald finished the last of his Riesling and contemplated the next day. Strasbourg to Paris to Mirabel to Dorval to Halifax to his international-law classes at Dalhousie. All in the service of Liechtenstein on the European Court of Human Rights.

"Love the work over here, love the people," he said. "Hate the jet lag."

He went early to bed at the Sofitel.

In April 1986, Macdonald made an even longer, more circuitous journey. It led him from Halifax hop-scotching across the Pacific and Southeast Asia to Peking. In the previous few years, he'd frequently visited China as an adviser to the country in its ambitious aims to establish a legal-education system.

"Can you imagine?" Macdonald says of his China trips. "They're planning on turning out one million lawyers in the next twenty years or so."

The purpose of Macdonald's April 1986 journey was to receive an honour. He was to be made an Honorary Professor of Peking University. Macdonald was only the fourth person to have such a tribute bestowed on him. The other three were high-powered scientists, and Macdonald was the first in law and the first from the Western world.

But by now, Ron Macdonald, Liechtenstein's man from Canada, was getting used to firsts.

James McRuer

The book was *The Path Through the Trees* by Christopher Milne. Its jacket glowed with bright children's colours and it lay open on James McRuer's lap. He was sitting in a stuffed armchair in the living-room of his apartment on the tenth floor of a building in Toronto's comfortable Deer Park neighbourhood. He had on a bow tie, a velvet smoking-jacket, and trousers that rode high over his waist. It was late afternoon in the spring of 1985, and James McRuer was coming up to his ninety-fifth birthday.

When he sat on the Ontario Supreme Court from 1944 to 1964, McRuer had a reputation as a stern customer. "Hanging Jim" some lawyers called him because he could be unbending and because, in his years on the bench, before Parliament did away with capital punishment, he was frequently obliged to sentence men convicted of murder to hang on the gallows.

"Those capital cases were a terrible strain," McRuer said from his armchair. He put the book on the end table at his side; the bright jacket faced up into the sombre light of the room. "You knew you had to pass the death sentence on a poor devil. But in about half the cases, you knew the hanging wasn't going to be carried out. Extenuating circumstances and that sort of thing came into it. You were required as the presiding judge to give your recommendations to the Minister of Justice. Should the man be hanged or not? You had to say what you thought. I can't speak for the other fellows on the bench in those years, what they felt about sending a man to be hanged. But for myself, I used to anguish very deeply over the decisions."

The skin on McRuer's face had a healthy pink tinge. Plenty of silver hair covered his scalp. His legs, he said, were giving him trouble, but his mind was strong and steady. And he had apparently picked up a more active sense of humour somewhere along about his eighth or ninth decade. Lawyers who appeared before him in court didn't recall McRuer as a man who had much use for a public laugh. But in his advancing years, even a subject as gruesome as hanging reminded McRuer of something funny that happened back in the days when he was perceived to be the last word in stony rectitude.

"I was the Chief Justice," he said, "and I laid down a rule that no judge in my court should try a capital case until he'd been on the bench for a year. If a murder trial came up in one of the new judges' courts, I'd ask an older judge to accept the assignment. Well, one year two new judges were appointed on the same day, Mr. Schatz and Mr. Walsh. George Walsh. A lovable curiosity as a practitioner, that's what George was, a very amusing fellow. But he should never have gone to the bench, because his nonsense didn't work there. You couldn't make jokes on the bench. At any rate, I had Schatz and Walsh into my office and told them about my rule in capital cases. That came as a great relief to Schatz. He told me he'd been dreading the prospect of sentencing a convicted murderer. But George Walsh was different. What George said to me was, 'Well, Chief Justice, I'll take them as they come!' "

McRuer's laugh was firm and high-pitched. He liked the story. He liked the memory of Walsh's one-liner. Walsh and Schatz died many years ago. McRuer was still alive and still sorting through his emotions from the days when he sent men to die.

"I sentenced the last man to hang in Canada," he said. "Perhaps not the last man precisely. There were two men who were hanged on the same night at the Don Jail over the river there in the east end of Toronto. One of the two was my man. I couldn't make any recommendation for mercy in that case. The man came from the criminal element in Detroit. He carried out the deliberate assassination of another man in Toronto. Killed him downstairs and then went upstairs and cut the throat of the man's woman. I remember the street it happened on, Kendal Avenue. And I remember his name, the last man who hanged. Lucas, that was his name. A black man."

McRuer was right about Arthur Lucas's background. He grew up poor and a thief in Detroit. He spent time in jail for armed robbery, mail fraud, and pandering. But those troubles came when he was a younger man, and for twenty years, either smarter or luckier, Lucas had glided through Detroit's underworld without a single conviction. By his own admission, he turned a good dollar by running a string of prostitutes, and, according to the police, he also worked as a courier for one of Detroit's big-shot drug dealers, a man named Gus Sanders. In fact, it was the police theory that Lucas was doing a job for Sanders when he murdered Therland Crater and his friend Carolyn Newman at 116 Kendal Avenue in Toronto on the early morning of Friday, November 17, 1961. Crater, it seemed, was another member of Detroit's demimonde and he was hiding out in Toronto with Newman, whom he was working as a prostitute around town, while he waited to testify against Gus Sanders in a narcotics case back in Detroit. Lucas admitted that he'd visited Crater and Newman in the hours before their deaths, but it was strictly for a business discussion between a couple of old pals from the Detroit streets. Lucas and Crater shared a bottle of whiskey and explored the logistics of setting up a larger prostitution operation in Toronto. To a couple of experts like Lucas and Crater,

Toronto looked short on hookers, especially the sweet black kind they could bring in from Detroit. It was, Lucas recalled, a fruitful meeting.

Crater's body was found just before 7 a.m. on November 17 at the bottom of a flight of stairs on the first floor of the house on Kendal. Someone had shot him four times in the back from up close and, for good measure, had cut his throat on both sides. Carolyn Newman's body was upstairs in a bedroom. She had a telephone receiver in her hand, but she hadn't been able to speak into it. Her throat, like Crater's, had been neatly slit.

Toronto homicide detectives quickly latched on to Arthur Lucas as a suspect in the two killings. It was the people on the morality squad who steered them in his direction. They had noted that Lucas had been around Toronto for a few weeks, pimping his friend Lillian Boykin at a couple of bars, and they put Lucas and his activities together with Crater. Moreover, Lucas appeared to have left town in a suspicious rush around the time of the killings. The Toronto detectives began rounding up clues in the case and asked Detroit police to keep an eye out for their man. Within a few days, Lucas was back in Toronto, this time in custody, this time facing two murder charges.

The evidence against him was entirely circumstantial. Without an eyewitness who placed Lucas in the company of Crater and Newman immediately before or after the murders, the police relied on a collection of physical evidence, on tests from their laboratories, and on the overwhelming coincidence of certain circumstances. The gun that killed Crater was spotted on the ground near the Burlington Skyway — a highway that Lucas would have driven over on the route he took back to Detroit by way of Niagara Falls and Cleveland — and ballistics tests run on Lucas's right hand indicated that he could have recently fired such a gun. Bloodstains that police found on shoes and clothes in Lucas's Detroit apartment were of the same blood type, group B, as those of both Crater and Newman. Similar bloodstains showed up in Lucas's car, which, not so coincidentally as far as the police were con-erned, was registered in the name of the dope dealer Gus Sanders.

There was more. Police discovered a ring in the tangle of sheets and blankets on the bed where Carolyn Newman died. The ring was a flashy number with zircons and a piece of adhesive tape fixed on the inside to make it fit a finger that was too small for the original size. The ring and the adhesive tape belonged to Lucas. And, on the morning of the murders, the night clerk at the hotel where Lucas was staying in Toronto, the Waverley, not far from Kendal Avenue, reported that Lucas was up and around very early, in and out of the hotel, awake and active. From the police perspective, the case was taking on a tidy and pat persuasiveness.

Lucas told a different story, and he stuck to it from the moment he walked into the arms of the Detroit police until the end of his trial. Sure, he knew Therl Crater. They went back a long way together. And, yes, he visited Therl and his woman in Toronto. Had a nice evening of drinking and talk-ing. Lucas left his zircon ring at the house on purpose. Therl needed a little cash and the ring'd be good security for a loan that Therl could negotiate with somebody. Therl was a friend. The two of them, Therl and the woman, were alive when Lucas left their place and went back to the hotel to check out. That was early in the morning, around five o'clock, six maybe. He had breakfast at a Chinese café on Dundas Street and drove to Niagara Falls and Cleveland. Lucas had business in those towns. Checking up on some girls he was running down there.

Only Ross MacKay believed Lucas's version. MacKay was the counsel who defended Lucas at his trial and he repre-sented a curious choice as a defence lawyer in such a major case. He was bright enough, a man with a hip style, cool in the way that bebop musicians were cool. But MacKay was

young and inexperienced, not yet thirty years old, not quite
four years at the bar. MacKay was on the hustle to get a criminal practice launched, and when he heard about Lucas, about
the strange, taciturn black man in the Don Jail who was turning away senior lawyers as his counsel, he decided to visit
him. The accused murderer may have recognized something
kindred in MacKay, different colour and different business
but similar style. He insisted that MacKay defend him.

MacKay had little to work with, either in funds or in evidence. He used his own money to travel to Detroit and poke
around the black underworld. But nobody would talk to the
white boy from Toronto, and when MacKay returned home,
he carried with him the distinct impression that the big guys
in Detroit had decided to let Lucas hang out to dry.

The crown in Toronto spent forty thousand dollars in putting together its case. Henry Bull would conduct the prosecution. He was the star among crown attorneys, a veteran
who took no nonsense from young defence counsel. Intimi-
dation was one of his courtroom specialties. In mid-May 1962,
when Bull went into Chief Justice James McRuer's court for
Lucas's trial on the murder of Therland Crater, he brought
along plenty of technical evidence, and, among his witnesses,
he had one Lucas associate who was prepared to blow the
whistle on his old pal. The witness's name was Morris "Red"
Thomas. He was a rounder and heroin addict from Detroit,
and he offered two pieces of crucial evidence. Thomas told
the court that Lucas was well known around Detroit as an
errand-runner, drug retailer, and general handyman for Gus
Sanders, thus shoring up the crown's contention that the
killings were a hit-man operation carried out by Lucas on
Sanders's behalf. Thomas also identified the murder weapon
that was found near the Burlington Skyway. The gun, Thomas
said, belonged to Arthur Lucas.

In the absence of any other witnesses who could rebut the
evidence against his man, Ross MacKay put Lucas in the box.

He led Lucas through his story. It sounded consistent, maybe even plausible. MacKay had his hopes, but Henry Bull had something better. He had a chance to cross-examine Lucas. He was withering, derisive, and moralistic. He questioned Lucas at enormous length about his adventures in the prostitution business. Bull went after details. He had a jury of twelve respectable white men from Toronto and he'd show them what they were dealing with here, this glowering black man from Detroit and his sordid trade.

But in pursuing his line of questioning, was Bull going too far? MacKay thought so. He objected. He argued to Chief Justice McRuer that the evidence of Lucas's occupation was irrelevant to the case. It had no purpose except to generate prejudice against Lucas in the minds of the jurymen. McRuer overruled MacKay. He held that by calling Lucas as a witness, MacKay had opened him to the crown's examination of his criminal past. McRuer allowed Bull to continue. Indeed, McRuer got into the act himself in an effort to determine what sort of curious creature this Lucas person must be.

"You were running bawdy-houses?" Bull asked Lucas at one point.

"I never ran a bawdy-house." Lucas was indignant. He had his standards. "I was engaged in prostitution, placing girls in places away."

"What do you *mean* by 'engaged in placing girls'?" McRuer interrupted, showing his distaste at all this testimony of commerce in female flesh.

"Well, your worship," Lucas answered, getting down to a patient lesson in the basics of his profession, "a girl in prostitution, you are liable to go to a fellow's house who is running a house of prostitution, and you will ask him if the girl can work there, and that is considered 'placing in a place of work' if he agrees to accept the girl to work there."

"Did you make money out of this?" McRuer persisted.

"Yes, sir, I did."

"What sort of money did you make out of it? Big money?"

"At times, yes, pretty big money."

"How did you collect your money?" McRuer pushed on. "Did you get it from the girls?"

"Whenever she came home," Lucas answered, "she would bring the money with her that she earned, and in return, she gives it to her man."

"I am talking about *you*," McRuer said in a mix of incomprehension and annoyance. "I do not understand at all how you get the money. If a girl goes to a house with a man and collects money from him, then does she account to *you* for a portion of it?"

Lucas was in the witness-box for several hours, not attempting to justify his life, merely to explain it. Nothing he said seemed to help his cause. "I could tell the jury despised and disbelieved him," Ross MacKay said many years later. MacKay didn't like the way the trial had gone from the very start. There was the matter of Carolyn Newman's blankets. McRuer had ruled that the trial would be restricted to the murder of Therland Crater, but Henry Bull brought into court the bedding from Newman's room. It was saturated with her blood.

"There was no air-conditioning in the courtroom," MacKay remembered. "It was hot weather and the stench of blood was overpowering. My objection to his lordship was that the stink was making everybody in the courtroom sick to their stomachs. There's no doubt in my mind that the stench effectively denied Lucas a fair trial."

In MacKay's address to the jury, he concentrated on the absurdity of the notion that Lucas, a man who was vastly experienced in the ways of crime, would carry out such a clumsy killing after leaving all sorts of announcements of his presence in Toronto. "I asked the jury," MacKay said later, "whether the possibility of Crater's murder at the hands of a professional killer who had been watching the house for Lucas's departure that morning was not actually as likely, or even more likely, than the idea that Lucas, for no proved reason, would suddenly decide to kill his old friend and then set about it so ludicrously."

MacKay thought his address might have planted a doubt or two in the jurymen's minds. But he felt that Chief Justice McRuer did the defence no favours in his charge to the jury. "McRuer seemed to be brushing aside every point I had made," MacKay said. "In particular, he virtually disregarded the fact that Morris Thomas, the witness who did the most damage to Lucas's case, was a drug addict who might have had many motives for lying."

Whatever MacKay's feelings — it was hardly uncommon for a defence counsel fighting a difficult case to criticize a judge's jury charge — the twelve jurymen didn't share them. They needed only four and a half hours to arrive at a verdict of guilty. When McRuer asked them to leave the courtroom again and consider a recommendation for clemency, they were gone a mere eighteen minutes. "My lord," the foreman said on the jury's return, "we make no recommendation." In his report to the Minister of Justice, McRuer could find no reason for suggesting that Lucas's life be spared.

Three weeks after the trial of Arthur Lucas, Ross MacKay was back in the same courtroom, before a different judge, to defend a man named Ronald Turpin. Again MacKay was in over his head, again he had a client who was charged with murder. Turpin was twenty-nine and a petty criminal, a robber with a long jail record. He had held up a gas station in the east end of Toronto, and when a policeman went after him, Turpin shot the cop dead. At the end of Turpin's trial, despite Ross MacKay's best pleading, Turpin was convicted and sentenced to hang.

At a few minutes past midnight on December 11, 1962, guards led Turpin and Arthur Lucas to the gallows in the yard at the Don Jail. The guards tied both men at their hands and feet and dropped white hoods over their heads. The hangman placed Turpin and Lucas back to back and sprang the trap on the scaffold. A doctor put his stethoscope to the hearts of the two men. Thirty-five minutes went by before Turpin's heart stopped beating. For Lucas, it was forty-five, and those extra ten minutes made him officially the last man to die by execution in Canada. He was fifty-four years old.

Ross MacKay took fifteen years to recover from the results of the two trials. Before the executions of Lucas and Turpin, he was a heavy drinker. Afterwards, he was an alcoholic. He lost his family, his practice, his money. He lost his teeth in a skid-row fight. In the mid-1970s, he managed a restoration of his life and career that seemed to his fellow counsel to be just about miraculous. MacKay joined Alcoholics Anonymous and he put together a new criminal practice. He accepted difficult, high-profile cases. He acquired a reputation as one of the pre-eminent practitioners of the hard art of cross-examination. He wore smart blue suits, smoked long black cigarillos, and listened to his collection of modern jazz records. But his winning streak wasn't permanent. In late 1983, just past fifty years old, he died of cancer.

As to the Arthur Lucas case, James McRuer probably spoke the final word on the subject in the spring of 1985.

"There was one good thing about Lucas's hanging," McRuer said from his armchair. "It was the last. Parliament ended the death penalty, and sentencing a man to hang is one part of the administration of justice that judges need have no fear of now."

McRuer's memory, as he talked in his living-room, was as precise on events that had happened twenty years earlier as on those that went back fifty years.

He recalled the time when he was a counsel appearing

before the Supreme Court of Canada, and the Chief Justice, Sir Lyman Poore Duff, sent word that he wished to speak to McRuer in his chambers. "What he wanted to know was where I'd got my false teeth," McRuer said. "He noticed in court that mine fit very well and his didn't fit well at all."

That happened in the early 1930s.

And he remembered the details of an intricate judgment he wrote in a commercial action, *Brown et al.* v. *Beleggings-Societat N.V.* The case involved the effect of an edict which the Netherlands government issued during the Second World War on millions of dollars' worth of securities, and McRuer's decision filled forty-four printed pages in the case reports. "The case was the biggest jigsaw puzzle I ever had to put together," he said.

That happened in the early 1960s.

Both events remained equally vivid to McRuer. So did almost everything else of large or small moment in his rich life. He was a man who had seen the introduction to Canada of the motor car, income tax, the radio, and woman suffrage, and he didn't appear to have forgotten a single piece of personal history in almost a century.

"I was assistant crown attorney in Toronto for four years commencing in 1919," he began one anecdote about an anti-combines prosecution he conducted. By 1919, McRuer had been called to the bar, suffered wounds in a war, married his first wife, and begun a family. The combines case was against some British Columbia brokerage and jobbing houses that were rigging the market in fresh fruit. "We seized the books of fifty-two companies," McRuer remembered. His successful prosecution of the companies came as a landmark victory in early combines cases.

"It was regarded with great respect in Ottawa," McRuer said. "They'd sent me and my family all the way out to Vancouver for a year and a half to prosecute it. I believe I was also regarded with great respect in Ottawa."

McRuer returned to Toronto and began his own firm. It was small, busy, and eclectic. It handled commercial work and real estate transactions. But McRuer stuck to litigation, and he founded a dynasty of counsel in the firm. He passed on his own skills to a young man named Andrew Brewin, and, years later, Brewin taught the same skills to another young man, Ian Scott. On the surface, the set of relationships seemed unlikely. McRuer was a devout Liberal. Brewin joined the CCF and served as an NDP member of Parliament. Scott was another Liberal; in 1985, he won election to the Ontario Legislature, and when the Liberals formed the provincial government, he took the attorney general's portfolio. What linked the three men, McRuer to Brewin to Scott, was their shared excellence in the courtroom.

In 1944, McRuer made the move from lawyer to judge.

"I had no notion of going to the bench," he said. The light in his living-room had almost vanished as the late afternoon gave way to early evening, but the colours still glowed from the jacket on *The Path Through the Trees*. "The people in Ottawa said they wanted me to succeed Chief Justice Rose of the Ontario High Court. Rose was failing badly. The idea of the bench came as news to me. Very flattering, I thought. But, shortly after, before I was appointed, an opening came up on the Court of Appeal. The Deputy Minister of Justice phoned me from Ottawa. Would I take the place on the Court of Appeal? Well, what about our original plan? That's what I asked. The man on the phone said nothing would interfere with that. Yes, sure enough, I was on the Court of Appeal for no more than a year when they named me Chief Justice of the High Court. I didn't care for the Appeal Court. Too stuffy. You didn't get the real life of a trial in it. I told that to my wife. 'I never need to go to the theatre,' I said to her. 'I can see enough tragedy and comedy every day in my trial court.' "

McRuer sat as chief justice for nineteen years. He heard cases that made significant law; his 1960 judgment in *Regina*

v. *Canadian Breweries*, a prosecution under the Combines Investigation Act, is still one of the two leading decisions in merger actions. And he heard cases that made headlines. During his nineteen years, McRuer somehow turned up on almost all of the sensational murder cases in Ontario. No one thought it was a coincidence. McRuer liked the responsibility. Perhaps he liked the limelight, too. He heard the steamy Evelyn Dick case in Hamilton in 1947 in which a gorgeous young woman of random morals was acquitted of her husband's murder but convicted of manslaughter in the death of her infant son. Then there was the infamous Suchan-Jackson case in Toronto. Steve Suchan and Leonard Jackson were skilled at two enterprises, sticking up banks and escaping from prison. In 1952, at high noon on a busy Toronto street, they shot and killed an inspector of police. They were arrested, broke out of the Don Jail, were recaptured, were brought to trial, and, after their conviction, McRuer dispatched them to the hangman. McRuer heard all the cases, and he made a reputation as a smart, tough, demanding judge.

From 1985, however, looking back, McRuer felt almost benign about his past. The cases were memorable and important, deserving of rumination. But so was his life between cases. He liked to remember one time when he was out on circuit, hearing cases in Port Arthur, the county town at the western end of Lake Superior. On a Sunday afternoon during the assizes, a local lawyer invited McRuer to pass a few hours at his house.

"It was a Sunday social," McRuer said, struggling to keep a small, sly smile in check as he talked. "My host had a young man in to sing for us. Well, he possessed a beautiful voice, and afterwards I asked him if he was getting the proper training in Port Arthur. Hardly at all, he told me, and I said I'd speak to someone in Toronto on his behalf. Oh no, the young man said, he couldn't afford such an extravagance as Toronto. He was earning a mere pittance at his job. Nevertheless, when

I got back to Toronto, I spoke to the teacher I had in mind and we brought the young man down from Port Arthur. The teacher was just as impressed as I was. He took the young man as a pupil." McRuer ended the struggle with the sly smile and let it radiate from his face. "And that," he said, "was the beginning of Jon Vickers."

McRuer liked to lend a hand — as long as the recipients were worthy. From 1946 to 1957, he was president of the Canadian Save The Children Fund. And he had his own private and possibly idiosyncratic sense of historical justice. He put in many weekends over many years organizing his thoughts on the trial that led to the crucifixion of Jesus Christ. He used the four Gospels as source material, and he wrote down the results of his investigation. The Clarke, Irwin Company published them in 1964 in a slim book called *The Trial of Jesus*.

"The Hebrew trial had been a mockery of judicial procedure throughout," McRuer wrote. "Jesus was unlawfully arrested and unlawfully interrogated in secret by one of the highest ranking members of the court, one who was to sit among his judges. . . ."

McRuer's own court, the High Court of the Supreme Court of Ontario, grew steadily in quality during his years as its chief justice. "The judges of today," he said, "are a lot better than they were forty years ago. The standards have been greatly raised." McRuer didn't mind claiming a small share of credit for the upgrading.

"Sometimes I was consulted by the Minister of Justice in Ottawa on appointments," he said. "But the problem was, you couldn't prejudge lawyers on how they'd make out on the bench. I remember one occasion when the Minister gave me a list of four or five lawyers' names and asked me to rate them. I put one fellow at the top and he got his appointment to the bench. Well, he was a disaster. He couldn't make up his mind on the cases he heard. He kept delaying and reserving his decisions. Counsel were coming to me and asking why they couldn't get their cases decided. After I heard the complaints, I decided to start setting down this judge's cases for rehearing, the ones he hadn't decided. That shamed him, and within a couple of weeks the poor fellow would finally make up his mind and issue his judgments. The whole thing showed you couldn't always tell about your choice of judges."

In 1964, when McRuer was seventy-four, Ontario Premier John Robarts asked him to conduct an inquiry into civil rights in the province. "I jumped at the chance," McRuer remembered. He resigned from the bench and spent six years on an investigation of the rights of the individual in Ontario. He gathered a staff and looked intensively at twenty-two boards that governed provincial rights, every tribunal from the Ontario Police Commission to the Ontario Liquor Licence Board. In the end, McRuer produced a five-volume report that ran to 2,280 pages. The report recommended, in general, that more checks and balances be placed on the powers of tribunals that regulate citizens. The province set about the business of instituting the particulars of many of McRuer's suggestions.

"The work I did after I left the bench," McRuer said, perhaps surprisingly, "was more rewarding than the work I did on the bench."

McRuer never wanted to ease up in his life of work. There seemed no need to. In 1967, he accepted an appointment as vice-chairman of the Ontario Law Reform Commission. In 1968, seventy-eight years old and a widower, he remarried. In 1972, he took a trip to China. He brought back dozens of slides and threw a party at his apartment to show them.

McRuer kept busy, but the trouble was that time got ahead of his pace. The world seemed to run out of jobs for retired judges who lived into their nineties. McRuer's contemporaries died off. So did many of the senior counsel who had appeared before him during his years on the bench. He found less reason to leave his apartment. He was keen for news of the courts and of the world of judges and lawyers, and he made grand company for any visitor. But not enough messengers came to call.

"I didn't expect to live this long," he said in his living-room.

In the spring of 1984, it was seventy years from McRuer's call to the Ontario bar. His old firm gave him a small celebratory dinner. By 1984, the firm was called Cameron, Brewin & Scott, though Brewin had died a few years earlier, and a little later the firm was absorbed into Gowling & Henderson, a large and versatile firm based in Ottawa. The dinner took place in a dining-room at the University Club, a muted and elegant establishment across University Avenue from Osgoode Hall. The guest list included a few retired judges and counsel whose careers had touched on McRuer's.

"You've got a choice," Ian Scott said to McRuer after everyone had finished dessert and coffee. "We can pass on to liqueurs in the other room or you can make a speech."

"I want to speak," McRuer answered.

He talked, off the cuff, for about fifteen minutes. He gave off a kind of mellowness. He spoke of his days at the bar and on the bench. He said he recognized that his generation of lawyers, what was left of it, was in its last chapter and that many at the dinner, Scott and the others, had reached only the middle of their own stories.

"My contribution to the law is something I'm glad of," McRuer said at the end of his talk. "I had a full life at the bar. And I wish you the same."

There wasn't a hint of regret or self-pity in his voice.

The light had almost gone from McRuer's living-room. He switched on the lamp beside his armchair and picked up *The Path Through the Trees*. Its author, Christopher Milne, was the son of A. A. Milne and the model for one of the most loved characters in children's literature, Christopher Robin of the Pooh stories. Christopher Milne's own book dealt with his life after Christopher Robin, his service in the Second World War, his career as a bookstore owner in Devon, his love for Claire, his daughter who was spastic.

"I like this sort of book," McRuer said. "A book about a good man."

He began to read.

CHAPTER SEVEN

The Supreme Court of Canada

Tony Lamer began the morning of November 19, 1985, a Tuesday, the way he begins every weekday morning. He got up at a quarter to five. He doesn't need an alarm clock. He went to his desk and read and made notes for three hours. He shaved, ate breakfast, kissed his wife goodbye, and drove from his home in the Sandy Hill neighbourhood of Ottawa to his office in the Supreme Court Building just west of Parliament Hill. Tony Lamer is Mr. Justice Antonio Lamer, a judge on the Supreme Court of Canada since his appointment to the court on March 28, 1980, and he starts early on his long, hard, thought-filled days.

At the Supreme Court Building, he rode the elevator to the second floor, where the nine justices of the court have their chambers. It was 8:45 a.m., and it was still and quiet. It's always still and quiet on the second floor.

"The living mausoleum," Lamer says of the building where he spends so many of his hours. "That's what I called it when I first came here from Quebec. The phone never rings and you can't hear any voices. I'm an extrovert, and I thought I would never get used to this place. But now it's the opposite. Not so long ago I went to have lunch with my friend the Chief Justice of Quebec, and I was waiting in his office. Three lines of phones were all going and people came barging into the room. I said to myself I could never work in such an atmosphere. So you see how you change in many ways when you come to the court in Ottawa."

Lamer may have adjusted his work habits to the life of the Supreme Court, but he's held on to his natural ebullience. He's lively and candid in conversation, and his manner invites confidence and friendship. He is a man of medium height with a square, blocky build and a full, merry face that's dominated by a spectacularly dense moustache. The moustache and his hair were dark when he arrived on the court at age forty-six, one of the youngest men ever appointed, but both are now sprinkled with grey. Work at the court takes a toll.

The factums for the case that the court would hear later in the morning sat on Lamer's desk when he reached his chambers. The case was called *Thomas Larry Jones* v. *Her Majesty the Queen*. Lamer flipped through the factums. Jones, the appellant, was a pastor in the Western Baptist Church of Calgary. In the basement of the church, he made space for the Western Baptist Academy, a school that he ran as an alternative to Calgary's "secular" public schools. The academy had an enrolment of about twenty-five kids, including Jones's own three daughters. Alberta school inspectors agreed that Jones delivered a perfectly acceptable level of education to his students, but he operated without a document issued by the provincial Department of Education certifying that children not attending a regular school were "under efficient instruction at home or elsewhere". The point was that Jones refused to apply for such a certificate; the idea of applying offended his religious principles. He was charged under the School Act with three counts of truancy, one for each of his three daughters, and after the Alberta Court of Appeal directed a conviction, Jones appealed to the Supreme Court of Canada.

"The court!" the clerk cried into the courtroom. *"La cour!"*

It was 10:35, and everyone in the main courtroom of the

Supreme Court rose as the justices, wearing black gowns and vests and white collars, entered through the door directly behind their long elevated bench. Chief Justice Dickson led the way, and the others followed in an orderly jostle. There were seven judges altogether. Normally the court sits its full complement of nine, but on this day, Mr. Justice Bud Estey was off conducting a federal inquiry into the collapse of the Canadian Commercial Bank, and in order to sit an odd number and avoid a possible tie in voting on the court's decision, Mr. Justice Julien Chouinard was absenting himself from the Jones case. The seven took their seats in an order dictated by seniority. The most junior sat on the far flanks, and the others ranged closer to the Chief Justice, who occupied the middle chair, according to the number of their years on the court. Lamer, who ranks sixth in terms of service, sat on the left side of the court with Jean Beetz in between him and Dickson and Gerald Le Dain on his own right.

"May it please your lordships," the counsel for the appellant, Thomas Larry Jones, began his argument. He stood at a large, flat lectern directly in front of the justices. To his right, three other counsel waited their turn to speak in the case. One represented the respondent, the Attorney General of Alberta, and the other two, present on behalf of the Attorneys General of Ontario and Nova Scotia, had been granted intervener status in the case to argue against the sort of interference with provincial control of education that the Jones matter might have threatened. Behind the counsel, in the small public section of the courtroom, a man leaned forward anxiously to catch the argument. He had slicked-down black hair, and wore a spiffy three-piece suit and cowboy boots. He was the appellant himself, Thomas Larry Jones. He held a Bible in his hands.

"I would ask the court to define liberty in the broadest sense," Jones's counsel told the seven judges. "That would include the liberty of parents to educate their children as they see fit."

The argument from Jones's lawyer and the other three counsel, as it stretched through the morning, had a meandering, unfocussed feel to it. The justices, particularly Bertha Wilson and Gerard La Forest, broke in from time to time with questions gently, almost apologetically, expressed that attempted to clarify points. But for all the proper manners, a sense came from the bench that their lordships and her ladyship were not entirely satisfied with the way the argument was drifting. Lamer shifted uncomfortably in his chair. He whispered to Le Dain on one side and muttered to Beetz on the other. He couldn't contain his restlessness.

The reason behind the unhappiness became clearer when Lamer asked counsel a handful of tactfully worded questions. All of his prodding centred on section seven of the Charter of Rights. It's the section that guarantees to Canadians "the right to life, liberty and security of the person and the right not to be deprived thereof except in accordance with the principles of fundamental justice." Section seven amounts to a kind of mini-Charter of Rights all by itself. It promises to present the Supreme Court with many problems of interpretation over the years, and the judges keep on the lookout for cases that might assist them in their interpreting chore. Lamer gave the impression that the Jones case offered a solid opportunity to dig into section seven, but counsel on the case weren't responding to his nudging questions. Jones's lawyer didn't seem to think he needed a careful analysis of section seven to win his appeal, and the other three counsel resisted the idea that the case's circumstances called the section into play. Lamer slumped back in his chair with a final mutter to Beetz.

At five minutes past three — and with an earlier ninety-minute adjournment for lunch and office work — Chief Justice Dickson ended argument in the Jones case. The seven justices filed out of the courtroom's back door and walked to their conference room directly across the corridor. They sat around a large, circular oak table and began the ritual of discussion in the case they'd just heard. Each judge, begin-

ning with the most junior, La Forest, and working through
seniority to the Chief Justice, spoke his and her piece. Opinions on the case began to shake down. Dickson kept score on
his note-pad, and after forty-five minutes of informal and relatively unemotional talk he was able to assign one of the judges
to write the majority decision.

No one outside the circle of judges and their clerks would
know the identity of the writer, the nature of the decision, or
the possibility of a dissenting opinion until the release of the
finished judgment eight or ten months later. The proceedings in the Supreme Court's conference room are more con-
fidential and far less prone to leaks than meetings of the
federal cabinet. Indeed, they're leak-proof, and for the following months, while the justices went about their decision-
making process, everyone else in the Jones case would wait
— the counsel, the lower courts, the academics who were
pondering the thrust of section seven of the Charter, even
the man most affected by the case, Thomas Larry Jones, with
his slicked-back hair and the Bible in his hands.

Lamer was back in his chambers at four o'clock. The room
has a high ceiling, a large desk, and an arrangement of easy
chairs and a sofa in one corner for social visits. A huge Graham Coughtry painting hangs on the wall; it's from Cough-
trey's two-figure series of the 1960s and it shows a graceful
collision of reds and oranges. "The picture brings colour into
the room," Lamer said. "I need a little of that in here." Most
of the flat surfaces in his chambers were stacked with draft
judgments waiting to be read and research material waiting
to be turned into draft judgments. During the court's 1985
fall term, it would hear thirty-one cases in thirty-two sitting
days. That added up to a lot of judgments.

"The number of decisions you have to make on this court,
you can't spend months and months making up your mind,"
Lamer said of the work. "It takes a while for a judgment to
go through the writing and translating and printing and so
on, but the part about making up your mind comes fast. When

you're first appointed, you hear a case and you think, I can't decide that in a few days. But you have to, because you'll probably have something even more important the next day. So you develop skills and you build up an immunity against losing sleep over your judgments."

The factums in the two cases that Lamer and the rest of the court would hear the following day, November 20, occupied the centre spot in the swarm of paper on his desk. In one, the appellant had been convicted of murder in Victoria, B.C., and was asking the court to direct a new trial on the grounds that the first trial judge had improperly allowed the crown to introduce certain incriminating evidence. And in the second case, from Ontario, the appellant was the administrator of an estate who was asking to recover a sum of money from the crown. The deceased man whose estate was in question had made his living as a narcotics dealer, and not long before he was killed in a car accident, the police had grabbed his money and property in a raid under the Narcotic Control Act. The administrator claimed he was entitled to possession of the dead drug dealer's assets. Both cases, involving criminal law, were right up Lamer's alley.

"After I was called to the bar in Montreal in 1957," he said, "I practised criminal law. Back then, twenty-five years ago, the criminal bar in Quebec wasn't especially respectable. It had a lot of fly-by-nighters whose office was in their pocket."

Lamer practised his criminal law effectively — and respectably — and in the beginning, he also applied himself to politics. "I got involved very young and very intensively at the organizational level in the Liberal Party," he said. Then came the crunch. "I had to decide whether it would be the law or politics, because I couldn't do both," he said. "I deliberated for three days and I chose." Law got Lamer's call, and over the next few years, apart from his practice, he held down many other positions in the profession. National chairman of the Criminal Law Section of the Canadian Bar Association. Founder of the Defence Attorneys' Association of Que-

bec. Special counsel to the Minister of Justice for the re-
organization of the courts in Quebec.

In 1969, he took an appointment to the Quebec Superior
Court. He was only thirty-six. "I guess I was a trend-setter,"
he said. "Nobody so young went to the bench in those days."
In 1976, in another career switch, he was persuaded to take
over as chairman of the Law Reform Commission of Canada,
the body that was founded in the early 1970s for the task of
introducing new concepts to Canadian law. Lamer, ever the
practical fellow, organized needed studies on pre-trial procedures, contempt of court, and sexual offences. But he wasn't
completely delighted with his role at the Law Reform Commission. "I wanted to get back to judging," he says. He got
back in 1978 when he was appointed to the Quebec Court of
Appeal, and two years later he went to the Supreme Court
of Canada.

As a justice on the court, Lamer is a "progressive". It's his
own description.

"I believe in the evolution of the law," he says. "Here at the
Supreme Court, you can't come on gung-ho and shoot down
long-established principles that have been around for years.
But you mustn't fear to break new ground. A progressive
doesn't mean liberal or conservative. It means not being afraid
to change."

At the desk in his chambers, Lamer gave a few finishing
touches to a judgment in a case from British Columbia which
the court had heard a year earlier in November 1984. Lamer's judgment would be released on December 17, 1985, and
there was plenty of good reason for the year of work that
had gone into it. The case involved the seemingly simple wording of the B.C. Motor Vehicles Act which made it possible for
a driver to go to prison for driving while his licence was under
suspension even though he didn't know of the suspension.
But the issue in the case, behind the seemingly simple language, was tough and fundamental. Lamer had to decide
whether the provisions of the Motor Vehicle Act violated "the

principles of fundamental justice" guaranteed in section seven of the Charter of Rights. His judgment ran to forty-six pages of reasoned and historically exact analysis and reached a no-holds-barred conclusion.

"A law that has the potential to convict a person who has not done anything wrong offends the principles of fundamental justice," Lamer wrote, "and if imprisonment is available as a penalty, such a law then violates a person's right to liberty under section seven of the Charter of Rights."

Lamer finds that the judgment-writing part of his job, as in the B.C. Motor Vehicles case, doesn't come easily.

"I have to suffer," he said in his office. "I don't write all that well, but I enjoy it more now than when I started. One thing is that, functioning in two languages like I do, it takes time to change gears. If I wrote a judgment in English and then the same judgment in the same case in French, you wouldn't believe that one and the same person — me, in fact — wrote both. With a hybrid like I am, the whole approach and dynamics is different in the two languages."

By six o'clock, Lamer was ready to drive home. He'd been concentrating on the law for most of the thirteen hours since he'd come awake in the morning. He assembled a thick stack of files and documents to take from the office. He'd work on them early the next morning. He wouldn't touch the files that evening. He rarely works at night.

"That's my time for the family," he said. "We go and see friends or go to the movies, to the Arts Centre. Or, better, I talk to my wife and drink a bottle of wine at dinner."

Lamer laughed.

"Even we guys on the court are entitled to that once in a while."

Of all Canada's major institutions, the Supreme Court of Canada is the least known and understood by most Canadians. Its role has been not so much misinterpreted as ignored.

It is our court of last resort, the forum to which citizens and corporations and organizations and governments with a grievance or an unresolvable question must turn for a final reading of their rights and status before the law. It deals in civil matters and criminal, in Quebec's civil code and in the other provinces' common law. It possesses the potential to shift Canada's social directions and to influence its political drift. It is the arbiter of all that the federal and provincial governments set out to accomplish, and it holds the great and conclusive power of the referee.

All of which raises the question: why has the court been so little acknowledged until very recent years and so easily overlooked for the largest part of its history?

Much of the answer reaches back to the court's tentative beginnings at the time of Confederation. The British North America Act made no specific provision for a Supreme Court, apart from a passing mention in section 101 that Parliament had the power to provide for "the constitution, maintenance and organization of a general court of appeal for Canada". That left most Canadians who cared scratching their heads, even the Canadians who had drawn up the BNA Act. One of them, Sir John A. Macdonald, said of section 101 that "this provision is very important, very brief; and not a little obscure."

A hesitant Parliament finally got around to setting up the Supreme Court in a statute that was passed on April 5, 1875. It was a shaky start, made all the more tenuous by a series of private members' bills introduced over the following decades seeking to abolish the court or to restrict its jurisdiction. The bills failed in passage, but the court's stature, already low-grade, was hardly enhanced.

The reason for the initial reluctance isn't hard to figure out. Superior courts were already established in the provinces, and the Judicial Committee of the Privy Council overseas in London seemed to be serving splendidly as a court of final appeal for Canadian cases. With that apparatus in place, many Canadians wondered out loud if there was a need for yet another court. The provincial governments had an additional motivation for reacting nervously to the existence of a Supreme Court in Ottawa. The court was the creature of the federal government, and it might therefore be expected to produce rulings in the feds' favour and at the expense of the provinces. Or so the provinces feared.

It didn't help the court's prestige that in its first few decades, many men who came to sit on it either were not in the prime of their careers or didn't have much in the way of careers at the bar or on the bench in the first place. Part of the explanation for their presence on the court lay in politics. All of the early prime ministers used the court as a final resting-place for pals and old pols who had well served the party in power at the particular moment of appointment. In fact, the taint of party politics, though it grew much less pronounced with the years, remained a problem for the court and its respectability until the 1960s.

The other problem — ineptitude or laziness or both — may have been even more severe. Some of the earliest justices, though they appreciated the title and perks that went with their positions on the highest court in the land, didn't appear to have their hearts in the job. Sir Alexander Mackenzie, the prime minister under whose government the Supreme Court came into existence, was of two minds, both doubtful, on the value of the court's opening sitting. He wondered about the dedication that the first justices, including the Hons. Taschereau, Richards, Fournier, and Strong, brought to their work, and he expressed his feelings in a letter written immediately after the court ended the first sitting.

"The Supreme Court Session passed off all right," he wrote to Edward Blake, the Toronto lawyer and Liberal. "They rose on Saturday at 1-30 and Taschereau was off on the train at 2. He tried on Friday evening to get the Court to sit until 10 pm

to enable him to leave at 10-50. Richards refused and Taschereau told him angrily he would be avenged for that.
Fournier left on Monday. Strong is very angry and insists on
both men doing *some* work. Neither of the Frenchmen opened
their mouths from first to last but both *looked* very wise
which probably had the same effect on the audience as if they
were wise."

Henry Strong, the justice who was angry at Taschereau and
Fournier, spent most of his tenure on the court in a bad temper. Since he sat for twenty-seven years as a Supreme Court
judge, the last ten as chief justice, his irascible ways drove a
couple of generations of colleagues to distraction. Strong was
often at odds with his fellow judges; on one occasion he wrote
to the federal Minister of Justice complaining of the "extreme
senile irritability" of his brother, Mr. Justice John Gwynne.
Many observers of the court regarded Strong's remark as the
ne plus ultra of the pot calling the kettle black.

Strong took regular umbrage at almost everyone who
worked at the Supreme Court or appeared before it. He was
particularly bullying to one of the court's messengers, a poor
old chap whose lame leg and partial blindness made him an
easy target. And Strong's rudeness to counsel frequently
threatened to break into open warfare. One clash in the spring
of 1898 became infamous among the bar of the day. It came
about when the court's list of cases to be heard unexpectedly
collapsed, leaving an appeal involving counsel from Toronto
and Chatham, Ontario, next up for hearing. Strong announced
that the case must proceed on the following day. That gave
counsel, all of whom were in their offices in Toronto and Chatham, much less than twenty-four hours to find their way to
Ottawa. None of them made it, whereupon Strong peremp-
to-rily dismissed the appeal and rejected a motion to rehear the
case. A terrific and predictable howl went up from the bar. It
fell on deaf ears.

But that encounter didn't represent the low point in

Strong's dealings with counsel. The nadir was struck in 1901 when a barrister laid an assault charge against the Chief Justice. The two men had engaged in a brisk discussion in the Supreme Court's corridor over the notion of Canadian jurists wearing wigs in the English tradition — Strong opposed such an innovation — and when the talk escalated, Strong let fly with several oaths and a punch to the barrister's head. If the early Supreme Court sometimes took on the quarrelsome giddiness of a retirement villa for elderly eccentrics, then Henry Strong was its grouchiest and most rigid inmate.

By the early 1920s, the young prime minister, Mackenzie King, was appalled that the court had fallen into such disrepute among many barristers and that its judgments weren't always commanding the necessary respect. In looking for a new chief justice who might invigorate the court, he departed from the informal tradition of naming the most senior judge on the court, thereby passing over the next man in line, Mr. Justice John Iddington, who was eighty-three years old. King offered the post to Eugene Lafleur, a much esteemed Montreal counsel. Lafleur declined. Indeed, he declined more than once, a state of affairs that constituted an ignominious commentary on the court's standing among Canadian lawyers. King turned by default to one of the court's associate justices, Frank Anglin, though he wasn't entirely convinced that Anglin was the man for the job.

"Anglin," King wrote in his diary, "is narrow, has not a pleasant manner, is very vain, but industriously steady and honest, a true liberal at heart."

In the end, King decided that steadiness, honesty, and a true liberal heart overcame a narrow, unpleasant, vain manner and elevated Anglin to the chief justice's chair. But the whole unfortunate sequence of events spread gloom among the court's supporters.

Still, against great odds, and despite attacks from the outside and turmoil on the inside, the Supreme Court was gradually managing to shape a body of law that it could call its own. The court continued to labour in the shadow of the Privy Council in England, since it was required to follow English precedents in case law and since Canada's lawyers could always appeal Supreme Court decisions to the Council. What's more, the overwhelming majority of the court's cases were concerned with citizens' quarrels over matters of contract and property, and these cases were not exactly the stuff of which sweeping legal history is made. Nevertheless, the court went diligently about the business of building an important store of private law that would guide the lower courts of the country. It proceeded by steady empirical methods, basing its judgments on legal precedent and on basic institutions of government rather than on such flashier concepts as "equality before the law" and "due process", which the free-wheeling American Supreme Court used in arriving at its much more activist decisions. In a sense, the U.S. court was another problem for the Canadian Supreme Court, since it cast a dazzling light that blinded most observers to the more modest accomplishments of the court in Ottawa.

It was Lyman Poore Duff who took much of the lead in upgrading the court in quality and authority. He sat as a Supreme Court justice longer than any other man, from 1906 to 1944, the last eleven of those years in succession to Frank Anglin as chief justice. Duff was afflicted with personal problems that, taken altogether, would overwhelm most men. He suffered from alcoholism, impotence, and a chronic inability to balance his bank account. He was perpetually in debt, even to the taxi company that ferried him around Ottawa. But no matter what indignities and ailments he laboured under off the bench, on the bench he possessed formidable strengths and resources.

Duff was quick, clever, and blessed with a ferocious sense of industry. He was a student of the law. He loved it and knew how to apply it. He wrote with clarity and he wrote often, handing down decisions in every area of jurisprudence. He wasn't a man who took a broad and crusading view in his judgments. Rather, his interpretations of the law were strict. The law, he said in his decisions, must prevail, and if there was a clash between the law and a litigant's apparent rights, then the litigant could forget his apparent rights. Duff was a conservative in his judicial philosophy. There was nothing good or bad or surprising about such a stance. It was the norm. Virtually all Supreme Court justices of the court's first seventy-five years took a conservative approach in their application of the law, and Duff was no exception.

In the field thought of today as civil rights, Duff differed not at all from his colleagues in holding that, for minority groups of citizens, such rights were almost non-existent under the laws that the court was asked to interpret. Thus, at various times over his thirty-seven and a half years on the Supreme Court, Duff upheld pieces of legislation that would be considered discriminatory in the 1980s. There was the Saskatchewan law that prohibited white women from being employed by Chinese men, the order-in-council that kept Japanese workers off crown lands in B.C., the Quebec law that authorized the forcible closing of any dwelling if the occupant had been convicted of operating a common bawdy-house. Duff found there was nothing in his strict interpretation of the law that made any of these legislative acts improper exercises of authority by the bodies that enacted them. And very few Canadians of Duff's day questioned the correctness of his decisions.

On the other hand, whenever Duff's analysis of earlier case law logically led him in a more liberal direction, he followed it. Most conspicuously, the Duff court was called on to deal with the Press Bill, one of a series of bizarre legislative acts passed in the 1930s by William Aberhart's Social Credit government in Alberta. The Press Bill required that the province's newspapers print only those stories about the Alberta

government that a provincial board first approved. Duff
showed the way in striking down the Bill on the grounds that
it, or another Social Credit Act that it depended on, was
beyond provincial powers. It was ultra vires. But he also
slipped into his judgment a hint that "the capacity of the Province to restrict public discussion on public affairs must necessarily find some limitation by reference to the admitted
fact that the parliamentary institutions of the Dominion necessarily pre-suppose for their effective working such public
discussion." That judgment of Duff's, uncharacteristically
convoluted language and all, didn't stray too far from his
usual firm and commonsensical ways. But he managed to
bring the Supreme Court for the first time to a reasonably
strong civil liberties position, a glittering area of the law the
court would revisit more forcefully in later years.

Immediately after the Second World War, the court underwent large changes that brought to it new lustre and authority. The first change was physical. Almost from its beginning,
the court carried on business in a building that had once been
a stable and had never lost its horsy atmosphere. It was a
two-storey structure at the foot of Parliament Hill, and it had a
hardy and quaint look, just the sort of place where a hunting
man might happily keep his string of mounts. As a seat for
dispensing justice, it was an insult. It was cramped and incon-
venient, sweaty in summer, drafty in winter, afloat in dust
and prone to gusts of evil smells that reminded judges and
counsel of the building's origins.

In 1935, inspectors from the Department of Public Works
gave the building a once-over and concluded that "the building should be condemned as being injurious to the health of
the occupants and totally inadequate for the purposes for
which it is used." The report helped to pave the way for
change, and in the late 1930s, the government engaged a gifted
Canadian architect to give the Supreme Court a setting, grand
and imposing, that it had begun to earn.

The architect's name was Ernest Cormier. He was a Montrealer, and he had already designed a series of gracious buildings in his own city: the Palais de Justice, several churches, the best of the University of Montreal's edifices. Cormier favoured the Art Deco style of the period and he brought it to stunning realization in 1931 in a house that he built for himself on Pine Avenue in Montreal and that, years later, Pierre Trudeau purchased after his retirement as prime minister.

When Cormier took on the Supreme Court assignment, he mixed his affection for art deco with more traditional styles. The result was a three-storey building that seems at once playful and august. It sits on a bluff overlooking the Ottawa River, set back from Wellington Street on the front at just the right distance to give it a sense of lofty grandeur. The entrance hall, which is reached through a pair of intimidating bronze doors, is towering in scale and marble in material. It presents the sort of introduction that seems calculated to cut visiting counsel down to mini-size. But, once past the entrance, Cormier was thoughtful enough to scale the courtrooms to more human proportions. There are two courtrooms, one on each side of the entrance hall, given over mainly to sittings of the Federal Court of Canada, and a third courtroom, straight ahead and up two short flights of stairs, where the Supreme Court of Canada holds forth. These courtrooms are congenial and welcoming. They offer the elegant dashes of art deco that Cormier adored — the large chandelier in the main courtroom is especially riveting — and the overall impression is of the law's glory and solemnity nicely leavened with a touch of tasteful hospitality. In its combination of looks, the building seems entirely the proper setting for a Supreme Court's deliberations.

Not long after the court moved into its new quarters in 1946 — and not long before its old quarters were levelled to make way for a parking lot — it took a giant leap forward in autonomy when appeals to the Judicial Council of the Privy

Council were abolished. As of 1949, the Supreme Court was master in its own house, and its house accommodated all of Canadian jurisprudence. The justices of the court would continue to study precedents of the English law lords as guides in arriving at their own decisions, but they had no more worries that the English body could overrule their judgments. At long last, the Canadian court had the final say in Canadian cases.

Also by the 1950s, the problem of recruiting strong judges to sit on the court had largely faded. True enough, political patronage still tarnished the court's reputation now and again; Douglas Abbott, never a judge in a lower court and removed from legal practice by many years, proceeded in 1954 from a cabinet post in Louis St. Laurent's government to a seat on the Supreme Court. But, for the most part, good men accepted appointments to the court and unqualified men were rarely considered for the appointments.

A group of justices fairly regarded as liberal in outlook asserted themselves in the court's deliberations of the late 1940s and early 1950s. Ivan Rand was their pivot, a flinty, upright man whose sense of social justice proved to be a formidable instrument. It met its major test when the court was asked to consider a series of legislative bills passed by the Quebec government under Maurice Duplessis. The bills took dead aim at the Jehovah's Witnesses, attempting to interfere with their civil liberties and, incidentally, with the civil liberties of other groups who happened to find themselves caught in the same net. There were seven bills in all, restrictive in intent and in result, and, with Rand leading the way, the Supreme Court overturned each one.

That was the good news.

The bad news was that the court split into two or three different groups in deciding why each of the Duplessis bills should be declared improper and how civil liberties should be upheld. The confusion was understandable; the BNA Act offered no guidance on the matter of individual rights, and Canada as yet possessed no Bill of Rights which might establish standards of personal liberty. The court was on its own, and it didn't back away from its lonely challenge. It stood up for civil liberties, even if it wasn't united in stating the specific bases for its stand, and it showed no reluctance in taking a brand-new activist position.

Change came to the court in the 1960s. The liberal Rand reached the newly mandatory retirement age of seventy-five in 1959, and other experienced, clear-headed, and mildly adventurous judges left the court for one reason or another around the same period. James Estey of Saskatchewan died in 1956. Roy Kellock of Ontario retired in 1958, only sixty-four years old but apparently at odds with the Chief Justice, Patrick Kerwin, and possibly anxious to return to the bar, where he could — and did — earn a good fee as counsel. Charles Locke of Vancouver followed Kellock's example and quit the bench in 1962 to get back to a barrister's work. With the departure of these men the court took on a variation in feel and style.

Through the 1960s, it was more conservative than in the 1950s, just as intelligent and rather less predictable. Part of the explanation for its drifting nature was that nobody lasted long enough in the chief justice's chair to push the court in a particular direction. When Patrick Kerwin retired as chief justice in 1963, Robert Taschereau was appointed to the post. Bright and experienced as he was — he had arrived on the court in 1940 — he suffered from a serious drinking problem. He stepped aside in 1967 and John Cartwright took over. Cartwright was all good things in a man of the law, scholarly, courteous, the product of an Ontario establishment background who, *noblesse oblige*, became an unfailing champion of the ordinary citizen. But he had reached an advanced age when he arrived as chief justice and retired after only two and a half years. He was succeeded by Gerald Fauteux, also learned and a veteran of the court but a man who lacked the personality and intellectual vigour to assist his fellow judges along any specific route.

During this period of waffling at the top, the Supreme Court still produced many significant judgments in the private law area. Cartwright, all by himself, accounted for several decisions that gave assurance to counsel and the lower courts. But in one essential, the court of the 1960s proved a disappointment. That let-down revolved around the Bill of Rights. John Diefenbaker guided the Bill through Parliament, a proud document he and many others expected to become the vehicle that would expand civil liberties in the country. The Supreme Court took a look at the Bill of Rights and, alas, couldn't make much out of it.

The Bill was passed in 1960, and the first case invoking it reached the Supreme Court in 1963. The case had to do with a humble bowling-alley. Under the Lord's Day Act, a federal statute, the alley was compelled to shut down on Sundays. But the alley's proprietors contended that the new Bill of Rights took precedence over the Lord's Day Act and allowed people like them to observe Sundays in ways that they chose. Their way was to throw open their bowling-alley to customers who hadn't gone to church.

The Supreme Court listened to the argument, and the majority reacted to it nervously and narrowly. The basis of their decision was that, contrary to what Diefenbaker's parliamentarians might have thought, the Bill of Rights created no new rights and freedoms. It merely confirmed rights that existed prior to 1960. Thus, if an earlier piece of federal legislation — the Lord's Day Act in the immediate case — wasn't considered to have interfered with an old right and freedom — freedom of religion in this instance — then the Bill of Rights introduced no new element into the equation. The bowling-alley would have to remain closed on the sabbath as the Lord's Day Act required.

So much for the promised glory of the Bill of Rights.

The one ray of optimism for civil-libertarians came from John Cartwright's lone dissent in the case. He took the activist view and wrote in ringing terms that where a parliamentary statute collided with the Bill of Rights, the statute must yield. That was the sort of approach John Diefenbaker, civil-rights champions, and bowling-alley proprietors had been hoping for. But, as history later indicated, they couldn't count on the court's following the direction that Cartwright pointed out. They couldn't even count on Cartwright's continuing along in his own direction.

The next major test for the Bill of Rights came in the Drybones case of 1970. Joseph Drybones had been drunk one night in Yellowknife, and, since he was an Indian, he found himself charged and convicted under section 94 of the Indian Act with "being an Indian intoxicated off a reserve". Drybones, like all native people, was treated differently from other Canadians, from *white* Canadians; the latter, after all, couldn't get convicted of such an arcane crime as being "intoxicated off a reserve". There was one law for Indians and another for the rest of Canada, a situation that seemed to call into play the Bill of Rights.

When the Drybones case climbed to the Supreme Court, the nine judges split six to three, with Roland Ritchie, an independently minded Maritimer, writing the majority judgment. It turned out to be a shining moment for the Bill of Rights. Ritchie held that, by all that was sensible, when a piece of legislation differed directly with the terms of the Bill of Rights, the part of the federal legislation that differed became instantly inoperative. Specifically, in the Drybones matter, section 94 of the Indian Act, under which poor drunken Joseph Drybones was convicted, ran head-on into section five of the Bill of Rights, which guaranteed equality for all Canadians before the law. Drybones, an Indian, wasn't treated equally with other Canadians. Therefore, the Indian Act's section 94 was out the window.

Civil-rights proponents celebrated the judgment. But their

joy wasn't unconfined. The trouble was that one of the three
dissenters in the Drybones case was none other than the hero
of the bowling-alley case, John Cartwright. By 1970, he had
moved up to the chief justice's job, and, in a stunning change
of mind, he wrote in his Drybones judgment that he had been
badly mistaken in his earlier judgment. Parliament, he concluded, couldn't possibly have meant that the Bill of Rights
should make other federal statutes inoperative. It was all too
vague, Cartwright said — Parliament's intention, the meaning of the Bill of Rights, the whole muddled package.
Cartwright may have been right. What was undoubtedly
certain was that his judgment in Drybones contributed to the
confusion among his fellow justices, and the upshot was that
the court was never again able to say much that added strength
or meaning to John Diefenbaker's Bill of Rights.

As such justices as Cartwright and Fauteux were running
out their string on the court, another man was moving to
recast the Supreme Court from behind the scenes. He was
Pierre Trudeau, himself a lawyer and a teacher much learned
in the law. Trudeau was probably the first prime minister to
understand precisely the sort of judges he wanted on the court
in Ottawa. He went on the hunt for scholars and for men —
and, as it evolved, for a woman — who understood a thing
or two about constitutional law. Trudeau was smoothing the
way toward a Supreme Court that would think through the
changes in the country's constitution that he saw as a necessity. He made a mistake or two in his appointments. Two
justices from Quebec, both Trudeau choices, had short and
mostly unhappy tenures on the court in the 1970s. Louis-
Philippe de Grandpré found himself lonely in Ottawa, and
his successor, Yves Pratte, gathered more satisfaction from
the corporate world, sitting on the boards of Domtar and
Power Corporation, to which he returned after less than two
years on the court. But de Grandpré and Pratt were exceptions
among Trudeau appointees. The others fitted the mould he
had in mind, most especially Bora Laskin.

Laskin was many things that made him unique to the Supreme Court: a Jew, an academic, a lawyer with virtually no courtroom experience. There had been a few of the latter who reached the court but no men who were either Jewish or workers in legal academe, much less one who was both. Laskin grew up in Thunder Bay, Ontario, the son of an immigrant from Russia who ran a furniture store. He studied law at Osgoode Hall and Harvard, and he taught for twenty-eight years. Most of those years were in partnership with the great pioneer in Canadian legal teaching, Cecil A. Wright, at the University of Toronto Law School. Laskin's range of subjects was breathtaking, from property law in first year to constitutional law in second year to labour law in third year. That tour de force of versatility meant that on any given couple of days in the classroom, Laskin would shift from the law's dry techniques to an exploration of the political science behind judicial opinions to a searching inspection of due process and the rights of individual Canadian workers. Laskin was bound to be an odd duck when he took his appointment to the Supreme Court in March 1970 and when he moved up to chief justice in December 1973.

Two labels stuck to Laskin during his years on the court. One was "the great dissenter" and the other, taking in him and the other eight justices, was "the Laskin court". Laskin didn't care for either label. The first had at least some merit on the record. Especially in civil-rights cases, Laskin often dissented from the majority judgments of his brethren. The Murdoch case in 1975 was famous as an example of that propensity. Irene Murdoch was the wife of an Alberta rancher who, when she became the rancher's ex-wife after twenty-five years of marriage, claimed half the ranch as her fair share. Nothing doing, the majority of the Supreme Court held in a four-to-one decision. The four justices treated marriage as a straightforward legal contract, and since Mrs. Murdoch couldn't prove in legal terms that her work over a quarter-century of tending to her husband's needs around the ranch had increased his assets, she was out of court and out of luck.

Laskin dissented.

"No doubt," he wrote in a preamble to the judgment in which he suggested a route to recompense Irene Murdoch, "legislative action may be a better way to lay down policies and prescribe conditions under which and the extent to which spouses should share the property acquired by either or both during marriage. But the better way is not the only way; and if the exercise of a traditional jurisdiction by the Courts can conduce to equitable sharing, it should not be withheld merely because difficulties in particular cases and the making of distinctions may result in slower and perhaps more painful evolution of principle."

Eventually everyone—his fellow justices and the provincial legislatures which passed family law reform acts to protect people in Irene Murdoch's dilemma — came around to Laskin's view. But by then he had moved on to different areas of dissent on his court.

As for the other label, "the Laskin court", it made sense at least as a public relations designation. Laskin was the first chief justice to take his message to the public, and his message was that the Supreme Court of Canada was a body that Canadians owed it to themselves to understand. For a judge, Laskin was a highly visible presence. He made speeches. He gave interviews. He introduced television into the courtroom when he allowed cameras to record the handing down of the court's judgment in the patriation case of 1981, the judgment that led to the bringing home of Canada's constitution. And he answered criticisms of his court. In 1978, when some legal academics took a jab at the Supreme Court in general and Laskin in particular as showing a bias in certain directions, the Chief Justice responded with *le mot juste*.

"I have no constituency to serve," he told a conference of journalists, "except the realm of reason."

But "the Laskin court" wasn't Laskin's court in the sense

that he carried it down paths he wished it to follow. Perhaps Laskin was too bold, too daring, too far out in front. Perhaps the traditional conservatism of the Supreme Court was resistant to Laskin's swifter pace. Perhaps haste in the law is better made slowly and reasonably. Perhaps other and opposite views were equally valuable in the law. Whatever the explanation, Laskin's influence on the thinking of the other eight judges was an occasional thing, and nowhere did he and they run into more fascinating wrangles than in constitutional cases.

Laskin was a strong centralist. As a law school teacher and as a jurist, he gave the British North America Act an interpretation that favoured the exercise of strong federal powers. That brought him into occasional clashes with other justices whose analysis of the BNA Act made them lean toward the provinces. What added more complication to the difference in philosophies was that often, even when he and his colleagues reached agreement in certain cases that the federal government should prevail over the provinces, they disagreed on the reasons for their decisions. One group of justices, trailing after Laskin, would base their judgment on one section of the BNA Act, while another group would find their rationale in an entirely different section. These were situations that made for intrigue, exasperation, and a small dose of comic relief.

The fine mess over the jurisdiction in criminal prosecutions was both typical and special. It got its start routinely enough when a fellow from Alberta named Patrick Hauser was charged by the federal attorney general on two counts of possessing cannabis for the purposes of trafficking contrary to the Narcotic Control Act, which is a federal statute. Hauser's lawyers, a nervy bunch, decided to launch a constitutional attack on behalf of their client. They contended that the Parliament of Canada lacked the competence to enact legislation authorizing the Attorney General of Canada to prefer indictments for an offence, as he had against Patrick Hauser, under the Narcotic Control Act. According to the argument on behalf of Hauser, a proper construction of the BNA Act gave jurisdiction for narcotics crimes to the provincial attorneys general and not to their federal counterpart.

The case of *Regina* v. *Hauser* came before seven members of the Supreme Court of Canada on May 29, 1978. A glittering array of counsel was on hand, John Robinette for the federal government and representatives for the attorneys general of nine provinces who were keen to test and expand the limits of their jurisdiction. Counsel went at the fray for three days, and the feeling in the courtroom was that the seven justices were buying the federal argument. When the court retired on the afternoon of May 31, Robinette and most of the other counsel would probably have bet a dollar or two on the prospects of a judgment upholding federal jurisdiction over drug offences. Little did they know they would be destined to wait almost a year until the judgment was released on May 1, 1979, to collect on their wagers.

The explanation for the hold-up lay in a shift of views behind the scenes at the Supreme Court Building. Mr. Justice Brian Dickson weighed in with the first surprise. He spent many months in research and rethinking, and at last produced a very long and beautifully crafted piece of writing that, to the consternation of all but one of his fellow justices (Yves Pratte, who concurred in Dickson's judgment), came out on the side of the provinces.

Dickson took the view that there is a basic division of labour which may not be implicit in the Canadian constitution but which is rooted in history. The division breaks down this way: the legislative responsibility in the criminal field is federal and the prosecuting responsibility is primarily provincial. Parliament in Ottawa may define the crimes and the procedural rights, but the provinces have the major role in law enforcement, because the provinces are closer to the people and because criminal law requires a grass-roots sensitivity. Thus, answering the constitutional questions raised in the Hauser circumstances, Dickson held that it wasn't within Parliament's competence to authorize the federal attorney general to lay charges under the Narcotic Control Act.

When Dickson's judgment was circulated among the other judges, Mr. Justice Louis-Philippe Pigeon was caught by surprise. Pigeon, a sound and thoughtful judge who was in the last of his thirteen years on the court, firmly believed that the authority to prosecute under the Narcotic Control Act belonged to the federal government, and he rushed to write a rebuttal to Dickson. The judgment that resulted proved to be a most peculiar document.

Pigeon might easily have concluded that the federal government derived its authority in drug prosecutions from section 91(27) of the BNA Act, which gave the feds jurisdiction over the procedure of criminal matters. That would seem convincing. Instead, Pigeon hied off in a different direction. He relied on the residuary power bestowed on the federal government by the BNA Act to pass laws that were for "the peace, order and good government of Canada". Pigeon's reasoning was that the Narcotic Control Act grappled with a genuinely new and pressing problem — illegal drugs — which didn't exist in 1867 when the BNA Act was written. The Narcotic Control Act couldn't be put under the class of "matters of a merely local and private nature" which the BNA Act assigned to the provinces. It came under peace, order and good government. It was a proper exercise of federal authority, and Canada's Attorney General could proceed against Patrick Hauser.

Pigeon's judgment, peculiarities and all, was joined in by three other justices and thereby became the majority judgment in *Regina* v. *Hauser*. But that left one of the seven justices who sat on the case unaccounted for, Mr. Justice Wishart Spence, a veteran who was approaching the end of his fifteen years on the court, and he proceeded to write his own judgment. He agreed that narcotics prosecutions were a federal matter, but he wasn't going for any of this peace, order and good government theorizing. He preferred section 91(27) of the BNA Act, the criminal-law power that was given to the federal government. That was good enough for Spence. And, what was more, he pointed out that narcotics was clearly a business which crossed provincial and national borders and that section 91(2) gave the federal government power over trade and commerce. As far as Spence was concerned, those two sections were the plain and clear end of the matter.

Thus, in the result, the sides stacked up in three groupings when the Hauser decision became public in May 1979.

Pigeon, joined by Ronald Martland, Roland Ritchie, and Jean Beetz, supported the federal authority in narcotics prosecutions under the peace, order and good government section of the BNA Act.

Spence upheld the federal jurisdiction under the criminal section and the trade and commerce section.

Dickson, joined by Pratte, in one of the most compelling dissents in recent court history, supported the provincial authority in drug prosecutions.

As for Patrick Hauser, he went back to Alberta to face the trial court once again.

But there was one more kicker to the story. Chief Justice Laskin did not sit on the Hauser case. He was ill and away from the court. Despite his absence, his side won the day. The court took a strong centralist position. But Laskin was far from happy with the *way* in which the desired result was achieved, and he let everyone know of his unhappiness in a novel and utterly unprecedented manner.

In mid-December of 1981, the case of *Brenda Ruth Schneider* v. *The Queen* came before the court. The case turned on the constitutional validity of a British Columbia statute called the Heroin Treatment Act. The Hauser case and the Narcotic Control Act came into issue in the Schneider case, if at all, in only the most peripheral sense, and yet Laskin, who had clearly been stewing since May 1979, used Schneider as an excuse to blow a little steam out of his ears over the judgments of his fellow justices in Hauser.

"There is one other point I wish to make," Laskin wrote in his very brief judgment in *Schneider*, "and it relates to the difficulties raised by the majority judgment in R v Hauser. . . . I do not hesitate to say that, in my view, the majority judgment ought not to have placed the Narcotic Control Act under the federal residuary power to legislate for the peace, order and good government of Canada. Unless we revert to a long abandoned view of the peace, order and good government power as embracing the entire catalogue of federal legislative powers, I would myself have viewed the Narcotic Control Act as an exercise of federal criminal power, and had I sat in Hauser, I would have supported the reasons of Spence, J. . . . There is, in my view, good ground to reconsider the majority basis of decision."

Laskin's signal couldn't have been plainer. If I get another chance at the issue you guys messed with in Hauser, Laskin was telling the court, just watch my smoke.

Laskin got his chance. It came a couple of years later in a case called *Regina* v. *Wetmore* which arrived before the court from British Columbia. The case concerned prosecutions under the Food and Drugs Act of Canada, and the issue raised was identical to the issue that was the subject of the mix-up over the Narcotic Control Act in the Hauser case: Does the Attorney General of Canada possess the authority to prosecute offences under this federal statute?

Laskin was as good as his warning words in the Schneider case. He wrote a judgment in *Regina* v. *Wetmore* that carried five other judges with him, leaving only Brian Dickson in lonely and consistent dissent, and he based his judgment, as he'd forecast, on section 91(27) of the BNA Act, the criminal-law power. Never mind the peace, order and good government authority, Laskin was saying, never mind any other powers under the BNA Act. It was the criminal-law power that provided all the support and justification that the federal government needed to push on with its prosecutions.

To add more heat to the whole simmering pot, a judgment in another case on the subject of criminal prosecutions appeared on the same day in October 1983 as the judgment in Wetmore was released. This case was called *Canadian National Transport* v. *the Attorney General of Canada*. It came from Alberta, and it raised the question of whether or not the federal attorney general could bring prosecutions under yet another federal statute, the Combines Investigation Act.

All seven judges who sat on the case agreed that the federal government had the power to prosecute under the Combines Act. But the seven split on their reasons for the decision. Three judges, led by Dickson, held that the federal jurisdiction derived from section 91(2) of the BNA Act which gave the feds power over matters of trade and commerce. But the other four, the majority, saw no need to bother with the trade and commerce section. Laskin wrote the majority decision. He took a passing swipe at Pigeon's judgment in the Hauser case, pointing out again that there was no need in Hauser to resort to the peace, order and good government power. And he rested the authority of the federal attorney general to prosecute under the Combines Investigation Act solely on the criminal-law power given to the federal government in the BNA Act.

Laskin had waited, and he had finally had his say in an area of constitutional law that he cared deeply about. He had fretted and stewed, and after four years of waiting for his chance to pounce, he had spoken his word. And, unless and until a case makes its way to the court and offers Brian Dickson an opportunity to revive his ideas on the subject, it will be the last word.

Laskin paid a penalty in health for such hard labours on

the court. In 1978, he endured open-heart surgery. His great friend and Ontario colleague on the court, Wishart Spence, urged Laskin to slow down his pace. But Laskin couldn't resist his job or the burdens it brought. And by the early 1980s, his flagging energy was beginning to affect his character and performance in court.

Until then, only one habit of unwary counsel who argued in the Supreme Court bothered Laskin, who was the most kindly of judges.

"My lords, at this point in time . . ." a counsel would say in his presentation.

"*At this point in time?*" Laskin would bark. "What's the matter with *now?*"

He couldn't stand lazy jargon.

But after his open-heart surgery, after trouble with his eyes, after other ailments brought on by his unforgiving fifteen-hour days, Laskin began to wear down. Afternoons in court were fatiguing for him, and he grew abrupt with young counsel who made errors in matters other than proper English. He was only seventy-one, still Chief Justice, when he died of pneumonia and additional complications at Ottawa Civic Hospital on March 24, 1984.

Laskin left behind a proud legacy of original notions expressed in trail-blazing judgments, and he had the satisfaction of knowing that during his stewardship, the Supreme Court underwent three changes that mightily increased its collegiality, its stature, and its work-load.

Laskin was himself responsible for the first change. He introduced a justices' lunch-room to the Supreme Court Building. A simple idea? Perhaps, but no one had come up with it earlier, conspicuously not in the days when crabby old men like Chief Justice Henry Strong engaged in slanging matches — "extreme senile irritability" — with fellow justices. The lunch-room became an invaluable forum for talk and fellowship among the judges of a civilized era.

The second change, much overdue, was ultimately the work of Parliament. It passed the necessary legislation, long begged for by members of the court, that gave sense and scope to its docket of cases. Before the legislation of 1975, the Supreme Court was at the mercy of litigants. Any dispute in which the wrangle involved an amount in excess of ten thousand dollars could proceed to the highest court as a matter of right. Much of the time of the justices was being consumed in deliberations over traffic accidents, broken contracts, and disputed wills, over quarrels that were regional, parochial, and, for a final appellate court, frequently pointless.

With an amendment to the Supreme Court Act, Parliament altered the rules. After 1975, monetary criteria counted for nothing, and the court could decide for itself which cases would receive leave to appeal to it. "With this change," Laskin said at the time, "the court can at last exercise control over its own docket." Freed of restriction, the Supreme Court moved more heavily into areas of public law. It heard an increased number of appeals in constitutional matters, in criminal cases of national importance, in the interpretation of statutes and government regulations, and in cases where at least two provinces were affected by the outcome. The impact on the court represented a large leap in action.

"Claims are now being advanced that would not have been dreamed of twenty years ago," Brian Dickson said in a speech in 1979. "Claims by married women, environmentalists, native groups, children, consumers' groups, athletes, all seeking relief from the court."

This process was accelerated by the third crucial event of the Laskin years, the judgment in the 1981 patriation case which opened the way for the passage in the following year of the Constitution Act with its entrenched Charter of Rights. If Brian Dickson was impressed by the range of cases that were beginning to come along in 1979, he braced himself for the avalanche after the Charter of Rights arrived on the scene.

In practical terms, the Charter guaranteed that any citizen who decided that the actions of his fellow citizens somehow infringed on his rights could ask the courts to examine those actions, even if they were expressed by the majority, even if they were laid out in a piece of legislation, and declare them in violation of a provision of the Charter and therefore unconstitutional. Business at the Supreme Court would never again be quite the same. Henceforth its justices would be more challenged, pushed into a brighter public spotlight, and loaded with the heavier responsibility of sorting out the rights and freedoms that Canadians feel they're entitled to.

Cases invoking the Charter began to hit the court in the spring of 1984, and the justices were no shrinking violets in handing down their decisions.

The cases took in a broad collection.

In one, the court decided that government agents acting under the Combines Investigation Act who grabbed files and documents in a raid on the *Edmonton Journal* were in violation of the Charter guarantee against unreasonable search and seizure. Brian Dickson, who succeeded Laskin as chief justice, wrote that the combines search had "a breathtaking sweep . . . it was tantamount to a licence to roam at large."

In another case, the court dumped on the controversial Bill 101 from Quebec. Bill 101 said that only children with at least one parent educated in English in Quebec could get English schooling in the province. But section twenty-three of the Charter says that children of Canadians educated in English or French anywhere in the country have the right to English or French education in any province where the numbers warrant. The court ruled that Bill 101 had to yield to section twenty-three.

And in yet another case, the court held that the federal Lord's Day Act — the same legislation that the bowling-alley proprietors challenged unsuccessfully under the old and now defunct Bill of Rights — offended the religion section of the

Charter. "If I am a Jew or a Sabbatarian or a Moslem," Chief
Justice Dickson wrote, "the practice of my religion implies
my right to work on a Sunday if I wish."

The Charter cases signal a new era for the court, a time
when its justices are compelled to juggle law and history and
political science, a dash of psychology, and a lot of divination
of the mood of the country under the Charter.

"We will have to understand and give expression to the
underlying values which gave rise to the Charter," Brian
Dickson said on the morning of July 15, 1985. He was speaking in Cambridge, England, to a group of Canadian and
English lawyers, judges, and academics, and he was in a mood
to be reflective. "In other words," Dickson went on, "we will
have to understand, in Alexis de Tocqueville's phrase, 'the
spirit of the age'."

It's a tall order, but what puts the odds in favour of the
court's success is that the eight men and one woman who sit
on it in the mid-1980s, measured in terms of intelligence,
devotion to duty, generosity, and pride, make up the best of
all groups of judges in the history of the Supreme Court of
Canada.

Willard Zebedee Estey — Bud to everyone who's met him
once — is the quickest, funniest, most rambunctious member of the court. He makes jokes on any subject. Ask him about
the rule requiring judges on the court to live within forty
kilometres of Ottawa. "That," he says, "is my definition of
capital punishment." About the meetings in the conference
room after the court has heard arguments in the courtroom:
"I leave my shoes untied, and when the Chief is looking for
someone to write the decision, I lean over to tie them." Or
about his feelings for the work on the court: "It beats chop-
ping down trees for a living."

Estey was born in Saskatoon in 1919 and still has the lean,

weathered face and wiry body of a prairie man. His father, James, was a crown prosecutor for twelve years, a founding member of the law faculty of the University of Saskatchewan Law School, and a justice of the Supreme Court of Canada for eleven years. The son followed in the father's footsteps, though there were some significant departures along the way for Bud Estey.

After law school and service in the RCAF during the war, he went east. "I thought Toronto was going to be the great centre of commerce," he says, "and I thought that'd get me the most interesting law." He was right. For almost twenty-five years Estey reigned as the holy terror of the commercial litigation bar in Toronto. "I liked tax law and copyright law," he says. "It was pure and clean, and when you got into inter-corporate battles, it was always related to a stake worth fighting for."

Estey left the bar for the bench in 1973, first to sit for a couple of years on the Ontario Court of Appeal, next to spend a year as chief justice of the High Court, and then to move up to the top job, chief justice of Ontario. On September 29, 1977, only nine months in place as Ontario's chief justice, he took an appointment to the Supreme Court of Canada. It was a shift in career that apparently grew out of a mild controversy. Wilfred Judson had stepped down as one of the Ontario judges on the Supreme Court in July of 1977. Chief Justice Laskin wanted his old friend from the Ontario Court of Appeal, Charles Dubin, to replace Judson. People in the Department of Justice were plumping for another candidate. The wrangle got so testy, so the story goes, that Prime Minister Trudeau stepped in to resolve it by asking Estey to accept the post.

Estey agreed, but he wasn't sure he wanted the Supreme Court. Several years later, he still wasn't persuaded the move to Ottawa was a good idea.

"The Ontario Court of Appeal was one of the most enjoyable jobs I ever had," he said. "Perhaps that was partly because all of its business came from one area instead of from all over the country the way it does on this court. Everybody who appeared in front of me or alongside me was an old friend or a new friend. The action was hot and heavy, cracking out those oral judgments, and I was busier than a one-armed paper-hanger with the itch. Or, again, maybe the trial division is the best place to be. You can do something for the beleaguered litigant that you can't do up here. In fact, sadly, often we have to send a lot of things back for retrial, which to me is like amputating your own foot. You just know the pain and expense of a new trial for the litigant.''

Estey found that the change from Toronto to Ottawa called for adjustments on several levels. For one thing, the range at the Supreme Court of Canada was so markedly different. "You deal with the two systems of law up here, common law and civil law," he said. "And we common-law lawyers always have an inferiority complex when it comes to civil law. It's a symmetrical kind of thing, whereas the common law has the scattergun approach." According to Estey, even the personality of the city, Ottawa, has an effect on transplanted Torontonians. "It's a town jammed with civil servants," he said. "They're an awful lot different from the sort of people you run into walking up Bay Street."

Estey gets around any problems that the change of pace in Ottawa has brought partly by keeping on the go. He plays tennis with his law clerks in the summer and skis on Saturday mornings at Mont Ste. Marie in winter. He's chairman of Hockey Canada and charges around the country on the occasional weekend to make the moves that he hopes will produce a gold-medal team at the 1988 Winter Olympics in Calgary. And when the federal government asked him to conduct the inquiry into the failure of the Canadian Commercial Bank in the summer of 1985, he jumped at the chance, even though Chief Justice Dickson prefers his judges to stick close to the courtroom.

For all of his outside activities, however, and for all of his good-natured grousing about the differences from the good old days on the Ontario bench, Estey, the brightest of men, inevitably acknowledges with much joy that, for a judge, the Supreme Court of Canada is the place where the historical action is going on today. And when he talks about the court, he puts its present situation in tidy perspective.

"Each era up here has its own swing," he said. "My father was here when appeals to the Privy Council were abolished. Everybody said that was the great time to be on the court. Then, during the heyday of the Cartwright era, it was supposed to be the great time because the court was beginning to shed the domination of Lord Watson and Lord Haldane and all the other English law lords and their precedents. Now they say it's the great time because the court is getting the constitutional confrontations between the two levels of government. In one sense, every era is the same, just a parade of human nature in the framework of adversarial debate about how to run a country. But, really, it's different today because the country is pulling itself into new configurations, and it's fascinating to sit on the court and watch them bubbling in front of you like the cauldron that Macbeth's witches stirred.

"The kind of ore going into our mill is changing," he went on, shifting metaphors. "Citizen-versus-citizen litigation is disappearing from our docket. Not many patent cases any more, no contract cases, no tax cases. Now we're into the exploration of the meaning, reach and extent, importance, application, and usefulness of the Charter of Rights and all the mysterious words in that mysterious document. We're living in the thunder and lightning of constitutional debate."

Gerald Le Dain is the man who first attracted the applause of many Canadians and the scorn of many others when he came up with the suggestion, either sensible or outrageous, that the simple possession of marijuana be decriminalized instead of remaining an offence punishable by as much as seven years in prison. He advanced the idea after he'd finished conducting an exhaustive federal inquiry in the early 1970s into the non-medical use of drugs. There are two points worth noting about Le Dain's recommendation. One is that, for all the Canadians who'd never heard of Le Dain, it obscured his remarkably varied and accomplished career. And the other is that, over a decade after Le Dain's suggestion, the simple possession of marijuana is still an offence punishable by seven years in prison.

It wasn't for Le Dain's expert views on non-medical drugs that Pierre Trudeau appointed him to the Supreme Court on May 29, 1984. It was, among more persuasive motives, for his moxie in the field of constitutional law. The man whose place Le Dain was taking, the late Chief Justice Laskin, represented the court's strongest constitutional voice, and while Le Dain was no Laskin — nor was anyone else in sight — he came close. He had worked at constitutional law as an academic (teaching at both McGill and Osgoode Hall law schools), as counsel (arguing cases on behalf of Quebec before the Supreme Court in the 1960s), as an adviser (instructing the Attorney General of Quebec on constitutional issues from 1963 to 1967), and as a judge (sitting on the Federal Court of Canada from 1975 to 1984).

In looks, Le Dain suggests an aging rock impresario. He has thick, longish silver hair combed over his head from the left side, a strong, no-nonsense face, and the kind of eyes that spot the funny stuff before anyone else. He was born in Montreal and has jammed in enough careers to occupy a half-dozen ordinary men. Service overseas with the Royal Canadian Artillery from 1943 to 1946. Practice in a couple of Montreal law firms. Dean at Osgoode Hall Law School from 1967 to 1972. Teacher. Counsel. Judge. He's bilingual and equally at home with the common law and civil law.

As to his position on the Supreme Court spectrum, left to

right, an old colleague on the staff at Osgoode Hall, Harry
Arthurs, probably best summed up Le Dain by not placing
him in any spot on the spectrum. "You can't view him as a
man of extremes," Arthurs said. "He's not an extreme liberal,
not an extreme conservative, not extremely pro-federal or
extremely pro-provincial. I see him as a man in the middle."

A look at some of Le Dain's judgments leads to a similar
conclusion. On the one hand, while he was a member of the
Federal Court, he held in a 1983 case that decisions of the
federal cabinet are in principle subject to the Charter of
Rights. And, on the other hand, he held in a 1985 Supreme
Court decision (to vigorous dissent from Brian Dickson) that
random spot-checks of cars by Toronto police operating under
a program to reduce impaired driving were a perfectly legitimate police activity. To some academic observers, the first
decision tilted to the liberal side, while the second leaned in
the direction of judicial conservatism. To Le Dain, both grew
logically out of his analysis of the materials at hand. Maybe
that makes him the judge in the middle.

William McIntyre was a judge who was stationed — and
prepared — in the right place at the right time. When Wishart
Spence retired from the court in late 1978, the Trudeau government decided that a justice from Western Canada would
be a politic choice in more ways than one. The new man would
have to be preferably a Liberal, satisfactorily versed in criminal law, an area in which a new voice was needed on the
Supreme Court, and reasonably bilingual. Enter Bill McIntyre. He had been active in the British Columbia Liberal Party
in earlier years before he went to the B.C. Supreme Court in
1967. His law practice in Victoria had covered plenty of
criminal law. And he had taken extensive instruction to make
himself able in French. McIntyre filled the bill, and he received
the nod to the Supreme Court at age sixty on January 1, 1979.

In appearance, McIntyre might be the fellow in the easy chair at the officers' club. He has a heavy, jowly face, a formidable body, and a low, authoritative voice. He comes honestly by his military air. During the Second World War, he fought his way with the Canadian army from the invasion of Sicily north through Italy. After the war, he returned to his home town of Moose Jaw, Saskatchewan, and started up in law, but he soon moved west to British Columbia, where he practised for twenty years. He sat on the trial division of the B.C. Supreme Court for almost six years and on the Court of Appeal for about the same length of time before his summons to Ottawa.

On the Supreme Court, he has shown that he is hardly a johnny-one-note of the law. His expertise goes far beyond criminal law, and his generally accepted categorization as a middle-of-the-road judicial thinker doesn't begin to tell the whole story. McIntyre demonstrated his wider range in a tantalizing little case that came along less than a year after he reached the Supreme Court. The case was called *Private R. C. MacKay* v. *Her Majesty The Queen*, and it represented a sort of last gasp for the Bill of Rights. The court hadn't found much to praise in the Bill of Rights through the 1970s, and, with the single exception of the Drybones decision in the case involving the inebriated Indian, the Bill hadn't proved to the justices that it had any strength as a protector of Canadian civil liberties. But in McIntyre's judgment in Private MacKay's case, a conscientiously crafted piece of work, he indicated that there just might be ways of breathing life into the Bill, though, to be sure, with the appearance of the Charter of Rights a few years later, the exercise became entirely academic.

Private R. C. MacKay had been stationed with the Canadian armed services in Victoria. He was caught in the act of peddling drugs on the base and hauled before a military body called the Standing Court Martial, which found him guilty of six charges and gave him sixty days' detention. MacKay appealed to the civil courts, and one of the grounds he raised was that his trial by court martial, rather than by a civil judge, offended the section of the Bill of Rights that guaranteed every Canadian equal treatment before the law.

When the case reached the Supreme Court, the nine judges split three ways. Roland Ritchie wrote a judgment rejecting MacKay's argument and dismissed the appeal, and he was joined by four other judges. McIntyre wrote a judgment to the same effect and was joined in it by Dickson. Chief Justice Laskin produced a dissent with which Estey agreed. Laskin's point was that, just as Joseph Drybones was treated under the law differently from other Canadians because he was an Indian, Private MacKay had been treated differently because he was a soldier. There couldn't be two ways of trying people on the same offence, one way for soldiers and another for everyone else, and the difference meant that MacKay's drug conviction by court martial violated the Bill of Rights. Laskin's judgment, consistent as it was with his civil-rights posture, had a half-hearted feel to it. He was tiring of the fight and seemed to have given up on the Bill of Rights.

By comparison, McIntyre's judgment came across as a refreshing point of view. The way he figured it, there was no violation of the Bill of Rights in trying Private MacKay by court martial so long as there was a persuasive reason for treating him differently from other Canadians who dealt in drugs. Supposing MacKay had been arrested in the act of selling his drugs in downtown Victoria off the army base, well, perhaps under those circumstances he should have been tried in a civil court. But a different set of rules applied, McIntyre reasoned, when MacKay was caught dealing narcotics in an army camp. That introduced a special kind of justice.

"Trafficking and possession of narcotics in a military establishment," McIntyre wrote, "can have no other tendency than to attack the standards of discipline and efficiency of the service and must clearly come within the jurisdiction of the military courts."

McIntyre wasn't rejecting the Bill of Rights. He was approaching it in a reflective way, producing an acceptable rationale for his decision to set it aside. Perhaps, his judgment implied, if earlier judges had looked at the Bill in a similar way, it might have led a different life.

In the last week of November 1985, Bertha Wilson and her husband John checked into the Park Plaza Hotel in Toronto. They were on their way to the small, sunny Caribbean island of Montserrat for a holiday from the Supreme Court. But first Wilson had some chores to perform at the University of Toronto Law School, which is located in an overcrowded and extended old mansion, once owned by Sir Joseph Flavelle, a block south of the Park Plaza. On Tuesday and Wednesday, Wilson delivered the two Goodman Lectures, the most prestigious public occasion on the law school's calendar, and on Thursday she took the Clara Brett Martin Workshop, an event named after the first woman called to the bar in Ontario. In between speeches and workshop, Wilson was tireless in a round of conferences with students and at lunches and dinners in her honour. She stood still for anyone who cared to buttonhole her, and when she talked and responded, speaking in her soft Scottish burr, she said things that enlightened the most savvy of the law students.

On the balance of cases heard by the Supreme Court: "At the beginning, we gave almost automatic leave to Charter cases. We felt we had to take a lot of them, and we had many, many criminal cases, too. That meant private-law cases got short shrift. So, not long ago, we put all of our cases through the computer to see what sort of work we'd been doing. When it showed the results — plenty of Charter work and criminal cases and not much private law — we decided we'd better get on the look for more of the private things, contracts and torts and other arguments between citizens. It sounds like an awfully primitive way to go about it, but that's just how it happened."

On the responsibility of making Charter decisions: "This isn't a role that the judiciary sought out. It was foisted upon us. But the government and the public must have some degree of confidence to give it to us. It isn't a political role in my view, but still, we have to fix on norms that will be acceptable to the community."

And on her pioneering roles as a woman entering the law and moving to the bench: "The law was a masculine preserve when I went into the field, and I rather went in knowing that I was the one who was going to change. The framework that's still in place is oriented toward men, and the structures of the court system have been developed by men. Now the thinking's come around to the point that it's time for the structures to change in ways that are more appropriate for women. Still, I don't think I'll see that in my time."

Bertha Wilson doesn't fit the usual figure of a pioneer. She's too serene, too cheerful, too downright friendly. Standing at the lectern for the University of Toronto Law School's Goodman Lectures, tidy brown hair, sensible, approachable manner, crisp white blouse with a big bow at the neck, she could have been just the nice woman who's the most popular aunt in everybody's family. But her inner qualities are beyond question: mental toughness, fierce sense of responsibility, determination. Almost everywhere she's gone, she's been a first. First lawyer to establish a research department in a Canadian firm. First woman on the Ontario Court of Appeal. First woman on the Supreme Court of Canada. She was the first woman to deliver the Goodman Lectures.

At the very beginning of her legal career, she may also have been the first woman to face down the brilliant and crusty dean of the Dalhousie Law School of the 1950s. The story of the encounter was first written by Wilson in a special 1977 issue of *Ansul*, Dalhousie Law School's magazine. The year was 1953, as Wilson tells it, and with her husband busy at his duties as a naval chaplain and with no kids to occupy her, she was in her early thirties, five years in Halifax from her native Scotland and not keen on idleness. She decided to give law a shot, not out of ambition to practise the legal profession but as an expansion of her education. She called on Horace Read, the renowned dean at Dalhousie Law.

"Have you any appreciation of how tough a course law is?" Read asked Wilson, very unhappy to have an older, married woman on the premises. "This is not something you do in your spare time. We have no room here for dilettantes. Why don't you just go home and take up crocheting?"

Wilson insisted. Read yielded. And Wilson found in law a revelation. "From the first day I entered law school," she writes, "I knew that law was my thing. I sopped it up like a sponge."

After her call to the bar and after her minister husband took a Presbyterian congregation in Toronto, she went to work for Osler, Hoskin and Harcourt. It's among the two or three top Toronto law firms in size and prestige and clientele. Wilson gave it an extra dimension. She went into the firm's back rooms and started a research section. She read the cases and developed a systematic catalogue of material that provided the firm's litigation counsel with a reliable supply of ammunition for battles on behalf of their clients.

"She had a fantastic mind for the law," Ed Sexton says, a man who should know, since he's the head of Osler, Hoskin's litigation department. "And she had the concept of how to organize the precedents and other stuff so that they were instant and authoritative. Because of her, we were ahead of the other firms."

It's a measure of Wilson's skills that today, a decade after she left Osler, Hoskin, her old job is handled by five lawyers and a computer.

In 1975, when Ottawa went looking for a first woman to place on the Ontario Court of Appeal, Wilson's reputation within the profession made her an ideal choice. With, however, one reservation — she'd never argued in a courtroom. She underlined the point at her swearing-in ceremony. "I hope you will forgive me if I confess an element of unreality," she said. "Other than on the occasion of my call to the bar, this is the only time I have worn a gown."

The absence of litigation experience in her curriculum vitae made no difference. She became a superior appellate court judge and displayed in particular two qualities. She was a superb writer — lucid and to the point — and she had, as one academic put it, a "contemporary feel" in her judgments. She was strikingly sensitive to the problems of citizens at the most basic and human levels. Though she was frequently in dissent, she hit on ways of making the law work for little girls who wanted to play on boys' hockey teams, for East Indian women who felt colleges discriminated against them, for common-law wives who thought they hadn't got a fair financial shake in the separation from their men. Wilson was just the sort of judge — good writer, adventurous thinker — to catch Pierre Trudeau's eye when he decided the time had come for a woman to break into the men's club at the Supreme Court of Canada. She was named to the court on March 4, 1982.

In Ottawa, Wilson's work has continued to manifest the same solid virtues — the sensitivity to social issues, the good old grass-roots understanding. In March 1984, she wrote in the case of six worshippers at a Catholic church in Stellarton, Nova Scotia, convicted of disorderly conduct when they insisted on kneeling during communion in defiance of the local bishop's directive to stand at communion. Wilson's judgment struck a typical note of horse sense.

"These six may be obstinate, insubordinate and disobedient parishioners," she wrote in holding that no crime had been committed in the Stellarton church, "but I find it difficult to see them as criminals. I may say I find it equally difficult to see their fellow parishioners as informants instigating criminal proceedings against them. Reasonableness and a spirit of accommodation do not appear to have been features of either side's conduct."

And Wilson still has the penchant for the daring dissent that she exhibited on the Ontario Court of Appeal. As Peter Russell, the Toronto political scientist, says, "She's nobody's follower. She can go into the big cases and take on the big guys."

The 1984 case of *Perka* v. *Her Majesty The Queen* offered a prize example. It was a case with a wild and woolly set of facts and it turned on the highly technical point of necessity as a defence to a criminal charge. The accused men in the case were ambitious drug smugglers. They set off from Colombia in South America on a ship called the *Samarkanda* with a load of marijuana worth about six million dollars in the wholesale market. Their destination was Alaska, but when the *Samarkanda* ran into engine trouble and high seas, they were forced to put in at a cove on the west side of Vancouver Island. Canadian police swooped in, seized the cargo of dope, and arrested all hands on charges of importing cannabis into Canada for the purposes of trafficking. The defence lawyers for the drug smugglers argued that their clients had no intention of doing business in Canada. Faulty engines and foul weather compelled them to land on Canadian territory. Thus, the question that the Supreme Court was called on to deal with boiled down to this: if an accused person has no alternative under a particular set of circumstances except to act in a way that is otherwise illegal, can he raise the necessity of his actions in defending himself in court?

Brian Dickson wrote the majority judgment in the Perka case. It was a long, polished piece of reasoning. It invoked Aristotle, Hobbes, and Kant and it wove a skilful path through common-law jurisprudence. It was Dickson at his most lyrical, and it concluded that there existed two sorts of necessity. There was necessity as an excuse and necessity as a justification, and in Dickson's view, only the former, necessity as an excuse, was available under certain conditions as a defence in a criminal case.

Dickson's judgment, directing that the accused, acquitted at the first trial, should be retried, seemed the last word on the tricky subject. But Wilson, intellectually bold, proceeded to challenge his conclusion. "My concern," she wrote, "is that [Dickson] appears to be closing the door on justification as an appropriate jurisprudential basis in some cases, and I am firmly of the view that this is a door which should be left open." Dickson was far more experienced in this corner of law, but Wilson insisted on pushing her point.

She too took a whirl at the philosophers, the judicial heavy thinkers, and the precedents, and when she came out at the other end, she concluded that, to the contrary, there were grounds where necessity as justification ought to be applied. No one else sitting on the case joined in Wilson's opinion. She was in solitary dissent. But her reasoning had a strength and density that suggested the judgment might be one of those dissents that judges turn back to for future re-evaluation.

Wilson had gone into a big case and taken on, in Dickson, the biggest guy of all.

Gerald La Forest of Grand Falls, New Brunswick, has the look of the new kid on the court. When argument gets rolling in the courtroom, he slouches low in his chair and chews on his black pen. He questions counsel in a quick voice, and he radiates a sense of alive eagerness. Everything about his manner says he can't believe his fantastic good fortune to be where he is. La Forest is closing in on sixty, but with his black hair, open face, and lanky body, it's easy to take him for many years younger. He arrived on the Supreme Court on January 16,

1985, as the representative from the Maritimes replacing Roland Ritchie, whose failing health took him away from the court in the fall of 1984.

La Forest boasts dazzling credentials for his job: Rhodes Scholar, federal deputy attorney general, member of the Law Reform Commission of Canada, dean of the University of Alberta Law School. He's bilingual and has written several books, including the definitive text on Canadian extradition law. He sat on his province's Court of Appeal, and he has five university degrees.

Still, when he began his career in the law, he found himself, five degrees and all, at home in Grand Falls (pop. 6,000). "Basically, I had to come back," he has explained. "I looked all over New Brunswick and couldn't find a job anywhere. So I put up a shingle and hoped it would be a good potato year." On top of everything else, he's got a sense of humour.

His stance as a jurist puts him, in the view of most court observers, on the liberal wing, but La Forest resists such categorization. He's like Antonio Lamer. He calls himself a progressive.

"We get cases affecting human values in many particular settings," he says, "so you can never be quite clear if a judge is a liberal or a conservative. I hope to be progressive."

Jean Beetz and Julien Chouinard met for the first time in the summer of 1951 on a ship that was crossing the Atlantic from Canada to England. It was natural that their paths hadn't crossed earlier. Beetz was a couple of years older, twenty-four to Chouinard's twenty-two, and from Montreal, while Chouinard had grown up in Quebec City. But the common purpose of their trip to England brought them together aboard ship: each had been chosen a Rhodes Scholar for that year. The period in Oxford was rewarding. "The great gift of the year to me," Chouinard said many years later, "was that I learned to develop a critical approach to every problem, to take nothing for granted." He might also have added that the time at Oxford solidified his friendship with Jean Beetz. Back in Canada, when Chouinard married, he and his wife used to have Beetz, a bachelor, to dinner each Saturday night, and Chouinard's children knew Beetz as "Uncle Jean". The two men's careers in the law ran along different paths, but, in the end, the friends came to their closest professional association when each was appointed to the Supreme Court of Canada.

Julien Chouinard has a seigneur's face, long and narrow, eyes slightly in shadow, heavy black brows, and silver hair. He tends to the conservative wing of the court and is its least chatty member when he's on the bench, asking few questions of counsel. Off the bench, he's one of the court's most charming members, and he's the only judge of the present court who's taken a flyer at politics on the practical level. He ran for the federal Parliament in 1968. He was a Progressive Conservative candidate, and he lost. For three years before running, he worked as Quebec's deputy minister of justice, and for seven years after losing, he was the secretary general of Quebec's Executive Council. In those roles, he served both the Union Nationale and the Liberal government, and it was the Trudeau government in Ottawa that named him to the Quebec Court of Appeal in 1975. Every political party approved of Chouinard, but the federal Conservatives approved of him the most.

In 1979, after Joe Clark led the Tories to power, it was rumoured that Clark would offer Chouinard a seat in Parliament and a post in the cabinet. Chouinard was in especially high repute around Ottawa at the time as a result of his efficient handling of the inquiry into the volatile *Gens de l'air* controversy stirred up by Quebec air-traffic controllers who objected to having to address French-speaking pilots in English. Chouinard's conclusion in August 1979 that bilin-

gualism in the air represented no threat to safety was em-
braced with alacrity by the Clark government. But Chouinard
resisted any attempts to coax him away from the bench and
into government. Instead, he accepted another offer from
Clark, an appointment to the Supreme Court on September
24, 1979.

Chouinard's friend, Jean Beetz, had already been on the
court for five and a half years. Pierre Trudeau named him on
January 22, 1974. Trudeau and Beetz went back a long way
together, back to the 1950s when both men taught law at the
University of Montreal. Except for a brief period in practice
in Montreal, Beetz has always applied his gifts in the law to
teaching, advising, and judging. Trudeau took him to Ottawa
for stints as assistant secretary to the federal cabinet from
1966 to 1969 and as constitutional adviser to the Prime
Minister's Office from 1968 to 1971. Beetz has the manner
that suits intellectual back rooms. He is soft-spoken, cautious,
and methodical. His looks are fine and aristocratic, framed
by a full head of silvery hair and a closely clipped moustache
and a beard that shades around his jaw.

Trudeau put him on the Quebec Court of Appeal in 1973
and moved him to the court in Ottawa a year later. Beetz
has continued his thorough ways on the Supreme Court. He
is its most deliberate writer, seemingly never satisfied with
his judgments until their logic is as close to unassailable as
a piece of judicial reasoning can stretch. He is, generally
speaking, strong on provincial rights and conservative on civil
liberties, though he's too complex to be entirely pinned down
by labels. In a perverse way, his judgment in the infamous
Dupond case demonstrated the curious workings of cause
and effect in Beetz's judicial style. The judgment has been
derided by academics and constitutionalists, and yet in a
strange way the final result of Beetz's decision has been aston-
ishingly salutary.

The case originated on November 12, 1969, when the Montreal City Council, afraid that the city was under siege from the FLQ and other radicals, passed a by-law that allowed the Executive Committee to prohibit any public assembly for a period of thirty days whenever it suspected that a parade or other gathering might "cause tumult, endanger safety, peace or public order." It was a sort of mini-War Measures Act, and a civil-libertarian named Claire Dupond challenged the constitutional validity of the by-law in the courts. The case reached the Supreme Court of Canada in April 1977, where Beetz wrote the majority judgment.

He upheld the by-law, and in the process he put the hammer to the notion that, under the British North America Act and the Bill of Rights, Canadians possessed anything that might generally be called fundamental rights and freedoms of speech, assembly, and association, of the press, or of religion. In fact, Beetz objected in his judgment to just such sloppy phrasing as "fundamental rights and freedoms".

"What is it that distinguishes a right from a freedom and a fundamental right from a freedom which is not fundamental?" he wrote in testy fashion. "Is there a correlation between freedom of speech and freedom of assembly on the one hand, and, on the other, the right, if any, to hold a public meeting on a highway or in a park as opposed to a meeting open to the public on private land? How like or unlike each other are an assembly, a parade, a gathering, a demonstration, a procession? Modern parlance has fostered loose language upon lawyers. As was said by Sir Ivor Jennings, the English have no written constitution and so they may divide their law logically."

From that disdainful beginning, it was a short jump in Beetz's judgment to several propositions that left the Canadian constitution, such as it was, for dead. The first Beetz proposition held: "None of the freedoms referred to" — of speech, assembly, association, press, and religion — "is so enshrined in the Constitution as to be above the reach of

competent legislation." Every freedom, in short, was vulnerable to an act of government and could be whipped away at
a whim. The rest of Beetz's propositions elaborated on the
first and ended with the flat assertion that "the Canadian
Bill of Rights, assuming it has anything to do with the holding of assemblies, parades or gatherings on the public domain,
does not apply to provincial or municipal legislation."

Beetz's blunt judgment carried Justices Martland, Ritchie,
Pigeon, and de Grandpré in agreement and drew furious
dissent from Chief Justice Laskin, who was joined by Justices
Spence and Dickson. Outside the court, it was described by
at least one critic as "the worst ruling produced in the 1970s".
But Beetz's judgment brought home a desperate truth: under
the constitution as it existed in the 1970s, there was little or
no justification in law for Canadian claims to fundamental
rights and freedoms. Beetz's put-down was so direct and so
single-minded that it demonstrated the need for a much more
explicit spelling-out of constitutional guarantees of basic
liberties. And in that roundabout way, Beetz accomplished
as much as any judge or politician or civil servant in pushing
the way toward the Charter of Rights.

On November 23, 1984, Brian Dickson considered the merits
of a movie with the inelegant title of *Dracula Sucks*. It was
hardly a film that Dickson would choose to see for himself.
It featured nudity, violence, simulated sex, and an ending in
which the hero, wielding sunshine as his weapon, knocked
off Count Dracula. The movie ran for several weeks in
Edmonton with a Restricted rating from the provincial censor
board, and it drew almost nine thousand customers before the
city police charged the owner of the theatre where *Dracula
Sucks* was playing with presenting an obscene film contrary
to section 163 of the Criminal Code. The judge who tried the
charge screened the movie and gave it as his view that "most

of the film was devoted to extreme tasteless violence and explicit unnecessary sex." He held that the movie was obscene within the meaning of the Criminal Code, which defines obscenity as "any publication a dominant characteristic of which is the undue exploitation of sex". The trial judge convicted the theatre owner, and the Alberta Court of Appeal upheld the conviction. The case was appealed to the Supreme Court, where seven judges heard argument on November 23, 1984. That's when Brian Dickson — the most upright of men, Chancellor of the Church of England Diocese of Rupert's Land from 1960 to 1971, a Canadian of impeccable taste — applied his mind to *Dracula Sucks*.

One of Dickson's most admirable qualities as a judge is the sense of clear-headed, thoughtful detachment that he conveys in his decisions. He has many virtues on the court. He writes eloquently. He may be the best administrator in the Supreme Court's history. And he puts in a working day that would stagger most men who have, as he has, passed their seventieth birthday. But what emerges from his judgments with more impact than any of his other characteristics is a mood of unruffled reasonableness. He's silky and perceptive and never loses sight of the point at the end of a judgment. His steadiness didn't waver in the task of using a movie as seamy as *Dracula Sucks*, as foreign a film could be to Dickson's own experience, to say something lasting and helpful about the state of censorship and obscenity in Canada.

The trouble with the trial judge's conclusions on the worth of *Dracula Sucks*, as Dickson saw it, was that the judge had applied his own subjective standards of taste. That was wrong. Obscenity must only be measured by community standards of tolerance. But, having said as much, Dickson was left with the slippery problem of spelling out just exactly the criteria by which community standards of tolerance are calibrated.

"What matters," Dickson wrote, "is not what Canadians think is right for themselves to see. What matters is what

Canadians would not abide other Canadians seeing because it would be beyond the contemporary Canadian standard of tolerance to allow them to see."

Clear enough so far. Then Dickson got even more definitive.

"Since the standard is tolerance," he wrote, "I think the audience to which the allegedly obscene material is targeted must be relevant. The operative standards are those of the Canadian community as a whole, but since what matters is what other people may see, it is quite conceivable that the Canadian community would tolerate varying degrees of explicitness depending upon the audience and the circumstances."

Dickson might be offended if he saw *Dracula Sucks*. The trial judge was certainly offended. But perhaps many of their fellow Canadians would regard *Dracula Sucks* as a swell evening at the picture-show. It was the community standard that counted in deciding whether the movie was obscene. Dickson set aside the trial judge's conviction of the Edmonton theatre owner and sent the case back for retrial. With Dickson's guiding judgment, maybe the next trial judge would be able to figure out how community standards of tolerance squared with *Dracula Sucks*.

Dickson has the manner and the looks that make him the very model of a chief justice. He's solid and stable, without a touch of stuffiness. He's gracious, polite, even genial, though it's plain there's steel somewhere back of the charm. His body has the heft of a man who's enjoyed a few roast beef dinners, and his face is a balance of force and calm. Dickson conveys an athletic sense, though he walks with a deep limp, a souvenir from the Second World War. He and the other men from his medium-artillery group were moving into place in the neighbourhood of Falaise in the fighting not long after D-Day when a fleet of British and American bombers flew over led by U.S. Pathfinders. The guide planes lost their bearings and the bombers dumped a load of bombs in the woods where the Allies were hunkered down. The men on the ground sent up signals in coloured smoke to warn off their own planes. But the alarm came too late for many of the soldiers in the woods. Some were killed, some were wounded. Dickson lost most of his right leg.

Dickson was born in Yorkton, Saskatchewan. His mother came from Ireland, where she was a fine horsewoman and one of the first women to graduate from Trinity College, Dublin. She took honours in Greek and Latin. Dickson's father worked for the Bank of Montreal. He managed at several branches in small Saskatchewan towns, and in the early 1930s the bank moved him to Regina, where Brian entered Central High School. He found himself in speedy company. Two of his classmates were Sandy MacPherson, destined in later years for a long run on the province's Court of Queen's Bench, and William Lederman, who would become one of the country's most innovative constitutional-law scholars.

"There was never any doubt who was going to stand first in the class," Dickson remembers. "That was Bill Lederman. The contest was over second place. With Sandy and me, it was pretty close to a dead heat."

MacPherson's father gave Dickson his first and lasting look at the life of a lawyer. The senior MacPherson was a prominent Regina counsel and politician. Dickson had immense respect for him.

"Murdo MacPherson was a great Canadian," Dickson says. "The year that John Bracken won the leadership of the Conservative Party, Mr. MacPherson gave him a good run at the convention." When Dickson the high school student came under the influence of MacPherson, the latter was Saskatchewan's attorney general. "Sandy and I used to do our homework at night in his father's government office," Dickson says. "Afterwards we'd go into the legislative chamber and lean over the railings and listen to the debates until all hours. It was very exciting to me, my first pre-law taste."

The Bank of Montreal packed the Dickson family off to

Winnipeg when Brian was finishing up grade twelve. Winnipeg became his home for almost four decades, but he didn't shake the attraction to the law that he'd felt in Murdo MacPherson's Regina. He graduated from the University of Manitoba Law School with the gold medal in 1938, and after the war he went to work for a leading Winnipeg firm, Aikins, Macaulay & Company. Dickson's life hit a useful and prosperous groove. He practised mainly corporate law. He married Barbara Sellars, daughter of a Winnipeg family that made its mark and fortune in the grain business and then spread to other industries. The couple had four children and pursued their interests in horses and in Canadian art. They bought a ranch outside Winnipeg and acquired some A.Y. Jacksons and some Lawren Harrises. Dickson sat on the boards of a number of companies, including a bank — the Commerce, not his father's Bank of Montreal — and took responsible roles in the Anglican Church. He contributed to his community.

The beginnings of his eventual move to the Supreme Court of Canada came in 1963 when he accepted an appointment to the Manitoba Court of Queen's Bench. "At first," he recalls, "I had some trouble with criminal-law trials." That was understandable, since Dickson had done virtually no criminal work in his practice. But he was a quick study, and in 1967 he moved up to the Manitoba Court of Appeal. Six years later, he sold his ranch to hockey player Bobby Hull and left for Ottawa. On March 28, 1973, he had been named to the Supreme Court.

If there's a pattern in Dickson's judgments on the court, it's a pattern of legal scholarship. He goes where the law takes him — and then, very often, a little farther. In the process, he's revealed a couple of fairly obvious tendencies. One surfaced when he opted for provincial rights over federal authority on at least a couple of significant occasions. The Hauser case was one instance; it involved the power of federal prosecutors in drug cases, and Dickson, in dissent, favoured prosecutions by the provincial attorneys general. And another was the 1981 patriation case, when he joined the majority in holding that the federal government needed the provinces' consent before it could amend the constitution.

In a second and even more marked tendency, Dickson's judgments are strong on civil liberties. That's a stance which, in his early years particularly, put him in frequent dissent. The *Gay Tide* case in 1979 offered a striking example. *Gay Tide* was a newspaper for homosexuals on the West Coast, and it wanted to run a brief advertisement in the *Vancouver Sun*: "Subs to *Gay Tide*, gay lib paper. $1 for 6 issues." The *Sun* refused the ad, and *Gay Tide* took its protest all the way to the Supreme Court, where it ran into more disappointment. Six of the justices supported the *Sun*'s right to turn away the ad. Laskin, Estey, and Dickson dissented, and Dickson's judgment wasted no words.

"I do not think," he wrote, "a newspaper or any other institution or business providing a service to the public can insulate itself from human rights legislation by relying upon 'honest bias' or upon a statement of policy which reserves to the proprietor the right to decide whom he shall serve."

In similar fashion, Dickson stuck up for a penitentiary prisoner whose rights had been violated by a disciplinary board and for a separated wife who claimed a share of the assets of a farming operation which she had worked on an equal footing with her estranged husband. None of these decisions and several others in a like vein stamp Dickson as precisely a knee-jerk libertarian. But they show him, more accurately, to be a judge who doesn't mind pushing at the edges of the law to accommodate the rights of individual Canadians against the workings of the state.

That propensity helped to make Dickson an obvious pick for the chief justice's chair after the death of Bora Laskin, and Pierre Trudeau named him to it on April 19, 1984. In one small sense, the appointment was a departure, since it interrupted the informal postwar custom of alternating chief justices between representatives from Quebec and representatives from the English-speaking provinces. Under that practice, Jean Beetz would have been the favourite for the post. But it seemed clear that Beetz wouldn't care for the job, partly as matter of inclination (Beetz apparently isn't keen on administrative chores) and partly as a matter of health (Beetz, though in fine trim today, suffered a heart attack after some vigorous exercise in the summer of 1982). In any event, Dickson was the stick-out choice among the justices on the court. He had the stature, the background, the record of accomplishment. He would have no trouble commanding the respect of counsel and of his fellow judges.

And there's also about Dickson, sitting now in the chief justice's office, a sense of inevitability. It's almost as if, away back when he caught a whiff of the law from Murdo MacPherson in Regina in the 1930s, he was destined to become chief justice of the Supreme Court of Canada. As his high school chum, Sandy McPherson, puts it, "Brian has the unlimited ability and the great sense of public purpose that makes him a natural for his job." Maybe he always was the natural for the job.

His chief justice's office occupies a corner in the Supreme Court Building, one window looking toward Parliament Hill, another toward the Ottawa River. It's a large, gloriously sunny room. It has a marble fireplace, an A.Y. Jackson on one wall, a photograph of a grandson in hockey gear, another of Dickson and his wife greeting the Pope. Dickson looks right at home in the surroundings. He looks ready to work the long days in the office and the nights and weekends at his farm, Marchmount, further west along the Ottawa River. "The reading never ends in this job," he says. That's all right. Dickson is the chief justice to handle it. He's the man to steer the Supreme Court through the most heavily responsible period in its history, to figure out the meaning and reach of the Charter of Rights, to act as guide to his colleagues on the court.

"Oh well, I'm just one voice in nine," he says modestly. But that doesn't tell the whole story. "If you influence your fellow justices as chief justice," he goes on, "it isn't done by proselytizing or by pulling rank. It's not by reason of force. It's by force of reason."

Dickson has already proved that he's the chief justice who knows plenty about reason.